From Indifference to Dialogue?
Estonian Young People, the School and Religious Diversity

ry

Religious Diversity and Education in Europe

edited by

Cok Bakker, Hans-Günter Heimbrock,
Robert Jackson, Geir Skeie, Wolfram Weiße

Volume 19

Globalisation and plurality are influencing all areas of education, including religious education. The inter-cultural and multi-religious situation in Europe demands a re-evaluation of the existing educational systems in particular countries as well as new thinking at the broader European level. This new book series is committed to the investigation and reflection on the changing role of religion and education in Europe. Contributions will evaluate the situation, reflect on fundamental issues and develop perspectives for better policy making and pedagogy, especially in relation to practice in the classroom.

The publishing policy of the series is to focus on the importance of strengthening pluralist democracies through stimulating the development of active citizenship and fostering greater mutual understanding through intercultural education. It pays special attention to the educational challenges of religious diversity and conflicting value systems in schools and in society in general.

Religious Diversity and Education in Europe is produced by two European research groups, in which scholars are engaged in empirical and theoretical research on aspects of religion and education in relation to intercultural issues:
* **ENRECA: The European Network for Religious Education in Europe through Contextual Approaches**
* **REDCo: Religion in Education. A contribution to Dialogue or a factor of Conflict in transforming societies of European Countries**

The series is aimed at teachers, researchers and policy makers. The series is committed to involving practitioners in the research process and includes books by teachers and teacher educators who are engaged in research as well as academics from various relevant fields, professional researchers and PhD students. It is open to authors committed to these issues, and it includes English and German speaking monographs as well as edited collections of papers.
Book proposals should be directed to one of the editors or to the publisher.

Olga Schihalejev

From Indifference to Dialogue?

Estonian Young People, the School and
Religious Diversity

Waxmann 2010
Münster / New York / München / Berlin

Bibliographic information published by die Deutsche Nationalbibliothek
Die Deutsche Nationalbibliothek lists this publication in the
Deutsche Nationalbibliografie; detailed bibliographic data
is available in the Internet at http://dnb.d-nb.de.

This research was supported by the European Commission (by funding
REDCo project) and the European Union through the European Regional
Development Fund (Centre of Excellence in Cultural Theory CECT).

The printing was kindly supported by the Evangelische Kirche
in Hessen and Nassau and by Herbert-Quandt-Stiftung Bad Homburg.

Religious Diversity and Education in Europe, vol. 19

ISSN 1862-9547
ISBN 978-3-8309-2288-9

© Waxmann Verlag GmbH, 2010
Postfach 8603, D-48046 Münster
Waxmann Publishing Co.
P. O. Box 1318, New York, NY 10028, U. S. A.

www.waxmann.com
info@waxmann.com

Cover Design: Pleßmann Design, Ascheberg
Print: Hubert & Co., Göttingen
Printed on age-resistant paper,
acid-free as per ISO 9706

FOREWORD

The place of the study of religion within public education, especially in publicly funded schools, has become a hot topic across Europe and on the wider international scene. This book, an engaging research report by Olga Schihalejev, represents a particularly interesting and valuable European case study. Of course, the book is extremely important for those considering the development of religious education specifically in Estonia, including teachers, academics, policy makers, politicians and religious bodies. Its contents should – must – be widely read and discussed in Estonia. However, the book is also highly valuable and relevant for those outside Estonia, whether in other parts of Europe or in other countries where the place of studies of religion in education is being discussed. The history of Estonia is unique, and that history will and should influence any Estonian discussion about the role of religion in schools. However, the questions faced by Estonia in considering this issue are essentially the same as those faced by other countries: Why are such studies important in today's world? What are the barriers to including studies of religion in the curricula of publicly funded schools? How might studies of religion be conducted so that their aim is to inform and stimulate discussion and reflection rather than either to propagate or to disparage religion? How might studies of religion be related to the questions and concerns of the young? What are the views of young people on whether or how religious diversity should be covered in schools? How do such studies relate to other areas of education concerned with values, such as education for democratic citizenship or human rights education? Such questions show why the Estonian case – one in which currently the study of religions is marginalised – is so interesting and important for non-Estonians. It provides a unique point of comparison with regard to questions like these. But Estonia also needs to be seen in the wider European context. It is, for example, a member of the European Union and of the Council of Europe, so any Estonian discussion of the place of religion in schools needs to be seen against wider European and international debates. No country today can be seen in isolation. From the outset, Dr Schihalejev's book sets the distinctively Estonian discussion firmly in the context of the wider European debate.

Why has the study of religion in public schools become such an important topic in Europe and internationally? In many countries, but especially in those where there has been a sharp distinction between religion and state – and Estonia is one of them – religion essentially has been regarded as a private matter. Estonia is one of the 47 member states of the Council of Europe. It is telling that before 2002 no Council of Europe educational project dealt with the study of religions in public education, precisely because religion was felt to belong to the private sphere. As acknowledged within the Council of Europe, it was the events of September the 11th, 2001 in New York and Washington that provided a wake up call for those habitually excluding religion from public – including educational – discussion (Jackson, 2010). 9/11 propelled religion into public debate. Thus, in 2002 the Council of Europe launched its first project on teaching about religions in schools. The rationale for this was concerned with the relationship of religion to culture. Everyone, regardless of whether they held religious beliefs or not, must surely appreciate that religion is simply *there* in the world. It was argued that, regardless of the truth of falsity of religious claims, religion is a part of life and culture and therefore should be understood by all citizens as part of their education. It was on this basis that the Council of Europe launched a project on the study of religions as part of intercultural education. There were several outcomes from the project. One was the publication of a reference book for schools, aimed especially at those countries with little or no study of religions in public education (Keast, 2007). But most importantly, the Committee of Ministers – the Foreign Ministers of all 47 member states, including Estonia – agreed to a policy recommendation that *all* member states should include the impartial study of religions within the curricula of their schools. The recommendation (Council of Europe, 2008) should be studied closely by educators, policy makers and politicians across Europe.

Independently from the Council of Europe, another major European institution concerned with human rights also considered the place of the study of religions and beliefs in public education. This is the Organisation for Security and Co-operation in Europe (OSCE). The OSCE was founded in the 1970s, and includes as participant states most European countries (including Estonia), plus the USA and Canada. The security brief of the OSCE includes the human dimension as well as the military/political and economic dimensions; hence it has an Office for Democratic Institutions and Human Rights (ODIHR). As with the Council of Europe, the ODIHR conducted a project to identify principles on which participant states could develop policy and practice for teaching about religions and non-religious beliefs in schools across its huge geographical region. The result was the publication of a standard setting document, the *Toledo Guiding Principles on Teaching about Religions and Beliefs in Public Schools*, named after the city in which the drafting team first worked on the text, and in recognition of Toledo's historical role in communication between those of different religions (OSCE, 2007). Again, this important document should be studied and used as a tool by educators, policy makers and politicians across Europe and North America and beyond.

However, the development of policy requires much more than the implementation of generic recommendations. Policy makers need detailed knowledge of what is actually happening 'on the ground', so to speak. In this respect, it is important to understand particular societies – their history, social composition, public attitudes, current educational practices and the views of students and teachers. This is where REDCo (Religion, Education, Dialogue, Conflict), a large scale inter-European research project involving eight countries,[1] is able to provide large amounts of relevant data at the national level to complement and inform European policy recommendations.

In the present case, Olga Schihalejev's extensive, mixed methods research, conducted as part of the REDCo Project, provides exactly the kind of data needed to inform public discussion and policy development in Estonia. It is written less than 20 years after Estonia regained independence, following nearly 50 years in which the country was part of the Soviet Union, and against the background of an educational system in which religion has a very minor role. Currently, according to Estonian law, schools only have to organise religious education classes if a minimum of 15 students or their parents make a request. Thus it is not taught in the majority of schools, and in those where it is, classes are often held out of normal school hours. Although the subject is non-confessional, it is widely perceived as promoting religion, and public awareness of the kinds of approach advocated by the Council of Europe and the OSCE is low. As Dr Schihalejev remarks, 'Insufficient legal status for the subject, the shadow of the former Soviet ideology in people's attitudes, the lack of qualified teachers and the overloaded curriculum make the organisation of religious education at a school level very difficult' (p. 55). Thus, the majority of students in Estonia acquire their knowledge, attitudes and views about religion by studying it in subjects such as history, civic education, and literature, although a few schools offer teaching about religion in subjects with titles such as 'history of culture' or 'worldview studies', rather than 'religious education', thus getting round the strictures of the current legislation.

Through a series of research studies, using both a quantitative approach and a variety of qualitative methods (including ethnographic interviewing and using video to study classroom interaction), Olga Schihalejev explores Estonian young people's attitudes to religion and religious diversity. Her research involved the investigation of their views on the role of schools in promoting dialogue and tolerance for different worldviews, and identified how religious education, as currently practised, affects these views. Her central research question was: 'What are the hindrances and potentials for developing tolerance towards religious diversity among 14 to 16 year-old Estonian students in the context of school, and of religious education in particular?'

Her detailed findings will be read in the book, but a few can be highlighted here. Religion was not a central issue for many Estonian young people, and the

---

1 England, Estonia, France, Germany, the Netherlands, Norway, the Russian Federation and Spain. The project took place between 2006 and 2009 and was funded by the European Commission as part of its Framework 6 programme. See Jackson et al. (2007) for accounts of the place of the study of religions in the education systems of the REDCo countries.

few involved with religion tended to keep their views private. For many, a secular worldview was seen as the norm. Students avoided conflicts about religious issues and were wary of entering into dialogue about religion with their limited skills and knowledge. In comparison to young people from other REDCo countries, Estonian students valued respect for religion less and viewed religious people more negatively. Religious students were found to be vulnerable in this climate. However, religiously attached students and those who studied religious education were more tolerant of others' views. Avoidance of religious topics, combined with little knowledge of religion, sometimes led to the unchallenged expression of bigoted attitudes. Students who did encounter religious diversity at school – even if they had negative experiences with members of different religions – tended to be more open to dialogue on religious issues than other students.

Students who did study religion appreciated this as much as their peers in the other REDCo countries. Interestingly, especially in relation to the recommendations of the Council of Europe and the OSCE, both students with and without a religious attachment believed that schools should provide them with objective knowledge about religions to prepare them for life in a pluralistic society. Those students who experienced religious education considered that it increased their tolerance towards others, and prepared them for dialogue with those having worldviews different from their own. Studying religious education did not make them more religious.

Dr Schihalejev's classroom interaction studies show that teacher centred instruction and content oriented aims were the main obstacles to dialogue. Lessons in which the teacher took the leading role did not encourage students to explore a topic, but led them to become dependent on the teachers' arguments. The current knowledge-centred approach was seen to discourage students from discussing their own views. Dr Schihalejev's findings should be of considerable interest to teachers and policy makers, as should her argument that a more dialogical approach could be fostered, concentrating on student interaction and with more agency given to students.

On an international level, the Estonian case is particularly interesting in terms of seeing possibilities for developing religious education against the background of a high degree of secularism in society. Moreover, the opportunity to get responses from young people with a range of possibilities for experiencing or not experiencing religious education at different points of schooling makes Estonia a valuable source for researchers in other kinds of setting.

While some of the REDCo countries had four or five researchers covering the fieldwork and research writing, most of the Estonian work was done by Olga Schihalejev, working under the supervision of Dr Pille Valk. This was a truly remarkable achievement on Olga Schihalejev's part, especially given the wide range of research methods used – something unusual even in a doctoral thesis. Pille Valk also led the whole REDCo project's quantitative research culminating with the publication of a very substantial, cross-European research report (Valk et al., 2009). It was a delight to see both Pille and Olga in their own Estonian environment when the whole REDCo team met at the University of Tartu in 2006.

At a personal level, I was honoured to be invited to co-supervise Olga Schihalejev's doctoral research at the University of Tartu. This was a very rewarding and inspiring experience for me, and included a period in which Olga came to the University of Warwick as a Visiting Fellow in Warwick Religions and Education Research Unit. Pille Valk became seriously ill and consequently, at the stage of thesis writing, my involvement as supervisor became more intensive than had originally been planned. Very sadly, Pille died in September 2009 and she is remembered very fondly by all the REDCo team. Olga Schihalejev's PhD thesis was examined in November 2009. This book is based closely on the text of the thesis, making Dr Schihalejev's excellent research on Estonia available to policy makers, teachers, students, scholars and researchers internationally. The book provides some fascinating insights into the Estonian story, raises important questions of international interest and, not least, offers a wonderful tribute to the work and memory of Pille Valk.

Robert Jackson

Professor of Education at the University of Warwick, UK, Director of Warwick Religions and Education Research Unit (www.warwick.ac.uk/go/wreru) and Professor of Religious Diversity and Education at the European Wergeland Centre, Oslo (www.theewc.org)

References

Council of Europe (2008) 'Recommendation CM/Rec(2008)12 of the Committee of Ministers to member states on the dimension of religions and non-religious convictions within intercultural education', available online at: https://wcd.coe.int//View Doc.jsp?Ref=CM/Rec(2008)12&Language=lanEnglish&Ver=original&BackColor Internet=DBDCF2&BackColorIntranet=FDC864&BackColorLogged=FDC864 (accessed 24 December 2009).

Jackson, R. (2010) Religious Diversity and Education for Democratic Citizenship: The Contribution of the Council of Europe, in K. Engebretson, M. de Souza, G. Durka, and L. Gearon (Eds.) *International Handbook of Inter-religious Education*, Volume 4: *Religion, Citizenship and Human Rights* (Dordrecht, the Netherlands: Springer Academic Publishers).

Jackson, R., Miedema, S., Weisse, W. and Willaime, J.-P. (Eds.) (2007) *Religion and Education in Europe: Developments, Contexts and Debates,* (Münster: Waxmann).

Keast, J. (Ed.) (2007) *Religious Diversity and Intercultural Education: A Reference Book for Schools*, (Strasbourg: Council of Europe Publishing).

OSCE (2007) *Toledo Guiding Principles on Teaching about Religions and Beliefs in Public Schools,* (Warsaw: Organisation for Security and Co-operation in Europe, Office for Democratic Institutions and Human Rights). (full text available online at http://www.osce.org/item/28314.html accessed 24th December 2009).

Valk, P., Bertram-Troost, G., Friederici, M. and Béraud, C. (Eds.) (2009) *Teenagers' Perspectives on the Role of Religion in their Lives, Schools and Societies: A European Quantitative Study*, (Münster: Waxmann).

TABLE OF CONTENTS

LIST OF CHARTS, FIGURES AND TABLES

Tables

Figures

Charts

ABBREVIATIONS

EHIS   Eesti Hariduse Infosüsteem [the Estonian Education Information System];
OECD   the Organisation for Economic Co-operation and Development;
OSCE   the Organisation for Security and Co-operation in Europe;
q.   question in the quantitative questionnaire;
REDCo   Religion in Education. A contribution to Dialogue or a factor of Conflict in transforming societies of European Countries?
REKK   Riiklik Eksami ja Kvalifikatsiooni Keskus [the National Examinations and Qualifications Centre of Estonia];
UNESCO   the United Nations Educational, Scientific and Cultural Organization;
Φ   measure of effect size;
$\bar{x}$ statistical mean.

ACKNOWLEDGEMENTS

This book is based on my doctoral thesis, submitted to Tartu University in September 2009. The book is dedicated to the memory of my colleague and supervisor Dr Pille Valk and to those students and teachers who participated in the research. on which the book is based. Additionally there were organisations and people who in various ways helped the book in front of you to be published.

The European Commission funded the REDCo Project (Religion in Education. A contribution to Dialogue or a factor of Conflict in transforming societies of European Countries?) and thus covered the expenses of the research and made possible a productive co-operation between researchers from different countries and institutions. The European Regional Development Fund (Centre of Excellence in Cultural Theory) funded the extensive period during which the thesis and the book were written. The Protestant Church in Hesse and Nassau (EKHN) in Darmstadt and the Herbert-Quandt-Stiftung in Bad Homburg generously covered the expenses incurred in publishing the book.

I would like to thank deeply my colleagues in the REDCo team who provided me with their feedback and inspiration, especially Professor Wolfram Weisse, Professor Thorsten Knauth, Anna Körs, Dr. Ina ter Avest, Dan-Paul Josza and Marie von der Lippe; also my English REDCo colleagues, Dr. Judith Everington, Dr. Kevin O'Grady, Dr. Julia Ipgrave and Dr. Sean Neill from the Warwick Religions and Education Research Unit for their feedback and their help in dealing with some of the secrets of the English language.

I would also like to thank the referee Professor Brian Gates and the opponent of my thesis Professor Hans-Günter Heimbrock for their careful reading and critical remarks which helped me to improve the book.

Further, I would like to commend the interest, encouragement, and great job of my co-supervisor Professor Dr. Robert Jackson. His role was expected to be minor in the beginning, but he offered more than I would ever have hoped after the terminal illness of my main supervisor, Dr. Pille Valk. Bob Jackson welcomed me to the University of Warwick as a Visiting Research Fellow in March 2009; this opportunity helped me to focus on the beginning and the structure of my thesis. He found time in his busy schedule to provide me with quick responses and an insightful evaluation of parts of my thesis. He also agreed to write the foreword to this book and assisted with language editing as the thesis took shape as a book.

Most importantly, special gratitude goes to my husband Rein, who was the first and the last one to encourage, support, and love me throughout all these years; and to our children Ruth and Sandra, who put up with a string of trips abroad, lost weekends, and odd working hours. Without such a loving and caring support group, it would have been impossible to accomplish this work.

Above all, thanks to God who is behind all these daily mysteries.

1. INTRODUCTION

1.1 Motivation, scope and structure of the book

The aim of the book is to explore the attitudes of young people in Estonia to religion and religious diversity, their views on the role of the school in promoting dialogue and tolerance among representatives of different worldviews in a secular context, and to investigate the ways in which religious education alters their views on these issues.

The main research question of my study was: What are the hindrances and potentials for developing tolerance towards religious diversity among 14–16 years old Estonian students in the context of school, and of religious education in particular?

Empirical research had a dual perspective which included both of the subjects' own views and an analysis of observed teaching situations. To answer the main research question the following research tasks were established:

a. I explore what role students themselves give to religion in their own lives and in human relations;

b. I investigate students' attitudes towards religious (and worldview) diversity and their experiences, expectations and evaluations of it;

c. I seek to establish the extent to which religious education might have a role in educating students about religious diversity and how this alters their views of religion;

d. I study the main potentials and hindrances for dialogue about different worldviews in the classroom practices of religious education.

These questions are answered first by the means of qualitative research, where students' views were collected and the language that they used in speaking about religion and religious diversity was analysed. On the basis of this information, a quantitative questionnaire was developed and the views were checked using a much bigger sample.

Having obtained data on the views held by students, I then investigated the main potentials and hindrances for dialogue about different worldviews in the classroom practices of religious education. This was done on the basis of participant observation and the analysis of interaction patterns in the classroom, focusing both on incidents exemplifying both successful dialogue and failures in lessons. This part of the research was conducted by videotaping lessons and then analysing student interactions.

The book has an exploratory character; it is intended to explore the field and collect data, not test a theory. It provides the basis for the future development of better approaches to the study of religion in education and as a reference point for future empirically based theories.

In the following section I present arguments for the relevance of my study in a European context and the reasons for my personal interest in the study. These two perspectives are linked by a European research project, which permitted me to conduct the research. The structure of the book is presented in section 1.1.3.

1.1.1 Relevance of the study in European context

European societies are growing more and more diverse. Although the influx of immigrants into Estonia has not been very large in recent years, cultural and religious diversity is not a new phenomenon in Estonia either. Across Europe, the promotion of tolerance in a diverse context is seen as highly important, and religions can both facilitate mutual understanding and generate conflict. A liberal theologian, Hans Küng, whose strong arguments for dialogue among representatives of different religions have inspired many inter faith initiatives, has pointed it out very clearly:

> *"Religion can contribute to human liberation as well to human oppression. Religions can be authoritarian, tyrannical and reactionary; they can produce anxiety, narrow-mindedness, intolerance, injustice, isolation. But religions can also have liberating effects, oriented out on the future and beneficial to human rights. They can dissemi-nate trust in life, generosity, tolerance and solidarity, social commitment, spiritual renewal, social reforms and world peace."* (Küng, 1991, 46)

Thus the key question is: "How can we promote 'trust in life' instead of intolerance and narrow-mindedness?"

Different organisations promoting inter-religious dialogue have been established as one of the responses, the first probably being, the World Council of Churches (WCC) in 1948; many other organisations followed, e.g. The World Conference of Religions for Peace (WCRP) in 1970; the International Council of Christians and Jews (ICCJ) in 1975, the United Religions Initiative (URI) in 2000, the Institute of Interfaith Dialogue in 2000, the European Council of Religious Leaders (ECRL) in 2002. These are just some among numerous examples of inter faith dialogue promoting open and respectful exchange of views.

The multi-cultural and multi-religious character of European societies has demanded a shift in policies to foster mutual understanding among people of diverse backgrounds. In this context, the high importance of teaching about religions and beliefs in public education has been noted by prominent international institutions, such as the Council of Europe (2004; 2007; also in Wimberley, 2003), the Organisation for Security and Co-operation in Europe (OSCE, 2007), the European Union, UNESCO, and the European Commission (for a detailed account see Jackson, 2008b, 153–156). Such bodies not only encourage dialogue between young people of different religious faiths, but also with those who believe in non-religious philosophies, such as secular humanism (e.g. OSCE, 2007).

A political philosopher and public intellectual, Michael Walzer, highlighted that a strong commitment to democratic citizenship and to the politics of difference has special relevance in a diverse society, which in turn encourages people to seek a sympathetic understanding of different groups. He argues that learning democratic citizenship is best begun in childhood and that education plays an essential role in it:

> "… that is why education is so important – school learning (also practical experience) aimed at producing the patience, stamina, tolerance, and receptiveness without which the strain [democratic culture of criticism and disagreement] will not be understood or accepted." (Walzer, 1998, 160)

Given the fact of societies with many religious and secular worldviews present within them, there is always possibility for disagreement and conflict. Although conflict can be seen as the opposite of peace, it is not necessarily the opposite of dialogue, since "issues of conflict can produce good dialogues" (Jackson & Skeie, 2008, 8). On the contrary, as one can see from classroom interaction in different European countries (ter Avest et al., 2009), disagreements and conflicts make dialogue necessary and possible and can be part of exploring the other and oneself, although the outcome of such dialogue is not necessarily to reach shared opinions. Of course, there are other categories of 'difference', such as ethnicity and culture, which need to be taken into account in dialogue. Thus, not only education about religions and beliefs should be fostered, but also intercultural dialogue in the context of schools – many of which are increasingly 'multicultural' in character – should be promoted (Council of Europe, 2008).

There are two influential papers which stress the importance of promoting dialogue to reach the aim of mutual understanding among representatives of different religions and worldviews: *The Toledo Guiding Principles on Teaching about Religions and Beliefs in Public Schools* published by the Organisation for Security and Co-operation in Europe (OSCE, 2007) and in May 2008 the Ministers of Foreign Affairs of the 47 member states, including Estonia, of the Council of Europe launched the *White Paper on Intercultural Dialogue: Living Together As Equals in Dignity* (Council of Europe, 2008). The *White Paper* provides various orientations for the promotion of intercultural dialogue, mutual respect and understanding. It contends that passive tolerance is not sufficient to face the demands of a plural society, and that dialogue must promote active tolerance:

> "However, pluralism, tolerance and broadmindedness may not be sufficient: a pro-active, a structured and widely shared effort in managing cultural diversity is needed. Intercultural dialogue is a major tool to achieve this aim, without

which it will be difficult to safeguard the freedom and well-being of everyone liv-
ing on our continent." (Council of Europe, 2008, 13)

The special attention to interreligious dialogue is given more precisely in section 3.5 "The Religious Dimension" (Council of Europe, 2008, 22–24). The
document recognises the importance of studying religions in the framework of
general education also in section 4.3.2 "Primary and secondary education" for
promoting mutual understanding. In the recommendations for learning intercultural competencies the inclusion of teaching about and understanding of religions and nonreligious convictions is made explicit:

> "*An appreciation of our diverse cultural background should include knowledge
> and understanding of the major world religions and nonreligious convictions
> and their role in society.*" (Council of Europe, 2008, 45)

The awareness of religion in education as a potential for conflict as well as
dialogue prompted the European Commission to include religion as a possible
area for research within the framework of the FP6 Specific Programme "Inte-
grating and Strengthening the European Research Area", Priority 7: "Citizens
and Governance in a knowledge-based society", special area 7.2.1: "Values and
religions in Europe". My thesis was written on the basis of my work in a joint
European comparative project REDCo (Religion in Education. A contribution to
Dialogue or a factor of Conflict in transforming societies of European Countries?) The project began its work in March 2006 and ended in March 2009.
Nine institutions from eight European countries participated in it: the University
of Hamburg (Germany) as a project leader, the University of Münster (Ger-
many), the University of Warwick (England), the University of Tartu (Estonia),
the École Pratique des Hautes Etudes (France), the Free University, Amsterdam
(The Netherlands), the University of Stavanger (Norway), the Russian Christian
Academy for Humanities in St. Petersburg (Russia), and the University of
Granada (Spain). The book reports research conducted in Estonia for which I
was specifically responsible, which contributed to the overall outputs of the
REDCo project. The book includes work that I specifically contributed to the
project as a PhD student under the supervision of Dr. Pille Valk and Professor
Robert Jackson. Project findings were reported in a range of books, including
Jackson et al., 2007; Knauth et al., 2008; ter Avest et al., 2009; Valk et al.,
2009; van der Want et al., 2009.

Several articles were published reporting my work in the project and formed
the basis of the sections of my thesis. The third section, about the qualitative
study among young people in Estonia, is based on two articles: *Meeting diversity – students' perspectives in Estonia* (Schihalejev, 2008b) and *Kohtumine
endast erinevaga – õpilaste arusaam* [Meeting difference – students' perspec-
tives] (Schihalejev, 2008a). The fourth section, about the quantitative study, is

based on the article *Options beside 'and no Religion too' – perspectives of Estonian youth* (Schihalejev, 2009d). The fifth section about classroom interaction is based on the articles *Prospects for and obstacles to dialogue in religious education in Estonia* (Schihalejev, 2009f) and *Dialogue in religious education lessons – possibilities and hindrances in the Estonian context* (Schihalejev, 2009c). There were some articles reflecting other results of my research which were not used in the thesis. These include a qualitative research study about teachers' responses to diversity in the classroom, their struggles, challenges and joys which is discussed in *Challenges in creating respect for diversity: Teachers' perspectives* (Schihalejev, 2009a) and *Portraits of the Estonian respondents* (Schihalejev, 2009e). These articles, concentrating on teachers, stayed out of the focus of my thesis, and therefore this book, which concentrates on students' views. Also omitted from the thesis and the book are two articles that compared the results of studies done in Estonia and Russia, one about the qualitative and the second about the quantitative study (Kozyrev & Schihalejev, 2008; Schihalejev, 2009b). These are not included as they highlight the differences between the findings of the studies done in the two countries.

The hot debates around religious education (see section 2.2.1) in Estonia have shown also the relevance of the topic here. The main argument against religious education has been a suspicion that a subject could influence students **into** religion. However, one of the key arguments for religious education (or education about religions and beliefs) from European institutions and the United Nations is its potential for shaping more tolerant attitudes and increasing social cohesion. The investigation about students' views about religion and religious diversity, if compared to their experiences with religious education, can challenge or support such arguments for and against. The findings can contribute to a more informed dialogue and to planning new developments in religious education. The findings of the research have already contributed to some changes in a syllabus for religious education (see section 2.2.2).

Review of the literature

No research conducted in Estonia has explored the views of young people, especially those of 14–16 years of age, on religious diversity. However, several studies, usually conducted among adults, are relevant to my thesis. There are some quantitative studies on religion of the Estonian population (Hansen, 2001; Kilemit, 2000; Estonian Council of Churches, 2001; Liimann, 2001; Kilemit & Nõmmik, 2003). Lea Altnurme, in her dissertation, has explored the religious life of individuals by using biographical interviews (Altnurme, 2006) and also in her edited books (Altnurme, 2004 and 2007). However, her focus was on adults and concentrated only on religiously affiliated people. Her master's thesis (Altnurme, 1997) is of some importance to me as it investigates the students' views about God.

Some small scale studies have been done about beliefs by undergraduate students (e.g. works about religious beliefs: Sirge, 2008; Vavilov, 2007; Toompuu, 2007); and also about atheistic beliefs (Remmel, 2005), but samples are from one school only and none of them is about views on religious diversity. Some studies have been done about views on religious education (Saar, 2005; Valk, 2003; Nõmmela, 2007; Pärkson, 2006) among teachers, parents and students from upper secondary school.

In my study I have drawn on the empirical and theoretical research done by Pille Valk who developed a contextual model of religious education for secular schools (2002b). In her thesis she explores the historical and societal context of religious education in Estonia. Her thesis covers theological reflection about religious education in the secular schools in Estonia. Valk argues that an appropriate grounding for the Estonian context is provided by the principles and anthropological and synthetic models of contextual theology as described by Bevans (1992). These models demand investigation of the attitudes, views and beliefs of people and finding a common ground for dialogue with contemporary people. The focus of my study follows the same stream of argument where the understanding of the context and people in this context is a central question. Valk has also investigated the views of students, teachers and head teachers on religious education (Valk, 2003).

While others have studied religion and religious education, my work focuses on students' readiness for active tolerance; their views about religion and their experiences with religious education are used as potential variables for their attitudes to a different worldview and readiness to engage in a dialogue with people of a different religious or non-religious background.

1.1.2 Personal motivation

The topic is relevant not only on a policy level, as discussed in the previous section, but it is also of high relevance for me in two respects. In improving curricula of religious education and writing teaching-learning resources, it is of great importance to know how young people perceive religion, how they respond to the diversity they meet, and how they feel about any education on religious issues received in school. The question, 'how can school promote social cohesion of students with different religious backgrounds instead of segregation and exclusion?' was highly important and interesting for me, and one of the reasons why I joined the project. Although I will focus on the contribution of religious education in promoting tolerance and respect towards others, I do not want to say that religious education should not also contribute as well to a student's personal development.

In the following I will give an overview of the structure of the book.

1.1.3 Structure of the book

There is always a question of what to include in a thesis or a book and what to leave out. Religious education in Estonia represents a secular religious studies approach (see section 2, especially section 2.2.3). Also my study falls into the framework of the study of religions, and thus theological reflection is outside the scope of this study. My study is exploratory and does not intend to give a theoretical contribution to related topics. Thus I will not introduce an extensive rationale of theoretical concepts, but will give only a brief account of the theories directly used for my empirical studies and put the main emphasis on the results of this empirical research.

My aim is to explore hindrances and potentials for developing tolerance towards religious diversity among 14–16 years old Estonian students in the context of school, and of religious education in particular. It includes investigation about young people's attitudes to religion and religious diversity, and the role school has in promoting dialogue and tolerance among representatives of different worldviews. This is done in the framework of constructive epistemology and a sequential exploratory strategy was applied using a mixed methods approach, combining different qualitative methods with a quantitative survey.

In the first section, which broadly covers conceptual and methodological issues, I give reasons for the relevance of the topic in the European context and for myself as an educator. Three keywords as used in the study – tolerance, dialogue and religious education – are presented and discussed. The main emphasis of the section is on a discussion of methodology, theoretical stimulus for the research and the rationale behind choosing specific research methods for data collection and data analysis. Details of the use of methods are given at this point so that readers can appreciate the range of research methods used, as well as be able to consider the strengths and weaknesses of all the empirical methods in one place. More specific and technical details describing samples are not discussed here, but are placed at the beginning of sections presenting the results of the study. The first section concludes with the timeline of the research and the ethical issues that had to be taken into consideration in conducting the research.

The second section describes the context in which the study took place. It gives an overview of the religious landscape, general education, and the current position of religious education in Estonia. The main emphasis is put on recent trends regarding religious education in Estonia and its position on the map of religious education in Europe. This section explains the social and political context of the research, thus providing important information to interpret the data collected in the course of the fieldwork.

The three following sections are dedicated specifically to my empirical studies. To answer the main research question, 'what are the hindrances and potentials for developing tolerance towards religious diversity among 14–16 years old Estonian students in the context of school and of religious education in particular?', it is necessary to know about the views held by students themselves.

The third section presents the results of a qualitative study among students on their own attitudes about, expectations of and experiences of religion and religious diversity in their personal lives and in human relations in general. Young people are asked about situations in which they recognise religious and worldview diversity and their views on the value they place on this diversity. The section also explores how they value and the role they see for religious education. The open questions give space for students' own wordings and interpretations, and also enable them to explore the way they speak about religion in the context of their own life-world and of those who held different positions from their own. The study was done among 73 students from three schools, different in their geographical location and language of studies, and included both students who studied religious education and those who did not.

The quantitative study is presented in the fourth section. On the basis of the results of the qualitative analysis, questions for a quantitative survey were worked out. Here, some of the hypotheses of the qualitative study were checked and research questions were tested on a bigger sample. The main research question was: 'What role can religion in education play concerning the way students perceive religious diversity?' The sub-questions were:

1. What role has religion in students' life and in their surroundings (important others, peers, family)?
2. How do students consider the impact of religions: do they contribute more to dialogue or more to conflict?
3. How do students see religion in school and the impact of religion in education?

Also, regarding the research questions, it was decided collectively by the REDCo quantitative research group to use the following hypotheses to find out about the meaning of religion and religious diversity in relation to its potential for dialogue:

1a) Religious students are less tolerant than non-religious students.
1b) Religious students are less open to dialogue on religious issues than non-religious students.
2a) Students who have encountered religious diversity in education are more tolerant.
2b) Students who have encountered religious diversity in education are more open to dialogue on religious issues.

The sample consisted of 1208 students from 21 different schools in different parts of Estonia. Students varied in their religious affiliation, type of school attended (urban and rural, municipal and private), and with different models of (when offered) religious education.

26

The fifth section discusses the limitations and potentials for dialogue in religious education classes on the basis of observations and analyses of interaction during lessons. In order to answer the main research question, an analysis of observed teaching situations needed to be included in the study. Together with data on the views held by students, it enabled me to study the main potentials and hindrances for dialogue about different worldviews in the classroom practices. The section reports my examination of what happens in a classroom, by observing and analysing patterns of interaction in religious education lessons in two schools. Video–ethnographic data collection was combined with stimulated recall. Incident–analysis, stemming from conversational analysis, was used to interpret the data. The section discusses the limitations and potentials for dialogue in religious education classes on the basis of observations of lessons. I investigated how the nature of the teacher's questioning and responding to students' answers contributes to the dialogue in the classroom. I also explored how students' readiness to engage in dialogue is influenced by the responses to their contributions.

In the last section I triangulate the results of my different studies and make suggestions for policies regarding education about religion in the context of Estonian education in the light of these empirical findings.

1.2 Terminology – keywords

The aim of this section is to define and map my assumptions about the concepts used in the book rather than to give an account about the historical and philosophical development of the concepts. First, the term 'tolerance' is explored by distinguishing 'active' and 'passive' tolerance. Such a distinction leads to the second concept, 'dialogue', which is explored next. The main influences on my understanding of 'dialogue' are the philosopher Hans-Georg Gadamer and the educationalist Paulo Freire. Finally, the term 'religious education' and the classification to which religious education, as practised in Estonia, could be applied are discussed.

1.2.1 Tolerance

Being tolerant is considered important by many people in Europe, as they live in societies where neighbours, colleagues, children and spouses have different beliefs and cultures. The larger the differences in a society or a neighbourhood, the more pressing is the need for tolerance. Differences do exist also in more homogeneous societies; as religions and worldviews have never been monoliths, but have an inner diversity and are ever changing, while responding to the contexts in which they are present. With regard to the representation of people who are adherents of 'religions', Jackson recommends an analysis based on the relationship between individuals, the groups they belong to or are associated with, and the wider religious tradition, rather than assuming that religions are homogeneous systems of belief (Jackson, 1997; 2004b).

Tolerance is a word often used in official documents, in many academic studies and is regarded as having central value in education. However, the meaning of 'tolerance' varies greatly. The meaning of tolerance in an educational context, as understood by teachers and national curricula in Norway and in theories of tolerance, is explored by Geir Afdal in his book *Tolerance and Curriculum: Conceptions of Tolerance in the Multicultural Unitary Norwegian Compulsory School* (Afdal, 2007). He points to the great diversity of opinions about the term 'tolerance':

> *"Not only is there disagreement of what tolerance is, there is also disagreement how to describe the disagreement."* (Afdal, 2007, 87)

I will not present here a comprehensive overview about the meanings of tolerance but chart the one used in my research.

The political philosopher and social critic Walzer in his book *On Toleration* (2004) describes what a democratic society requires if different groups are to live together in peace. He confines toleration to the collective level, looking at toleration as a prerequisite for the peaceful coexistence of people with different religions, cultures, and ethnic identities. In his preface, Walzer writes: *"Toleration makes difference possible; difference makes toleration necessary"* (1997, xii).

The object of tolerance (the tolerated) can be an individual (for example, Heyd, 1996; Gray, 1991; Rawls, 1971), a group (e.g. in MacIntyre, 1985; Sandel, 1998; Walzer, 1997) or an opinion (e.g. Churchill, 1997). In political sciences the subject is usually the state/society and the primary object is either the individual or the group. The teachers and also educational documents studied by Afdal, navigate smoothly between these levels. The teachers emphasise more the individual as an object of toleration, recognizing the individuality of each student (Afdal, 2007, 188). The main shortcoming of Walzer's conception for implementing it in education is his focus on groups; as such a view does not take seriously the inner diversity of religious groups. Regarding a student in his developmental rapidly changing years, and having often a rather loose idea about the religion he or she belongs to as a representative of a particular religious group, is even more problematic. Together with teachers whom Afdal studied, I argue that in an educational setting it is more appropriate to speak about respecting individuals, not groups, as students cannot be regarded as representatives of a particular religious body, but rather as multi-layered individuals influenced by variety of contexts. Also Walzer, addressing the school context, speaks about individuals rather than about groups. He argues that strengthening democracy requires that people *"learn to think of one another as fellow citizens and to accord to one another the rights that democratic citizenship entails"* (Walzer, 1998, 156).

Although in his book *On Toleration* Walzer writes about toleration of groups, and avoids intentionally the individual level, I find his list of forms of toleration very useful as the point of reflection about different levels and forms of tolerance, whether the subject or 'tolerator' is the individual or group and the object of tolerance is a group, an individual or an idea. Walzer identifies five forms of toleration:

1. a resigned acceptance of difference for the sake of peace, as it was found in the 16th–17th centuries;
2. a passive, relaxed, indifferent attitude to difference: 'it takes all kinds to make a world';
3. moral stoicism, a recognition that the 'others' have rights 'even if they practise these rights in an unattractive way';
4. openness to others, curiosity, willingness to listen and learn;
5. enthusiastic endorsement of difference; acknowledgement that existence of differences is a necessary condition for human beings to make choices and feel their autonomy to be meaningful. (Walzer, 1997, 10–11)

The first three forms of tolerance, which are based on scepticism and indifference, could be classified as passive forms of tolerance, requiring no dialogue. Gabriel Moran believes that indifference could support tolerance only if people do not to communicate with each other.

> *"Perhaps indifference would breed tolerance if people did not have to interact with each other. ... There is a different path that tolerance could have taken and eventually must be developed, a toleration based on understanding rather than indifference."* (Moran, 2006, 45)

Throughout my paper I use tolerance in a very broad sense, as a way to recognise and live peacefully with difference. If I distinguish passive from active tolerance, then passive tolerance corresponds to the first three forms of toleration according to Walzer. Active tolerance corresponds to the fourth and fifth forms of tolerance and by definition requires encounters with differences. This leads to the next key word which is 'dialogue'.

1.2.2 Dialogue

Active tolerance by its definition implies being in dialogue with difference. What does dialogue mean? Although there are many influential theologians (e.g. Martin Buber, Franz Rosenzweig, Ebenhard Jüngel, Michael Barnes), and philosophers (from Socrates and Plato to Mikhail Bakhtin and Paul Ricoeur), for whom dialogue has been at the centre of their thinking, I cannot cover all of them and must restrict myself to the introduction of two philosophers for whom dialogue has been of great importance in their philosophical stances and who have influenced my own understanding of dialogue: These are Paulo Freire, who introduced dialogue to the field of education; and Hans-Georg Gadamer, a philosopher and social theorist who used dialogue as basis for understanding and hermeneutics.

Paulo Freire (1921–1997), the Brazilian educationalist, in his *Pedagogy of the Oppressed* (Freire, 1972), asserts the importance of dialogue and uses the notion of 'critical dialogue'. Dialogue is one of the central elements of Freire's pedagogical method. For him dialogue is a key to practise freedom and to 'liberate the oppressed', to 'empower the powerless' and to make changes to existing structures. For him, dialogue is a part of human nature and the main impetus for transformation. Freire argues that dialogue, which is usually practised in pedagogy, is vertical, the so called 'dialogue of elite'. He criticised such pedagogy, where the teacher has power and students must deposit ready-made answers; he regards this as 'banking' pedagogy. The student must only listen while the educator 'deposits' knowledge. This form of education puts those who know and those who do not in different categories. Freire argues that knowledge is banking of information, which can be gained by monologue, but it is a critical reflection of one's own experiences and strategies if done in dialogue. Freire viewed true pedagogy embodied in dialogue as a horizontal relationship, in which both parties have the capacity to reflect and if reflection is missing, he claims it to be 'domestication':

> *"But to substitute monologue, slogans, and communiqués for dialogue is to attempt to liberate the oppressed with the instruments of domestication. Attempting to liberate the oppressed without their reflective participation in the act of liberation is to treat them as objects which must be saved from a burning building; it is to lead them into the populist pitfall and transform them into masses which can be manipulated."* (Freire, 1972, 52)

He opposes pedagogies which are not deeply rooted in dialogue and believes that 'anti-dialogical' education is a manipulation and therefore cannot be accepted. In the third section of the book, Freire describes what he means by dialogue. He sees words as a means to change reality (Freire, 1972, 75). There are certain elements without which dialogue cannot occur:

- Dialogue is based on love, respect and tolerance. *"Dialogue cannot exist, however, in the absence of a profound love for the world and its people"* (Freire, 1972, 77); love is a condition of dialogue and dialogue itself. He sees domination and usage of power structures as an opposite of love. He be-

lieves that without love and a wish to liberate people from oppression no dialogue is possible.
- Dialogue cannot exist without humility, openness to others; one should not
  perceive oneself as the holder of truth.
- Faith in people is an *a priori* requirement for dialogue, but it does not mean
  being naïve; trust is albeit established by dialogue. (Freire, 1972, 77–80)

Freire argues that dialogue is more than a mere act. It is, rather, an approach to
students or an overall framework of teaching.

> *"The dialogical character of education as the practice of freedom does not begin
> when the teacher-student meets with the students-teachers in pedagogical situa-
> tion, but rather when the former first asks herself or himself what she or he will
> dialogue with the latter about."* (Freire, 1972, 81–82)

In relation to the concept of tolerance, Freire's concept is not very helpful, as it
is more involved in changing existing power structures, and does not focus on
promotion of a society with harmonious relations. Yet, if we take the Freirian
notion of dialogue as rebellion against an intolerant society, some of his ideas
could be applied to an education that promotes tolerance. In conclusion, Freire
introduces dialogue as a pedagogical relationship to enter rather than simply as
a method. In dialogue participants change existing [oppressive] power structures
by reflective encounter and mutual respect. Maybe one of the most important
issues in Freire's work for my purposes is the relevance of dialogue as a way to
turn a traditionalist educational context into a reconceptualist one, not to prepare
students to live in the world of yesterday, but to shape and live in the world of
tomorrow.

The second person I want to introduce is the philosopher **Hans-Georg
Gadamer** (1900–2002). Together with Freire, Gadamer argues that dialogue is
essential for human existence. For Freire, the aim is to transform the context in
which one lives. For Gadamer the aim is to transform one's own understandings. While Freire believes that dialogue is a means to give freedom to students,
Gadamer believes that dialogue is a means to understand the world around
oneself; he emphasises a dialogic structure of human understanding.

Gadamer presents an alternative concept of human knowledge to one found
in subjectivism as well in positivism, stressing that knowledge is not a fixed
entity to be grasped or something 'out there' waiting to be discovered; neither is
it an arbitrary unit. Rather, it is an aspect of a process that arises from interaction. Each human person has her or his own 'horizon of understanding', which
always includes prejudices. Gadamer applied the notion of horizon, as 'the
range of vision that can be seen from a particular vantage point', to the mind.
Doing this he points to the fact that understanding is always limited, but it is
possible to speak about the broadness of one's horizon. If it is small, then understanding is limited to what is nearest (Gadamer, 1975, 269). The prejudicial

character of understanding means that, whenever we understand, we are involved in a dialogue that encompasses both our own self-understanding and our understanding of the matter at issue. Prejudices, in Gadamer's view, work as prerequisites or building blocks in the everlasting process of creating new interpretations of reality.

An encounter with other understandings is essential in building up one's own understanding. In dialogical encounter with the other, one tries to relate the horizon of the other to his or her own horizon and to put one's own understandings under scrutiny. Gadamer sees a conversation as opening up oneself to the other person:

> "*A conversation is a process of two people understanding each other. Thus it is characteristic of every true conversation that each opens himself to the other person, truly accepts his point of view as worthy of consideration...*" (Gadamer, 1975, 347)

By such an encounter a person's understandings become intelligible and more complex, without necessarily having to agree with the other (Gadamer 1975, 270).

One of the reasons Gadamer has a special relevance for dealing with religious issues and for religious pedagogy, is his positive evaluation of the role of authority and tradition as legitimate sources of knowledge. Dialogue is not only a question of the present moment, it is a continuum. Inasmuch as understanding always arises against the background of our prior involvement, it always occurs on the basis of our history. Gadamer sees dialogue as having a dimension of 'dialogue with a tradition', the encounter with the past and the understanding of the tradition to which one belongs. Meaning-making is continually combining old and new understandings, a fusion of horizons within a person (Gadamer 1975, 273).

Freire and Gadamer both argue for the need of change in understandings, but Freire sees prior understandings as prisoners and as manifestations of oppressive power structures to be freed by dialogue; for Gadamer the past can be a building block for the transformation of understandings. If Freire's approach is revolutionary, then Gadamer's approach is transforming and better suited to promote active tolerance, as it takes seriously history and other people, as well as one's own presuppositions. It is an open-minded enquiry which is based on and promotes tolerance and tries to widen horizons by taking others' views as worthy of consideration. Thus, not every conversation is dialogue, according to Gadamer; but genuine dialogues promote active tolerance. Dialogue is a three-fold enterprise, consisting of exploration of one's own horizons of understanding, that of the other(s) and that of the phenomenon.

A working definition of 'dialogue' for the purpose of this research is developed from Hans-Georg Gadamer (1975), but also incorporates and applies the more practice-centred ideas of William Isaacs (1999) and David Bohm (1997). Dialogue is understood here as a joint exploration of thinking towards wider horizons of understanding of oneself, each other and the phenomenon under examination. It is a shared inquiry and a means to explore assumptions, meaning and social effects, where new forms of understanding may emerge. In this sense dialogue consists of three components: exploration of one's own ideas; discovery of the ideas of another human being; and examination of the subject. Such a definition does not demand final agreement and even does not have to be 'soft', and may involve conflicting issues; controversial topics are not simply put aside as unsuitable. Dialogue is not opposed to conflict, but rather to monologue or silence.

In the analysis I distinguish among several aims of dialogue:

- a debate which attempts to prove a view is right or more correct;
- an aspiration to understand each other, find meaning in what is said;
- a search for common ground, readiness to change one's own point of view.

The last two forms of dialogue are not aimed at reaching 'the right solution' but recognize dialogue as an ever-changing way to understand oneself and reality, rather than as a purposive attempt to express some viewpoint(s).

1.2.3 Religious Education

Religious education can be seen as a wide concept, including religious education given in the organisations of the faith communities or in families (*Religionspädagogik* in German). In this book I use the term 'religious education' as a subject focusing on religious issues, as taught in the context of publicly funded and private schools (*Religionsunterricht* in German). But even given the context of school, the subject can be understood very differently. In the following I will discuss the terminological debate about 'religious education'. The classification of the subject 'religious education' as taught in Estonia is presented in the second section in the course of my description of religious education in Estonia.

There are three possible ways to translate 'religious education' into Estonian: *'usuõpetus'*, *'usundiõpetus'* and *'religiooniõpetus'*. The first is used in the Estonian legislative acts for the subject. The first part of the compound *'usuõpetus'* comes from the word *'usk'*, what can be translated as 'belief', 'faith' or 'religion'. In the Estonian language, words easily make up compounds and thus can have certain connotations. The word *'usk'* is used in everyday life as synonymous with religion (*'islami usk'* = 'Islam', *'ristiusk'* = 'Christianity'), but also for trust in oneself (*'eneseusk'*). It can be loaded with negative meaning for a generation raised in the Soviet era – a religious fanatic is always *'usuhull'* or *'usufanaatik'*, never *'religioonihull'*. Other words with negative connotations are used with the word: '*kergeusklik*' = 'credulous', '*ebausk*' = 'superstition'. The word itself has no negative connotation *per se*, but the reason is that it is just the most common and oldest word used. For example, theological faculty is '*usuteaduskond*', theology is '*usuteadus*', co-follower of a religion is '*usuvend*' or '*usuõde*'. The word '*usuõpetus*' ('religious education') can be easily understood as '*usu õpetus*' – 'teaching to believe' (Valk, 2002b, 28) and thus has strong connotations of indoctrination.

Many schools and teachers of religious education prefer the term '*religiooniõpetus*'. Indeed, the Association for Teachers of Religious Education has recently changed its name accordingly. '*Religioon*' is a foreign word, used mainly in scientific language and it is more connected to 'world religions'. '*Religioon*' seems to have a less negative connotation in general. Some evangelical Christian movements which stress the need for a personal relationship with God use the word as an antonym to the right way of believing, as an outwardly and formal way of performing rituals.

The third option, '*usundiõpetus*', is used in the new (draft) syllabus. '*Usund*' is used for world religions, but also for indigenous religions. The term is very similar to '*religioon*'. It is not usually used for personal religion, but shows some distance; '*usundilugu*', for example, means 'history of religion'. '*Usundiõpetus*' thus reflects an emphasis on world religions and on the impersonal 'information' aspect of the syllabus for religious education.

A similar difficulty can be seen also in the ambiguity of the English term 'religious education' – is it education for being more religious? Is it religiously taught education? Or does it have some other meaning? Alternative names for the subject have been proposed and/or used. Some of them try to resolve the ambiguity of the adjective in the phrase 'religious education' by replacing it with an alternative, as in the use in South Africa of the term 'religion education' (Chidester, 2002). Some other alternative terms stress its inclusive character as in 'integrative religious education' (Alberts, 2007). Some official documents have used the term which could be used for wide variety of education about religion, including education on these issues in history, literature and other subjects, as in 'teaching about religions and beliefs' (OSCE, 2007) and 'education about religions and beliefs' (Alliance of Civilizations, 2009). Some commentators feel that such terms put too much stress on knowledge and give little space for personal development. The name can stress also the wider framework of intercultural education as in 'the religious dimension of intercultural education' (Council of Europe, 2004). The terminology about the subject, particularly in relation to the Estonian debate, will be considered in more detail in section 2.2.3.

1.3 Methodology

In this chapter I will discuss the methodological framework of and methods used for my study. Both 'philosophical' and 'technical' decisions are discussed here, as they were interdependent. The arguments behind selecting methods for data collection and data analysis are discussed here, while samples are discussed in more detail at the beginning of the corresponding sections (3–5) in order to make a more direct link for the interpretation of data.

First I will explain the wider epistemological framework in which the study took place, showing how this framework has influenced my understanding of data and the stance I took as a researcher. Then I will discuss the methods of data collection and describe briefly how the data analysis was undertaken. The timeline for the research will also be presented. Finally the ethical issues concerning the study will be discussed.

1.3.1 Methodological framework

1.3.1.1 Mixed methods' approach

The research was done in the framework of constructive epistemology and a sequential exploratory strategy (Creswell, 2003) was applied for a mixed methods approach. The views of young people on religion and religious diversity are interwoven with the value systems held in school, society and in youth culture and influenced by developmental issues, and there is also an interrelation between educational and personal interests. Such a complexity requires using varied methods in order to triangulate the outcomes from several pieces of research. The need for this approach has been pointed out by Campbell (1957) and more recently by Creswell (2002), Flick (2004), and Niglas (2004). For me, as a novice researcher, it has been a challenge to deal with such an overwhelming amount of data. However, each set of methods was appropriate to the studies, and the triangulation of data has increased the reliability and validity of the findings. The findings obtained through different instruments could be compared and triangulated. In some cases different studies have provided illustration or clarification, and in other cases raised questions or added information to the findings of different sub-studies. A mixed methods approach has enabled me also to fine-tune instruments of data collection (as described in section 1.3.2).

1.3.1.2 The framework of social constructivism

By relying on a social constructivist approach, I cannot assume that the data gathered during the study consists of given facts; data result from social interaction, during which meanings are constructed and reconstructed (see Blumer (1986), Searle (1995), Gergen (2002), Burr (2003)). In the framework of social constructivism the person cannot be seen as separated from his or her context. In interviews, the interviewees opposed, for example, the critique raised against religious education, even though I did not ask about these topics directly. They brought thoughts, dilemmas, emphases and controversies from their daily discourses at school or in the media. However, the interaction of thoughts works not only between the context and the person, but also between the interviewee and interviewer; data are often created during the interviewing process, as scholars such as Garfinkel (1967), Cicourel (1974), Silvermann (1993), Alasuutari (1995) and Holstein and Gubrium (2002) have pointed out. In several interviews, respondents said explicitly that they had not thought about the issue before, which does not mean that they did not have an opinion. They constructed their meanings during and because of the interview, so the results were not ready-made constructions but the collaborative result of an interview.

Similarly, just as meaning is constructed by mutual influence, the object of study cannot be separated from the analysis. Data are always results of interpretations in constructivist epistemology.

Positioning of the researcher

I positioned myself as a 'stranger' (Simmel, 2002), without identifying myself with any group in the school (i.e., teachers, students, staff). This enabled me to move between various groups without having superordinate or subordinate relations to any of them and to have also an emic perspective gained from participants and a more distanced and analytical etic perspective as well (Pike 1967; Headland et al. 1990). This allowed me, as the researcher, as well as the participants, to look at situations from another perspective. I presented myself and approached lessons from the perspective of a university researcher, and did not claim to be able to blend into the group of students as the difference in age was too obvious. Moreover, I found it impossible to identify more with children than with adults, although I could still empathize with the way in which students were thinking. My role as a researcher could not be defined as a non-participant, given that mine and the camera's presence, unofficial, informal talks before and after lessons, and official interviews inevitably had some influence. For example, by asking students and teachers about the way in which they or others behaved in class, I forced them to analyse and verbalise their behaviours and their impact on others. In this sense, I was not a person who simply collected data, but rather one who participated in creating the 'reality' under study. Such 'subjectivity' as part of the research process is an advantage of qualitative study. To be subjective does not in this case mean presenting unreflective presuppositions, but rather reveals as much argument as possible to support the conclusions and to give others the opportunity to refute them (Pink, 2001).

1.3.1.3 The interpretive approach as a stimulus

Within this constructivist framework I used the interpretive approach, as worked out by Robert Jackson (1997), as a stimulus and a means to reflect on the processes of my research. Three key concepts, as described below, assisted in clarification of issues in theory, methodology and pedagogy. The approach was seen in terms of questions to be reviewed throughout the research.

The interpretive approach was initially developed during ethnographic studies of children and young people (e.g. Jackson & Nesbitt, 1993; Nesbitt, 2004). The interpretive approach draws on methodological ideas from cultural anthropology, recognising the inner diversity, fuzzy edgedness and contested nature of religious traditions. Individuals are seen as unique, but the group tied nature of religion is recognised, also the role of wider religious traditions providing identity markers and reference points is recognised.

The interpretive approach, as described by Robert Jackson (1997; 2004a; 2004b; 2005; 2008a and elsewhere) is equipped with three issues, – the representation of religions in their inner diversity, developing skills of interpretation and providing opportunities for reflexivity. How these principles influenced my methods is discussed more in detail in the following section (1.3.2). Here I will present briefly the most important principles used in my study, derived from the interpretive approach.

The first principle is concerned with **representation**: this means seeing religions as a part of living human experience which responds to the present context and develops throughout the lifetime (as opposed to the idea of unchangeable, homogeneous and uniform systems of belief). Representation involves also understanding that religions are represented by unique members, who are affected by many influences, both cultural and personal. Often, these individuals, although unique, belong to groups of various kinds (such as sects, denominations, or ethnic groups), and group membership may be very influential on the individual, for example as a source of concepts and attitudes. The broadest reference point is the religious tradition, with its multiple sources of authority. Religious identity may be analysed in terms of the relationship between unique individuals, groups and the wider tradition. It is the analysis of the hermeneutical relationship between individuals, groups and the wider religious traditions that brings religious material, as it were, to life. Jackson's discussion of this way of looking at religions led to the formulation of a number of questions which were very useful to me and other researchers in the REDCo Project.

The questions under this section I asked myself included: How well am I portraying the way of life of those I am studying so that I avoid misrepresentation and stereotyping? Am I giving sufficient attention to diversity within religions? How far am I aware of the perceived relationship (or lack of relationship) of individuals studied to the background religious and cultural traditions? (Jackson suggests how the key principles of the interpretive approach might be expressed as a set of questions in Jackson, 2008a, 9). In my study I paid attention to the inclusion of different perspectives and respondents with diverse cultural and personal backgrounds. The respondents were viewed as unique individuals, not only in their social context, but also in relation to time, which means that in another situation and time they might answer in another way than they did at the moment of my study. Different parties of the study contributed different perspectives and created a mosaic of readings. In school-based fieldwork, interviews were used to reconstruct students' personal approaches to religion. Classroom interaction was also studied from the perspective of the learners and teachers. To avoid misinterpretation I decided to include interviews and to use the method of stimulated recall for analysing videotaped lessons. This gave voice to the interpretations of those involved in lessons.

The second principle is concerned with **interpretation**: this means understanding that I (in this case as a researcher) cannot set aside my own presuppositions, but rather should compare them constantly with new concepts gathered from the fieldwork. The questions under this section I asked myself included: How well am I 'translating' the other person's concepts and ideas (or comparing the other person's language/concepts with my own nearest equivalent language/concepts) so I have a clear understanding of them? How far am I able to empathise with the experience of others after I have grasped their language/concepts/symbols? Have I considered the impact of power relations on processes of interpretation? (Jackson, 2008a, 9) This aspect had a central role in influencing my specific data collection methods and methods of analysis as well as the interview techniques I used, which required explanations and arguments from respondents, not only in the phase of data collection but also through their feedback during data analysis. The religious language used by those whom I was studying was at the centre of my concern. In the first phase of the fieldwork the key term 'religion' was not imposed on respondents; instead they were asked about their views and understandings. During interviews, possible interpretations of understanding were asked from each interviewee (*"Did I understand correctly that you meant ..."*).

The third principle is concerned with **reflexivity**: this means being self-aware in relation to the data, being both sensitive to the meanings expressed by others and maintaining critical distance towards my own thinking and the material under study. The questions in this section included: How far am I aware of the impact of my own cultural background/values and beliefs/gender/ research role/power etc. on the research process or development of pedagogical ideas? How far am I relating the data of the research to my own current understandings of difference? How far am I giving attention to the evaluation of my research methods? (Jackson, 2008a, 10). A combination of ethnographic and educational approaches to religious education, bringing together hermeneutical and empirical methods, and starting from the qualitative study of views about religious diversity, made space for a reflexive analysis of material and methods used. Reflexive activity is intimately related to the process of interpretation. To ensure reflexivity, I first "interviewed" myself on the topics covered in the interviews, to become aware of my own presuppositions and ideas. Then these were compared and contrasted with those of interviewees. The students who were videotaped and the teachers who were interviewed were asked to distance themselves and to reflect upon their own views, ideas and values as seen on the videotape or experienced in their lessons.

1.3.2 Methods of data collection and data analyses

During the project the strong need for using a combination of qualitative and quantitative methods (see above section 1.3.1) was felt and found to be valuable. Qualitative methods facilitated an understanding of the meanings and patterns of thinking of people under study, while quantitative methods gave some grounds for generalizations from patterns that emerged.

1.3.2.1 Views of students: qualitative study

Views of students. First I was interested in gaining insight into the role of religion in the lives of young people – how do they speak about religion in their own lives, about their contacts with religion and their views about religion at school? I wanted to study their vocabulary and the attitudes they expressed towards religion. Not much is known about the views of people younger than 16 on these issues. In order to study the significance of religion in the perception of young people, we addressed both individual and societal domains of religion and additionally paid attention to the question of religion at school and as a source of conflict or dialogue in human relations.

Our fieldwork always contained several steps which enabled me to fine-tune the methods. As we did not want to impose our own views on students but to investigate their thoughts, we started always with qualitative methods. The study about the views held by students was conducted in three steps. It started from extended individual interviews with students from one school, each about 20–45 minutes long. This gave an opportunity to grasp the way students think about religion in their school-life and relationships with others, but also to learn how they understood the questions. In the second phase of study, semi-structured written interviews with open questions, gave space for authentic reactions from the young people and opened up ways to grasp a large diversity of ideas. The third phase investigated the spread of these views in a bigger sample.

The first phase was a pilot study and consisted of eight in-depth oral interviews, with two boys and six girls, with and without experience of religious education and also with different home backgrounds in relation to religion. We took the decision to use semi-structured interviews, where the interview items guide the interviewer flexibly through the discussion with the interviewee. Open questions were used to create opportunities for authentic reactions from the interviewees. They helped to get an insight into how students think about religion. Given the space for further questions and explanations, some hidden aspects emerged, which would not have been revealed in a written interview.

The next question was whether to conduct group or individual interviews. Group interviews can stimulate students to consider thoughts that they would not have been aware of and so would enrich answers. However, there is a danger of group-pressure during a group interview. Some of the views can remain unarticulated and the responses would lose their individual nature. As Estonians tend to be very sensitive about religion, I decided to conduct individual interviews. This decision caused some inequality in terms of 'power' in the interview situation – as an adult researcher interviewing students. I tried to minimise the effects of this by choosing a time and place outside of the normal school routine, at the end of summer holiday in an informal environment. Such a decision proved to be fruitful and the young people spoke in a candid and open way.

The findings of the first phase profited me in two ways – they enabled me to understand some of the young people's perceptions of religion and religious diversity. They also helped with the main task for this phase of research which was to find ways to make improvements to the questions for written interviews in order to make them more intelligible for the young people. After oral interviews, different types of questions were formulated. Five 15-years olds were asked to complete them and to comment on the questions. The answers were compared to those of similar pilot studies in Germany, Norway and France. The questions were changed to make them more understandable and relevant for the age group. The final questionnaire, which is presented in more detail at the beginning of section 3, consisted of eight open questions, and was standardised for all eight countries to make the results comparable.

The aim of the second phase was to collect the views of students whose spectrum of opinions about religion would be as diverse as possible. Therefore the written interview was used to reach students from three schools since it would have been impossible, given the limited financial resources, to do this by means of oral interview. To obtain a wide variety of opinions I included Russian and Estonian medium schools, students who had studied religious education and those who had not. I introduced the research, its aims and participating countries to the students, and the students were encouraged to contribute to the research by answering frankly, providing examples if possible. Respondents could complete the questionnaires in either Estonian or Russian, depending on their choice and language of studies. As many young people were familiar with the use of computers, the option to use an internet-based questionnaire was offered. Two schools did not have an available computer room and students wrote using pen and paper. In one school students had the possibility to answer the questions via the internet. The qualitative questionnaire (Appendices 1–2) was completed by 73 students.

The answers of students who used the internet were longer and they had more explanations for their choices. It must be admitted that the oral interviews yielded more interesting and richer answers than written ones, where some of the responses tended to be very brief, such as: *"No"*, *"Can't say"*, *"Hard to remember"*. The reasons, in part, could be that students regarded writing responses as a boring and tiring thing to do or that the students just did not fully understand words but were afraid to reveal their ignorance. However, compared to oral face-to-face interviews, the written form gave more anonymity and freedom to decline to answer questions that students regarded as too personal (see also section 1.3.4 "Ethical issues"). Abstract questions gave space for different answers and interpretations but did not give an opportunity for students with more concrete thinking to answer at all. If the students had some basic knowledge of using computers, the option to use internet-based questionnaires should be offered to them. In future abstract and general questions could be combined with more concrete requests for reflection on a given situation.

Both oral and written interviews with students and teachers were analysed using similar methods. In the analysis I acknowledged that while my interpretation of the responses could not give an objective and comprehensive picture of reality, I would not be able to reach all the thoughts a respondent had on a topic; the data resulted from a process of social construction, often created in the course of interviewing, and open to changes.

Analysis of qualitative interviews looked for inner categories and ideas emerging from the interactions, using open coding methodology adopted from grounded theory (Strauss & Corbin, 1990). I took a 'bottom-up' perspective, starting analysis with the individual meaning of a sentence, then seeing it in the context of other answers given by the same respondent, moving to the context of school and then to the ethnic context. Following the agreed guidelines for data analysis, I analysed question by question focusing on similarities and differences. For finding these features I grouped codes found from the answers under key categories and identified the topics of interest to the research (dialogue, conflict, studying religion). In presenting my findings I illustrated the main patterns of meaning by using revealing quotations that would enable the reader to assess the relevance of my conclusions.

The second phase allowed an analytic insight into the problem under investigation, conceptualised as case studies, giving a focused snapshot of specific settings but not, of course, having validity as a national survey.

1.3.2.2 Views of students: the quantitative study

Data with more generalizability were needed to answer the research question. A questionnaire for the quantitative study was developed by using results and quotations from qualitative interviews and two steps of pre-tests. There was a pre-pre-test with 5 students to assist in the development of the quantitative study, and an additional group interview was conducted. Feedback on students' impressions was given to the team developing the quantitative questionnaire with comments on questions which students found difficult to understand and recommendations for lay-out. A pre-test for the quantitative study was carried out with 62 students and feedback on their impressions and their perception of the term 'religion' was given to the team designing the quantitative questionnaire. These included confusing items and recommendations for cuts. Because of the limited resources available, we had to utilize non-probability sampling methods, using purposive or judgemental sampling with certain criteria (Babbie, 2008, 204). Although the sample was not representative, it is still significant and rational and the findings have some degree of generalizability. Although the qualitative study had a value in its own right, the quantitative research also aimed to find how much the views found in the qualitative study could be generalised (Cohen et al. 2007, 142–144). On the basis of the answers given in the qualitative study, we chose quotations for statements in the quantitative study and students had to decide the degree to which they agreed or disagreed with their European peers. In the Estonian sample, 1367 students altogether, 1208 of them who were aged 14–16 years, from 21 schools participated in the main survey of the quantitative study. Similarly to other phases of fieldwork, students were encouraged to participate in the research by giving honest answers and taking advantage of the possibility to use space at the end of the questionnaire for further explanations behind their choices.

There were three main research questions for the quantitative study, each of which could be broken down into sub-questions.

What role does religion have in students' life? How important is religion for young people in personal terms, and is it consistent with their religious affiliation and religious practices? What attitudes towards religion do students have? How visible is it in their relations? How much do they have dialogue on religious issues and with whom? What reasons do they give for speaking about religion or for avoiding the topic? What are the main sources of information about religion? What variables reveal the differences on these issues?

How do students consider the impact of religions on human relations and society? Is religion seen rather as a source of conflict or a factor in building peace? What strategies do they value most in building peace between people with different worldviews?

How do students see religion in school and the impact of religion in education? What forms of religious education are appreciated by students? How far do they value education on religious issues provided by school? What do they value and what would they change? What differences are there between people with experience of different models or religious education?

We also developed hypotheses based on the qualitative study about tolerance and openness to dialogue according to religion and encounter with religious diversity at school and in everyday life. These are as follows:

1.a Religious students are less tolerant than non-religious students.

1.b Religious students are less open to dialogue on religious issues than non-religious students.

2.a Students who have encountered religious diversity in education are more tolerant.

2.b Students who have encountered religious diversity in education are more open to dialogue on religious issues.

The final version of the questionnaire used for the research was worked out by the team responsible for quantitative research and translated according to translation guidelines into the Estonian and Russian languages (the questionnaires in English, Estonian and Russian are given in Appendices 3–5).

1.3.2.3 Classroom interaction

To answer the research question it was not sufficient to use interviews and questionnaires but it was necessary also to look at what was actually going on in the classrooms. The aim of studying classroom interaction was to explore what potentials and limitations for dialogue could be identified in students' interaction at school in the context of religious education in Estonia. Classroom interaction in two contrasting schools is presented in the book. For better understanding, and in order to apply questions related to the 'representation' element of the interpretive approach, group-interviews with students by means of stimulated recall and semi-structured interviews with teachers were used.

The video-ethnographic method was utilised for data collection. In comparison to other methods, such as keeping diaries or audio recording lessons, videotaped material offers many advantages, especially in the precision and reproducibility of the information obtained. Instead of paraphrasing the contents of the lesson, videotaped material allows for precise transcriptions. In addition, video recordings enabled me to look at the events several times, each time concentrating on a single aspect of communication (such as mimicry, body language, tone of voice, movement, class arrangement, and acts of speech) and to incorporate them into the analysis of classroom interaction.

Certain technical decisions such as the type of camera(s) to use, place and time to videotape, and the perspective of the camera had to be made before the fieldwork started. Such technical decisions also influenced the information gained and shaped the analysed reality. Even before videotaping a series of decisions had to be made: should the study use many cameras or one and should professional or 'amateur' cameras be used; should the whole day be recorded or just a lesson or an incident; and should the focus of the video be on teachers or students (also in Henley, 2001)?

The first decision related to how to use a camera – as a facilitator of events (as, e.g., Rouch, 1995 or Denzin, 1989 see it) or in such a way so as to minimise the effect it may have on students? As the research aim was to explore patterns of interaction in *statu nascendi*, not to investigate the effects of the camera, the decision was made to reduce the camera's possible effects. Prior to videotaping, I visited classrooms without the camera in order to be able to compare lessons with and without the presence of the camera. In order to minimise the effects of the camera on the behaviour of teachers and students, I stood in a corner and used a small amateur camera. In addition, to minimise side effects, only one researcher was present in the classroom and I did not move around with the camera in the class as a rule so as not to interfere with the lesson.

In order to check the effects of the presence of the camera and myself, I asked students to comment on how the lesson differed from others and how the camera affected their behaviour. It was a surprise both for me and also for the students that they felt that the camera did not bring about major effects on their usual behaviour, except some students sometimes glanced towards the camera. It is unlikely that that the camera did not have any effect but, it seems plausible that the camera did not affect the behavioural patterns and the attitudes of students and teachers during their normal lessons. Some students reported that they hesitated more to volunteer with an answer in early lessons where the camera was present, but they forgot the presence of the camera quickly when they were involved in discussions. For others the presence of the camera made them sometimes flirt with it (eye contact with the camera), controlling their behaviour; as one student declared in an interview: "*I would not start to pick my nose*". The way students communicated was not influenced by the camera, according to students and teachers and my own observation.

As I was interested in the dialogue from the students' perspective, the camera was focused on students' interactions. Such a decision made it possible to follow the students' perspective, but it concealed some other aspects, such as teachers' movements and facial expressions. The reality was reproduced only partly and was most useful when teacher-centred methods[2] were applied. For example, in one of the schools, a significant amount of group work was used; consequently, it was not possible to obtain information on different groups' work using one camera while standing in a corner. In addition, in other lessons, many side conversations could not be reconstructed, as only one or two microphones were used in the classroom. In order to hear all of the 'asides' and to determine what was going on in the groups, each student would have had to be fitted with a microphone, a procedure that was not feasible.

The video camera was placed at the front of the class, focused on the students. As it was clear from the preliminary video sessions that it was very difficult to understand students' speech from the back of class, an audio recorder was placed at the back of the class. This additional recorder not only helped to clarify what was said publicly, but also provided access to valuable information about students' side conversations.

In order to have several readings and a meta-perspective on the same text, group interviews with students using the method of stimulated recall were used. After a lesson a selected sequence was shown to a group of students and they were asked to comment on their thoughts, feelings and the lesson. The method of stimulated recall was initially described by Bloom (1953, 161) and developed by several researchers in educational (Cook 2007; Henderson & Tallman 2006; Polio et al. 2006; Lyle 2003; Gass & Mackey 2000; Knauth et al. 2000; O'Brien 1993; Meade & McMeniman 1992; etc) and medical (Skovdahl et al. 2004; Barrows 2000; Elstein et al. 1978; etc) research fields, as a method to revive the memories and mental modes of participants about an event under investigation.

The teachers were interviewed about their aims and interpretations of their motivations behind the decisions they made. The analysis was enlarged by different readings on the lesson from the different perspectives of the members of our international working group. These processes helped to make the data richer and the interpretation thicker.

The transcription of videotaped lessons (what to write down, what not) influences what researchers have as data. In my transcription, not all the move-

---

2   In the teacher-centred method of instruction, the focus of the class is on the teacher. Students listen as the teacher lectures; during interactions, the teacher plays a strong moderating role, and students speak to the teacher. Student-student conversations, if they exist, are mediated by the teacher.

ments, facial expressions and voice moods were written down but only those helping me to interpret or questioning my interpretation. Relevant elements were written down and their relevance was checked during analysis. In this respect the positivist goals of attempting to obtain general theories of patterns ever working at school were abandoned. I rather wanted to explore the patterns existing in some religious education lessons in a particular context which could contribute to an understanding of deeper structures of school life. I started from my subjective pre-understandings of the lesson and proceeded by reflective analysis of the lessons and any background information that was available.

For the first step, I watched the videotaped material several times (the description of schools, classes, and number of lessons is provided in section 3). During each viewing, I focused on a single aspect of the data and inserted codes found from these observations into tables: these covered content or topics under study, teaching-learning methods used, duration, types of questions and answers given, facial expressions, interactions, any increase and decrease of interest among students, and questions and remarks that arose while viewing the material (see Appendix 7; the codes used are presented in Table 7 and an example of coding is provided in Table 8). This method served as a tool to sharpen my attention and identify units that needed further investigation. The sequences found in such a way are called 'incident suspicious units'. Only if the selected unit revealed something of wider significance behind it in a way which helped to answer the research question, did I call it an 'incident', as described below.

In the second step, the selected units were examined in the light of the research question and classified as 'incidents', a term coined by Knauth in identifying hidden aspects and structures – the 'tips of the icebergs'.

"Incidents are phenomena in the course of interaction. They represent structures which are lying under the surface of interaction." (Knauth, 2007)

Incidents are surprising, sometimes critical events and, most importantly, they are crystallisations of a problem which is related to the basic question of the research.

On the basis of Knauth's definition of an 'incident', I looked for hidden aspects representing the overall structure of interaction and pedagogical context, in relation to dialogue, that appeared or were hindered in the classroom context. A working definition of 'dialogue', as described in the section on terminology (1.2.3), was used here as an analytical tool for finding incidents. All incidents were identified and transcribed.

1.3.3 The time schedule of the research

The research conducted within the framework of the REDCo project was extensive, and the various studies proceeded in an agreed order. In the first year of the study we looked through the literature and started with hermeneutical reflection on historical, legal and contextual elements for religious education and religious diversity in Estonia (Valk, 2007b). My role in this early stage was as a supervisor for several students in the Theological Faculty of the University of Tartu who carried out content analysis of religion in the school textbooks and syllabuses. I organised and tutored the team in developing tools for research and fine-tuned their methods according to the subject under study, taking account of studies in other subject fields. These included Danilson (2007a; 2007b) who studied different textbooks on literature, Jansen-Mann (2007) and Laks (2007) who studied textbooks on history, Põder (2007) who studied textbooks on civic education and Uibopuu (2007) who studied textbooks on philosophy.

Starting from August 2006 I had sole responsibility for carrying out fieldwork in schools and continued to March of 2008. During the second semester of 2006 I conducted semi-structured oral and written interviews with students and fieldwork recording classroom interaction in one of the schools under study. I interviewed students and had informal talks with teachers. During the first semester of 2007 I conducted the fieldwork in the second school. In the second semester of 2007 I conducted semi-structured interviews with teachers, which are not presented in this book. In June 2007 I conducted the pre-pre-test of the quantitative study on the views of young people about religions, religious diversity and the role of school, followed by the pre-test in September 2007 and the main survey in January-March 2008.

1.3.4 Ethical issues

Throughout the research special attention was paid to ethical considerations. The Estonian Scientists' Code of Ethics (paragraph 2.6) states that a study must not violate the dignity of the participants; it must inform participants about the aims of the study, and must ask for their permission to participate in the research (Aavik et al. 2007, 224). Information should be stored confidentially. I adhered to these principles fully in conducting the research. In addition I adhered to protocols recommended in the international literature on empirical social research. These were as follows:

No harm to participants. Social research should never injure the people being studied, regardless of whether they volunteer to participate in the study or not. Speaking about religion is considered a very personal topic by many Estonians, and this was one of the reasons why I chose written, anonymous interviews instead of oral ones. During oral interviews special attention was paid to body language and verbal signs of the respondents to avoid crossing the individual barriers of confidentiality of the respondent. In wording questions for questionnaires, special care was taken to avoid the questions which would encourage labelling any groups. For example, in some research studies participants are asked to choose adjectives for special groups (e.g. Muslims, Buddhists, Christians, and Atheists). Such questions and tasks were felt by our research team not only as encouraging stereotyping, but also harmful for participants themselves, who could be offended by such tasks. Several respondents, after filling the questionnaire, stated that such documents could support the self-esteem of religious students who often feel marginalised at school. At the same time, many students without a religious background were annoyed by having to answer so many questions about a topic that they considered irrelevant to their lives.

As mentioned before, some students did not want to be videotaped during a lesson. They were not excluded from the lesson. They still participated in class, but were located outside of camera range.

The students and teachers were not only subjects of the study, but also active participants in the research. In order to have several readings and meta-perspectives on the same text, group interviews were conducted with students using the method of stimulated recall. After the lesson, selected sequences of the lesson were shown to a group of students, who were asked to comment on their thoughts, feelings, and on the lesson itself. The group interview using stimulated recall enabled students to reflect on the lesson and their patterns of interaction. The teachers were interviewed about the aims and interpretations of the reasons for the decisions they made during a stimulated recall session. In this way, as many participants stated, they thought that, far from being harmed by the research, they gained personal benefit from it by being able to reflect upon their own ways of acting and thinking and by being listened to and treated as worthwhile partners in the research. Every school in the quantitative study received personalised reports..

Voluntary participation. Students and teachers participating in the study were informed orally and in written form about the aims of the research and about their right to withdraw from it. Although the students did not take the opportunity to decline to fill in questionnaires, some of them withdrew from answering some of the questions. In addition, regarding the right to withdraw from the research, not only students, but also their parents were asked for permission of their children to be videotaped during the lessons.

Anonymity and confidentiality. In written interviews and questionnaires no names were requested, so both the people who read about research and I were not able to identify people from their answers. In reporting the data, codes were used to denote people and to give some background information about them.

Confidentiality was guaranteed for persons who were interviewed and video-taped by using pseudonyms (either chosen by themselves or by me). Although some efforts were made (by using codes) to avoid identification of the schools that participated in the study, it was not always possible to guarantee anonymity. For understanding the contextual setting of the qualitative research it was necessary to provide some background information about the schools. In a country as small as Estonia, it is possible for the teachers who participated in the research, and others who are curious, to identify which schools were used. The issue was discussed with the participants and they gave their permission to use and publish the data.

Before I move on to give a detailed account of the empirical studies, it is necessary to provide some contextual background about the Estonian religious and educational landscape. This will give valuable information for understanding and interpreting the empirical results. In the next section I will present the main characteristics of religious education embodied in the Estonian religious landscape and educational framework.

2. RELIGIOUS EDUCATION IN ESTONIA

In this section I will give the socio-political and legislative background of religious education in Estonia. I will begin with a description of the ethnic and religious composition of the Estonian population. In the following section I will explain the essentials of compulsory education, the legislative framework for religious education and will describe the status of teachers in general and of religious education teachers in particular. The reader will then be able to understand the status of religious education within the general education system. Interested readers can find a history of religious education in Estonia in the masters and doctoral theses of Pille Valk (1997; 2002b). The section on contemporary developments gives special attention to the recent debates over religious education in Estonia. I will present the aims, status and challenges to religious education in Estonia. I will also put the subject into the wider European context of religious education.

2.1 Background factors for religious education

When Estonia gained independence in 1920, a new model of religious education was introduced and Estonia became one of the first countries with a model of non-confessional religious education. The subject made a clear distinction between religious education in schools and catechesis in churches and included learning about world religions (Valk, 1997). Nevertheless, the major content was Christianity, with an emphasis on moral development and cultural heritage. Bible stories were presented from a non-confessional perspective, in an attempt to do justice to different denominations. Although religious education was voluntary, almost all students took the courses. Under the Soviet regime (1940–late 1980s) all religious instruction in schools was prohibited and in some places courses on scientific atheism were introduced. The restoration of independence in the early 1990s presented a new opportunity for religious education. The interrupted tradition of religious education stood between several forces: its historical roots – such as textbooks for religious education translated from Finnish (confessional learning resources, some of which were sometimes adjusted for the Estonian situation) and a rather sceptical view about the need for any religious education from many people, as will be seen in the following section.

2.1.1 The ethnic and religious landscape of Estonia

Estonia, as a gateway between East and West, has been a battleground between different forces for centuries. Danish, German, Swedish and Russian rulers have left their political and cultural impacts on the country. The first schools in

Estonia for non-Estonians were established in 1251 in cathedrals by German and Danish Crusaders. Lutheranism established itself in Estonia in the 1520s and under its influence the first schools for Estonians were established in 1545. During the following Swedish rule (middle of the 16th century to the beginning of the 18th century) the Lutheran Church had the status of state church. One cornerstone of Lutheranism was literacy, so that anyone would be able to read the Bible. The network of public schools that emerged by the end of the 17th century was in this sense a child of the Lutheran church, being to some extent an expansion of the confirmation school, in which religious education had a central role.

Russian communities, mainly consisting of traders and religious and political dissidents, have lived in Estonia for the last 1000 years (Estonian Institute, 1997). Many immigrants from the Russian empire made their home in Estonia from the 18th century, when the country fell under Russian rule. Prior to the Second World War, Russian communities in Estonia were small. After 1945, Soviet Russification dramatically altered the social and demographic landscape of Estonia. Estonia's 1.3 million inhabitants now comprise two large ethnic groups and more than 100 small minority groups. Today about one-third of Estonia's population consists of immigrants from the former Soviet Union, or their descendants. Most of them settled in Estonia during the Soviet period. According to the censuses of 1934 and 2000, the percentage of non-Estonians has grown from 12% to 31% (Riigi Statistika Keskbüroo, 1935, 47–53 and http://pub.stat.ee/). According to data from 2008, Estonians make up 69% of the total population;[3] Russians are the second-largest group at 26%. Other minority groups are much smaller: Ukrainians (2%), Byelorussians and Finns (both about 1%), and others each under 1%. On a regional basis, however, the composition of ethnic groups varies remarkably. In some north-eastern towns of Estonia the proportion of the Russian speaking population is almost 80%. Most of them are ethnically Russians but some people from other ethnic groups may use Russian as their first language as well. In contrast, on the Estonian islands, Russian speakers comprise only 1–2% of the population (Table 1). There are more people with a migration background living in Tallinn and the north-east of Estonia: 69% Russians and 20% Estonians live in Ida-Viru, while 93% Estonians and 4% Russians live in Viljandi county.

From the 11th century Estonia was under the influence of the Catholic Church. In the 16th century, Estonia became a Lutheran country. A significant movement towards the Orthodox Church took place during a crop failure in the 19th century, when Estonian peasants were encouraged to convert to the Orthodox faith with promises made by the Russian empire for land and for the socio-economic improvement of the converts. There was neither ecclesiastical structure nor any detached diocese for the Orthodox Church in Estonia until 1919,

---

3   All the statistical data about Estonia are counted according to the information on the Web page of Statistics Estonia. (http://pub.stat.ee/, accessed 16.04.2009).

but all ecclesiastical administration depended on the Archbishop of Riga. Nevertheless, a significant number of Estonians belonged to the Orthodox Church. According to the second census in Estonia in 1934, 78% of Estonians were Lutherans, 19% were Orthodox and 1% had no religious affiliation (Riigi Statistika Keskbüroo, 1935, 118–121).

Table 1: Proportion of Estonian speaking population (%)

County	2.01.2008	County	2.01.2008
Harju	59.6%	Pärnu	87.6%
Hiiu	98.4%	Rapla	93.3%
Ida-Viru	19.7%	Saare	98.3%
Jõgeva	90.3%	Tartu	83.0%
Järva	93.5%	Valga	82.7%
Lääne	87.8%	Viljandi	94.3%
Lääne-Viru	85.2%	Võru	94.5%
Põlva	94.8%		
		Total Estonia	**68.7%**

Estonia's religious landscape changed dramatically during the last century. It is highly secularised today – only about 25–35% of the population define their religious affiliation according to different surveys made in Estonia (Statistical Office of Estonia, 2002; Halman et al., 2005; Liiman, 2001). However, religious affiliation, even if it does not mean belonging to a specific religious community, seems to be connected with ethnic identity. Lutherans are mainly Estonians, while Russians feel more commitment to the Orthodox Church. There are also parts of Estonia (especially Southern and Western Estonia, and some islands), where Estonians belong to the Orthodox Church. It is interesting to note that, according to some surveys, Russian speaking people in Estonia are more favourable to religion, and particularly Christianity, than Estonians (Hansen, 2002, 112).

A number of other churches and religious communities (Baptists, Roman-Catholics, Jehovah's Witnesses, Pentecostals, Old Believers, Adventists, Methodists, Muslims, Mormons and others), even if not numerous in terms of adherents, add diversity to Estonia's religious landscape. As with ethnic distribution, religious affiliation is not dispersed evenly in all counties (Figure 1). One of the reasons for this is the fact that Estonians are less affiliated to religion than other ethnic groups in Estonia. Harju and Ida-Viru, where many Russian speakers live, have more religiously affiliated people, especially Orthodox (Chart 1). Ida-Viru is 33% Orthodox with 6% Lutherans, but Rapla county is 22% Lutheran and 3% Orthodox. Although most of the Orthodox in Ida-Viru county are Russians, in Tartu, Pärnu and Põlva counties there are many Orthodox Estonians. One of the reasons for the higher proportion of believers, and especially Lutherans in Saare, Põlva and Võru counties, could be the long lasting influence of the Moravian Church in these regions (Ilja 2006, 237; Plaat, 2003, 9).

Figure 1: Proportion of religiously affiliated people in different counties

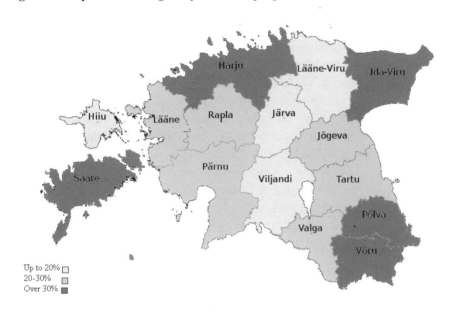

Up to 20% ☐
20-30% ☐
Over 30% ▓

Chart 1: Religious affiliation of the population of different counties

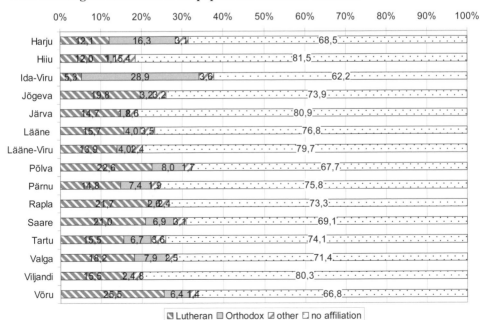

	Lutheran	Orthodox	other	no affiliation
Harju	12,1	16,3	3,1	68,5
Hiiu	12,0	1,1 5,4		81,5
Ida-Viru	5,3	28,9	3,6	62,2
Jõgeva	19,8	3,2 3,2		73,9
Järva	14,7	1,8 6		80,9
Lääne	15,7	4,0 3,5		76,8
Lääne-Viru	13,9	4,0 2,4		79,7
Põlva	22,6	8,0 1,7		67,7
Pärnu	14,8	7,4 1,9		75,8
Rapla	21,7	2,6 2,4		73,3
Saare	21,0	6,9 3,1		69,1
Tartu	15,5	6,7 3,6		74,1
Valga	18,2	7,9 2,5		71,4
Viljandi	15,5	2,4 8		80,3
Võru	25,5	6,4 1,4		66,8

☑ Lutheran ☐ Orthodox ☑ other ☐ no affiliation

53

The low importance of religion does not occur only in terms of belonging, but is also mirrored in beliefs and values. The Euro barometer survey *Social Values, Science and Technology*, conducted at the beginning of 2005, shows Estonia to be the most sceptical country in Europe with regard to belief in the existence of God. Less than one out of five declared that they believed in God (16%). At the same time more than half of Estonians (54%) believed in a non-traditional concept as 'some sort of spirit or life force' (European Commission, 2005). The study conducted by Estonian researchers shows that, among students, religion is valued as the least important factor, with a readiness for globalisation as the next lowest in priority (Rüütel & Tiit, 2005).

Thus, in general terms, the Estonian people are rather distant from traditional religion, although religion plays a more important role for other ethnic groups in Estonia. Usually, more religiously affiliated people are found in border areas and fewer in central Estonia. These geographical factors needed to be taken into account when planning a sample for a survey on religious issues.

2.1.2 The legislative framework and *status quo* of religious education

In this section I will explain the legislative frameworks for religious education in Estonia. I will take a closer look at how schools have adopted these frameworks in organising religious education. I will also comment on teaching in general and on being a teacher of religious education in particular.

The Constitution of the Republic of Estonia declares that there is no state church in Estonia. Membership of the church or religious associations is voluntary; schools and churches are separated. The essentials of compulsory education in Estonia are regulated nationally, but the schools still have some freedom in developing their own profiles and curricula within a given framework. The Parliament (Riigikogu) approves the laws regulating education, through which the main directions of education policy and the principles of school organisation are defined. The organisation and general principles of the education system in Estonia are shaped by the Education Act of the Republic of Estonia (Riigi Teataja 1992, 12, 192).[4] This states that basic education is the minimum compulsory general education. Compulsory school attendance begins when the child reaches the age of seven. Basic school is divided into three stages of study: stage I – grades 1–3 (7–10 year olds); stage II – grades 4–6 (10–13 year olds); and stage III – grades 7–9 (13–16 year olds).

After graduating from basic school, students can attend an upper secondary school, a secondary vocational school, or enter a profession (Ministry of Educa-

---

4   The last reduction became effective on the 01.09.2009, Riigi Teataja I 2009, 2, 4, also available online at: http://www.riigiteataja.ee/ert/act.jsp?id=13198443 (accessed 07.09. 2009).

tion and Research, 2007, 5–6). Upper secondary school (Gymnasium) is not compulsory. The target group of my research was students in stage III or in their first year of the Gymnasium.

The Government of the Republic (Vabariigi Valitsus) decides the national strategies for education and approves the national curriculum, which provides a list of compulsory subjects with a syllabus and study time for each subject (Riigi Teataja I 2002, 20, 116). Religious education is not a compulsory subject, so there are only general guidelines, but no national syllabus. Schools have the freedom to develop their own curricula for electives.

Religious education is regulated by the Basic Schools and Upper Secondary Schools Act. Schools are obliged to organise religious education classes, if a minimum of 15 students or their parents in one school stage are interested in the subject (Riigi Teataja I 1999, 24, 358).[5] Parents have to give their consent for children younger than 15 to take religious education.

The enforcement of this legislation is complicated. There is no way to gauge interest in religious education. The schools do not have an obligation to introduce it; parents have to ask if a school would be interested in offering religious education. Since it takes some effort to find a teacher of religious education, only a few head teachers are interested. There are several other lapses in the legislative framework, which result in a lack of clear definition of the obligations of schools to find religious education teachers, leaving the status of the 'voluntary subject' open to interpretation (Valk 2007b, 170). There is no alternative subject to religious education; students who have chosen religious education may have an extra lesson at the end of the school day and sometimes must wait for an hour or two. Insufficient legal status for the subject, the shadow of the former Soviet ideology in people's attitudes, the lack of qualified teachers and the overloaded curriculum make the organisation of religious education at a school level very difficult.

The majority of students in Estonia acquire their knowledge, attitudes and views about religion much as French students do. They do this by studying religion in their history, civic education, and literature courses (Willaime, 2007; Beraud et al., 2009). According to the information from the official website of Estonian Ministry of Education and Research, in 2006–2007, when most of my fieldwork was carried out, Estonia had a total of 601 primary schools and upper secondary schools.[6] Only a few schools offered religious education, usually in primary classes or for a year in upper secondary school, according to a letter from the Ministry of Education and Research (Vaher, 2009). Having about 6% of schools with religious education and about 10% of classes in each of them having an option to take religious education, it can be calculated that fewer than 1% of all

5 Põhikooli ja gümnaasiumi Seadus [Basic Schools and Upper Secondary Schools Act] available online at: https://www.riigiteataja.ee/ert/act.jsp?id=77246 (accessed 21.04.2009).
6 http://www.hm.ee/index.php?048055 (accessed 20.02.2008)

students in Estonia can take religious education classes, even if they wish to do so.

According to official statistics the number of schools offering religious education has decreased (44 schools in 2005/2006, 34 schools in 2008/2009). The most remarkable changes have taken place in primary and upper secondary schools: 27 primary schools offered religious education in 2005/2006, 18 in 2008/2009; 38 upper secondary schools offered religious education in 2005/ 2006, and 21 did in 2008/2009. The changes have not been so remarkable in other school stages: from 18 to 16 in the second school stage, from 16 to 14 in the third school stage (see Chart 2, according to Undrits, 2006; Vaher, 2009).

The official statistics, however, do not show the real situation. There is some variety in the terms by which the subject is organised. By the law it should be voluntary for students, so some schools offer religious education at the end of the school day. In addition to the few schools offering voluntary religious education, some schools have tried to solve the problem of religious illiteracy by giving a different name to the subject, such as 'History of Culture', 'World-view Studies', and 'History of Religions'. It is remarkable that in such cases schools do not have to follow the principle of voluntary learning and these courses could be compulsory. Parents' permission is not needed.

Chart 2: Number of schools with religious education in 2006 and 2008

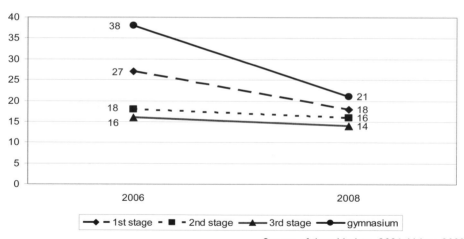

Source of data: Undrits, 2006; Vaher, 2009

As a result, some of the schools offering special instruction on religion avoid using 'religion' in the course title. This makes the situation rather confusing. At the beginning of 2009, I made a request to all 80 schools which, according to the Estonian Education Information System, offer philosophy, cultural studies or similar subjects. I received responses from only 42 schools. I could work out that the number of schools which offer courses in religious education was more than had been counted earlier – an increase from 34 to 50. Thus I can conclude that the number of schools actually offering these courses is certainly higher, especially upper secondary schools, than the official numbers would have us believe. The reasons for that can be found in the public debate over religious education, which is discussed in the next section.

In my study I distinguish between students who:

a) study at a school which does not pay any special attention to education about religion and which does not have religious education in any classes;

b) study at a school which does not have the subject, but, nevertheless, religious education is integrated into school life; students may regularly attend religious services in different churches or have a chaplain at school;

c) have studied religious education only a long time ago in primary classes, usually as a voluntary subject with content oriented to Bible stories and Christian festivals, but dealing also with students' values;

d) have studied religious education within a year of my research; in most cases it was a compulsory course about world religions.

Something must be said about teachers in Estonia. There is a bimodal distribution of teachers in terms of age and length of service according to the OECD report. The highest concentration of teachers is those with more than 15 years of service; however, approximately 20% of the teachers have less than five years of service, showing a high number of teachers leaving the profession (OECD, 2001, 68; Eurydice, 2008, 146–152). According to the statistics of the Ministry of Education and Research, 66% of teachers are more than 41 years old (the homepage of Ministry of Education and Research http://www.hm.ee/index.php?048055), which means that most teachers completed their basic teacher training under the Soviet regime. The state audit office reports that more than 1/3 of teachers are over 50 years old, while the number of young teachers is decreasing (Kivine, 2004, 8). Many educational officials argue for the integration of all religious topics into other subjects taught in school – such as literature, history, civic education, arts – thus removing the need for separate religious education. At the same time, most teachers have not been trained to deal with religion in their classrooms. None of the teacher training programmes, except those for teachers of religious education, have any compulsory courses on religious studies.

A full time teacher of religious education is exceptional in the Estonian education system. Some teachers work only 1–3 hours in a school having, for example, a church as their main employer; others teach subjects such as philosophy or history (Paesüld, 2005). As the requirements are high, the teachers are usually specialists, educated in both theology and pedagogy. While most teachers in Estonia received their education in the Soviet era, most teachers specifically of religious education completed their professional training during the last 15 years. Teacher training for religious education did not begin until 1989/1990 by the *Eesti Evangeelse Luterliku Kiriku Usuteaduse Instituut* (Theological Institute of the Estonian Evangelical Lutheran Church). This was the first institution to train teachers of religious education. During the Soviet regime the Theological Institute was a training college for pastors. After independence it began to train other church workers: Sunday school teachers, youth leaders, deacons, and teachers of religious education. When, in 1995, the first graduates completed their studies in the re-opened Faculty of Theology in Tartu University, it became possible to establish a teacher training programme for teachers of religious education at the University. There are two more confessional institutions for higher education that have prepared teachers of religious education: *Eesti Metodisti Kiriku Teoloogiline Seminar* [Baltic Methodist Theological Seminary], *Kõrgem Usuteaduslik Seminar* [Higher Theological Seminary of the Union of Evangelical Christian and Baptist Churches of Estonia], and an ecumenical private high school *Tartu Teoloogia Akadeemia* [Tartu Academy of Theology]. At present there are more than 250 qualified teachers of religious education, of whom approximately 40 are teaching religious education in schools (Paesüld, 2005).

2.2 Current developments

2.2.1 Public debates about religious education

The restoration of independence in the early 1990s gave a new opportunity for teaching religious education in schools. Some teachers and school headteachers welcomed this change. Several higher educational institutions started to prepare teachers for religious education; most of them were theological institutions. The first textbooks for religious education and handbooks for teachers adopted were translated from Finnish. Textbooks for primary education dealt with Bible stories (e.g. Alaja et al., 1994; 1995; Kankaanpää et al. 1994; 1995) and were meant for children coming from a Christian background. The textbooks for upper secondary school covered world religions (Mauranen, 1990), church history (Heininen et al., 1990), Bible studies (Pihkala et al., 1991) and dogmatics (Peltola et al., 1989); all of them were meant for children who have studied the subject for many years. Also a book on didactics of religious education (Tamminen et al., 1998) was confessionally driven. Little by little some textbooks written by Estonian authors, especially for non-confessional religious education in Estonia, were published for courses on church history and Biblical studies in the upper secondary school (Jürgenstein, 1997;
Jürgenstein et al., 1999), and all the core-courses relating to this proposal, were covered by teaching-learning resources and made available for teachers on-line

(Jürgenstein & Schihalejev, 2005; Schihalejev & Kaljulaid, 2003; 2004a; 2004b). Appropriate didactic materials for a non-confessional religious education in Estonia were published (Valk, 2007a; 2008).

The most heated public discussions about the necessity for religious education have taken place since the re-establishment of independence. Although there is some kind of general agreement on the need for 'learning about religion', there is no agreement on *how* it should be done (Valk, 2000; 2002b). When schools became open to religious education the shared understanding about its aims and contents were not clarified. Supported by translated textbooks, some people without pedagogical experience and professional skills made no clear distinction between the mission of a church and religious education at school. Unfortunately individual failures have been exaggerated and generalised and caused a strong opposition to religious education. At the same time, different high schools prepared teachers of religious education to eliminate such failures and the Council of Religious Education has worked on improving the syllabus for religious education (see 2.2.2).

There have been several attempts to establish religious education as a compulsory subject in all schools, but opposition in the media and in internet forums has been very strong. Pille Valk has called it "*a hot topic*" (2006), as there is no other subject that is so emotionally loaded. Efforts to defend the need for religious education in schools have been met with opposition from influential groups such as the Estonian native faith group (e.g. Heinapuu, 2004) and famous writers, columnists and artists (e.g. Kivirähk, 2006; Liiv, 2002).

The controversy over religious education has continued also over the last three years of my research. For example, religious education was prohibited as a mandatory subject at one of the best schools in Estonia. In this school, religious education had been taught as an optional subject since 1994. Soon religious education was recognised by the faculty and students as a needed and informative subject. With the introduction of humanities classes it was decided to make the subject of world religions obligatory for students of humanities for all three years of upper secondary school. A citizen of a town, not related to the school, wrote a letter complaining that religious education was being taught as a mandatory subject, thus violating the law. In response to the letter, at the beginning of 2006, the Chancellor of Justice prohibited the school from teaching religious education on a compulsory basis (Jõks, 2006a). In protest, students of the school collected more than 2000 signatures in favour of continuing compulsory religious education (Jürgenstein, 2006). In spite of this, the school was forced to interrupt the tradition. Religious education continued as a voluntary subject but nevertheless almost all students choose to take religious education in this school.

A similar pattern could be followed in other discussions – the people who are in opposition to the subject have no experience of the subject themselves

(Saar, 2005; Valk, 2007b, 178). In contrast, according to several studies, students who have studied religious education are very positive and supportive of the subject, even when they were required to take the course (Saar, 2005; Pärkson, 2006; Soom, 2007; Schihalejev, 2008a; 2008b).

In October 2006 and February 2007 two endeavours were made by a group in the Estonian Parliament to establish religious education as a compulsory subject for upper secondary schools. The proposition was rejected. Together with Allar Jõks (Jõks, 2006b), the previous Minister of Education, Mailis Reps, also opposed mandatory religious education (e.g. Reps, 2006). However, the new Minister of Education, Tõnis Lukas, has been in favour of a year of compulsory religious education in upper secondary school in order to give an overview of world religions (Lukas, 2008).

The latest debates were initiated at the end of 2008 by the Minister for Regional Affairs, Siim Kiisler, who proposed to make religious education compulsory for students in both secondary and upper secondary school: *"Taking into account how important religious education is in acquiring balanced and comprehensive education, we are of the opinion that religious education should be included in the national curriculum as a compulsory subject"* (Kalamees & Koorits, 2008). This time the Minister of Education was cautious in making any promises or expressing his own views. The Estonian Academy of Sciences expressed its objections very quickly. Richard Villems, President of the Academy, dedicated half of his speech on the general assembly to that issue. He underlined that religious studies are appropriate only in the context of the study of history; special studies of religion could be accepted only as non-confessional voluntary subject in upper secondary school and should not be allowed in any form in the basic school.

> *"But religious education as a distinctive subject should not exist in basic school, especially in the earlier stages, not even as an optional subject, because children of this age, at least the majority of them, are not yet safeguarded enough against, alas, a quite likely opportunity that instead of receiving religious education they are served the views of 'our own church', or of whatever other confession or a sect. The things that are acquired in history lessons are totally sufficient."* (Villems, 2008, 6–7)

As I have noted above, two main factors contribute to this opposition. First, as described in 2.1, Estonia is highly secularised. Second, fifty years of the Soviet totalitarian occupation and atheistic regime, which forbade religious education in schools and also in religious communities, has resulted in a lack of knowledge of religion. Opponents of religious education claim it to be 'an agent of the Church' which hopes to increase its membership and force students to believe. The teachers of religious education, most of whom are Christian, are not considered to be able to present Christianity or world religions in an objective way.

2.2.2 The national syllabus for religious education

There is an advisory syllabus for religious education at the national level. Developing a national religious education syllabus to meet a situation where some schools offer the subject only in the first grades, some only in upper secondary school, and where there are exceptional schools with religious education in all of the grades, is a complicated task. Although schools may not follow the contents of the subject as explained below, they share the aims of the subject as described in the national syllabus.

The representatives of the churches have co-operated in the work of the Council of Religious Education and worked as an advisory board in developing the current version of the national syllabus for religious education in 2002–2006. It adopts a contextual approach to religious education, which means that it has to take into consideration the social and cultural environment of religious education (Valk, 2002b). It is emphasised that the subject should not be proselytising. It must present different worldviews, but with cultural and historical reasons to justify a greater emphasis on Christianity rather than on the other world religions. The Estonian Council of Churches has signed a protocol of joint interests with the Estonian Government, including religious education (The Estonian Council of Churches and the Government of the Republic of Estonia, 2002). Below are the objectives for religious education in Estonia:
1. to provide knowledge of different religions as a means towards religious literacy and understanding cultural heritage
2. to develop an open identity and readiness to dialogue across different religious and non religious beliefs
3. to support students' moral development
4. to support development of students' worldview and critical thinking
5. to develop social awareness and responsibility.[7]

The advisory syllabus proposes four more fixed core courses and optional courses with more freedom to choose the precise content. It recommends starting in primary school from more familiar material – children's values, festivities from the folk calendar and selected Bible stories. In the second school stage the core course is ethics, while possible optional courses deal with the cultural impact of religions in Estonia. The third core course is about world religions and their cultural impact. This is designed for upper secondary school, and this section, 'Humanity and religion', deals with phenomenology and philosophical questions. In practice, religious education in primary school often focuses on Bible stories and in secondary school on the history of world religions and comparative religious studies.

---

7   The syllabus is availale on line at: http://www.us.ut.ee/orb.aw/class=file/action=preview/ id= 207358/Religiooni%F5petuse+ainekava.doc (accessed 21.04.2009).

Unfortunately the advisory syllabus presupposes that the subject is taught at all school stages. The real situation is different: religious education is only taught in primary classes or for a year at upper secondary school level. Although a recommended syllabus is available, headteachers and teachers of religious education are not bound to it but may create their own, so the content of religious education in various schools differs. Despite some dissimilarity between religious education in these few schools, where it is taught it is inter-religious and is targeted at developing religious literacy, open identity, creating a readiness for dialogue, and evaluating spiritual and moral values.

The new national curriculum, including syllabuses for individual subjects, has been developed in recent years and is still under construction, including improvements in the national syllabus for religious education. This is planned to be implemented in 2010/2011. First, religious education is included on the official list of subjects with an established syllabus in the new national curriculum.[8] It must go through different steps of revision and, as with other subjects, must be accepted by The National Examinations and Qualifications Centre (REKK). REKK is a governmental body administered by the Ministry of Education and Research. The new policy is a step towards a shared understanding of religious education in Estonia's schools. Second, many important changes have been made in the contents of the syllabus for religious education: the outcomes of studies regarding tolerance and freedom of belief have been worded more precisely and the need for mutual respect is made clearer than it was in previous versions. It includes recognising and coping with prejudice and discrimination and stresses dialogue with representatives of different religious and secular worldviews. More attention has been paid to world religions. For example, if in the previous version primary school students learned 'selected stories from the New Testament', then now they are expected to learn 'stories from different religious traditions'; before they learned about the ten commandments, but now they learn about ethical principles in different religions; also secular worldviews are included in discussing how worldview shapes values. More emphasis has been given to self reflection and analysis.

---

8 The draft syllabus is available online at:
   https://www.oppekava.ee/ainekavad_sotsiaalained (accessed 12.05.2009)

2.2.3 Positioning of Estonian religious education in the European context

There are several ways of describing and organising religious education. Usually different forms of religious education are distinguished as 'confessional' and 'non-confessional' (or 'interreligious') (e.g. Schreiner, 2000, 7; Willaime, 2007; also Jackson, 2008b). Peter Schreiner distinguishes the religious studies approach from the denominational approach (Schreiner, 2002, 91–93). In the following, I attempt to position Estonian religious education in a wider context. In doing this I will not give an overview about representative models of religious education as taught in different countries, but rather will focus on the difficulties of classifying models of religious education. I will highlight some of the most controversial examples from different countries in Europe, including examples of those where a clear distinction between different types of religious education is easier and others where it is difficult or impossible to make a distinction between different types.

The distinction can be made according to the law and policy statements at the national level – policy being determined by educational or religious bodies. The second distinction could be made according to the aims of and the third to the contents of the subject, as described in the syllabus. The fourth division is at the school level and deals with who takes the subject. It is therefore important to pay attention to the basis on which these distinctions are made.

Distinction according to the legislation

The distinction is often made according to legislation: who is responsible for the development of syllabi and textbooks, content of teaching, and the training and appointment of educators – the religious communities or educational bodies? 'Confessional religious education' is organised by and responsibility is given to religious bodies. There is a big variety of possible solutions under the umbrella of this label, church or churches having the authoritative role of supervision, sometimes combined with educational authorities, with regard to content of the subject and appointing teachers of religious education. 'Confessional religious education' may teach the 'religion of the state' (e.g. in Spain, Ireland, Italy, Poland, Rumania), the 'religion of the sponsor' (e.g. Holland, in which the religion of the group sponsoring the school is taught) and in other countries' confessional schools, 'the religion the student belongs to' (e.g. Finland, Croatia, Germany, Latvia, Alsace).

In 'non-confessional' approaches, which include the 'religious studies' approach to religious education, religious bodies have no role in public education, or occasionally a limited role (as in local Agreed Syllabus conferences in England, in which syllabuses are designed jointly by teachers, local politicians and religious bodies, but to non-confessional aims). Thus, there is a range of possible accommodations to this model. In some countries there is no distinctive subject for religious studies (as in France, Montenegro, Macedonia and Albania). Knowledge about religions can be dealt with in courses on history, literature or as a dimension of intercultural education or citizenship education. In other countries (e.g. Sweden, Denmark, Norway), religious education is provided exclusively by the state's educational bodies. Although in some cases (e.g. Iceland) religious bodies may be used as advisers, the educational bodies have the responsibility and the last word in composing the subject.

From the perspective of who decides the contents and approaches of religious education, Estonia is similar to the 'non-confessional' or 'study of religions' models. In Estonia religious education is organised by the state's Ministry of Education and Research, and the religious bodies have only a limited advisory function (see section 2.2.2).

Distinction according to the aims

There are some shortcomings with distinguishing religious education only on legislative grounds. Many authors (e.g. Diez de Velasco, 2008; Josza, 2008; Alberts, 2007; Crawford & Rossiter, 2006) have criticised the rigid distinction between confessional and non-confessional religious education made along the lines of the types of bodies with responsibility for organising the subject. They have tried to suggest other variables for distinguishing different models. The most important is that such a distinction does not indicate anything about the aims and the contents of the subject. This brings us to the level of syllabuses for religious education. Speaking about the aims, a distinction is sometimes made among three aims of religious education: teaching 'into', 'about' and 'from' religion (Grimmitt, 2000; Hull, 2001). Teaching 'into' refers to bringing students closer to the corresponding religion and to educating them from the perspective of that religion. Instruction stems from an insider's perspective and the teachers are expected to be representatives of that religion. This aim is appropriate only in the context of confessional religious education, although the other two aims can also be present.

Teaching 'about' religion promotes religious literacy, comprehension of different religious traditions, interpretation and sometimes reflexivity. It requires knowing about and understanding the beliefs, values and practices of different religions, and how religion affects individuals and communities. Religion is taught from the outside, from a descriptive and historical, often non-religious perspective. Learning 'from' religion is sometimes part of this model (as in England) and aims at students' personal, spiritual and moral development, at reflecting and building their own responses to religious traditions, but this element is not intended to inculcate religious faith.

"In the first two kinds of religious education, 'learning religion' and 'learning about religion', religion is taught for its own sake, whether as an object of faith to which the children are summoned, or as an object worthy of critical study. However, in the third kind, 'learning from religion' the central focus switches to the children as learners." (Hull, 2001, 5)

One can assume that the aims of non-confessional religious education vary from more content oriented 'teaching about' (e.g. in Norway) to more reflexive and child-oriented 'teaching from' in which the experience and identity of the students is at the centre of teaching and learning (as in Sweden, for example) and have elements of 'teaching into *tolerance*'. Some endeavours to develop curricular materials from a non-confessional comparative religious perspective could be found also oversees, in California, Iowa and Massachusetts in the USA (Hackett, 2007, vi) in Montreal in Canada (Ouellet, 2006) and in South Africa (Chidester, 2003). Still, there is no clear-cut distinction between the aims and organisation of religious education. As Peter Schreiner comments: "*This rough differentiation is idealistic because a good religious education should include elements from all these perspectives*" (Schreiner, 2007, 9). It should be noted that not only confessional religious education can be biased. Some non-confessionally organised religious education can contain bias and introduce students to an anti-religious worldview by focusing mainly on the negative impacts and potential misuse of religions.

Estonia is similar to the 'non-confessional' models with less emphasis on developmental aspects, having rather a content-oriented focus or mainly 'teaching about' different world religions (Valk, 2000).

Distinction according to the contents
With regard to the contents of religious education the simple answer would be that in 'confessional' religious education students mainly learn one specific religious tradition and in 'non-confessional' religious education they learn several religions without being nurtured into any specific religious tradition. But in a plural world more and more countries with a 'confessional' approach incorporate 'teaching about' different religions more or less into their sylla-buses. In those countries which have non-confessional forms of religious educa-tion there is debate about how many religions should be covered, and at what ages students should learn about them. Dan-Paul Josza (2007) distinguishes different models of religious education based rather on contents and philosophy of religious education.

Dan-Paul Josza (2007) distinguishes different models of religious education based rather on contents and philosophy of religious education. He argues that different models can be and are present within the same legislative framework. He considers the contents of the subject and groups religious education models according to this, and not so much to approaches 'into', 'about' and 'from'. In 'confessional' religious education Josza discusses the contents of religious education in more detail, as there are many forms of religious education which contain different religions, but in different proportions (Josza, 2007). He concludes that if the proportional representation of different religions is only a quantitative one "*without making a 'qualitative' difference between the religions per se, and especially without the aim to introduce the pupils into a specific religion*", then the approach is 'non-confessional'. In a 'confessional' approach the focus on one religion is above all 'qualitative', even if accompanied in general also by a 'quantitative' focus. If one religion is presented from a 'qualitative' point of view differently from the others, generally "*with the impetus at least to bring that specific religion more nearer to the pupils, in most of the cases to introduce them to that religion*", he would count it as a 'confessional'.

On the level of contents, according to the syllabus of religious education in Estonia, one can follow a greater emphasis on Christianity, because of the country's culture and history. In the revised syllabus more emphasis has been put on different religious and secular traditions. In any case, there is a quantitative difference, not a qualitative one. A critical and analytical approach to any of the religions studied is seen as a prerequisite.

Distinction according to the participants

As discussed above, the political-organisational framework and the aims of religious education have only a loose connection. Beside the responsible body and syllabus there is one further aspect, namely those who attend the lesson. There are some examples, where the state is responsible for the subject, even though it is directed towards students of one religion (usually Christians or Muslims) and to provide knowledge about that religion, as in case of special religious education for Muslim children in North-Rhine-Westphalia in Germany (Josza, 2008). By the definition given above it would still count as 'non-confessional' religious education. On the contrary, the Hamburg model of '*Religionsunterricht für alle*' would be classified as 'confessional' because it is organised by the Protestant Church, although it is designed to be attended by all students and to provide knowledge and to learn from a non-confessional perspective different religions (Knauth, 2008).

Josza develops a model of religious education also according to the target group. In the religious education model of 'confessional religious education' he distinguishes 'explicit confessional religious education' from 'general confessional religious education'. 'Explicit confessional religious education' is designed only for the students affiliated to that religious tradition. 'General confessional religious education' is designed for all students regardless of their religious affiliation. A model of 'non-confessional religious education' with students being separated according to their religion is termed 'separative non-confessional religious education'. The model where students are not separated according to their religion is called 'general non-confessional religious education' or simply 'non-confessional religious education'.

There is a difficulty with the scheme. Let us imagine two classes with the exactly same syllabus, a teacher and the approach. The students in one class come from a similar religious or secular background and in another class there are two children with a different religious background. Should religious education be classified in one class as 'general' and in other as 'separative'?

Although Estonian religious education definitely falls into the 'non-confessional' model, the appropriate 'cluster' for the Estonian case is missing also in Josza's scheme. As the students are not separated in Estonia according to their religion, but according to their own or their parents' will, it would not count as 'separative non-confessional' religious education in Josza's sense. The extension of the category to include the Estonian case in either the 'separative' or the 'general' model would not do justice to either of them, as the students come from diverse religious or secular backgrounds. Moreover, Estonian religious education is not inclusive, as not all the students from a particular class are represented; some of the students who attend religious education feel sometimes quite segregated because of that (see section 4). My suggestion is to add a category of 'elective non-confessional religious education' to label the model practised in Estonia.

Wanda Alberts introduces the term 'integrative religious education' and insists that one of the characteristics of such a subject is its non-separative educational framework which requires the concept for dealing with diversity in the classroom:

> *"The term 'integrative religious education' is used as an analytical category referring to a particular form of religious education in which the children of a class are not separated (...) but learn together about different religions."* (Alberts, 2007, 1)

In defining such a model she takes for granted the responsibility of the educational body and adds two distinctive characteristics about students who participate – all students – and about the subject matter – which includes various religions – without taking the perspective of any religion as a framework.

Religious education in Estonia is inconsistent in its form and aims. Although the subject in Estonia represents a religious studies approach and the students who study it come from diverse religious and secular backgrounds, it cannot be classified as integrative as Alberts describes it. Such a misfit could be one of the reasons why Kodelja and Bassler classified religious education in Estonia as an optional confessional religious education (Kodelja & Bassler, 2004, 17) The separation is not done as in 'confessional religious education' according to the religious affiliation of a child, but the subject is still separative, as not all the children attend it and they are separated according to their motivation to attend an additional lesson. There are a few schools in Estonia which practise integrative religious education in the way Alberts describes it and this is done illegally, as the law stipulates that the subject must be optional.

Thus there is no simple contrast between 'confessional' and 'non-confessional' religious education. As presented in the discussion above, the distinction about confessional and non-confessional religious education could be made on the basis of the system, aims, content and of what actually happens in religious education from the students' perspective. The system can be confessional, as in most parts of Germany, but the aims not so, as in Hamburg. The aims might be non-confessional, but the content could be confined to one religion. There are several forms of confessional religious education, from conservative religious education with a strict focus on a single religion and (a hidden or more explicit) syllabus to bring children nearer to one religion, to very liberal forms of confessional religious education with open and child-centred aims and striving for non-discrimination and sympathetic teaching about other religions. Similarly, some forms of non-confessional religious education tend to reduce religion to a cultural or historical phenomenon, whereas others see religious education as providing a safe space for respectful dialogue between religious and non-religious points of view. The students, who attend religious education, be it confessional or non-confessional, can belong to one religion, one denomination or philosophy or be of different religious and non-religious backgrounds. In the non-confessional framework of aims, participants might find that their own understanding of religion has grown and their faith is deepened. In another context, the aims might be confessional but the child might be turned off religion in the process.

Religious education in Estonia is non-confessional by its system, aims and contents. Those students who do choose to do it are taught together as a group. It seems a pity that the school cannot make the non-confessional subject officially available to all students since it aims neither to promote nor to denigrate religion; its aim rather is to understand religion. Some upper secondary level schools have decided that religious studies are an important part of education and have a mandatory course on world religions under different names. Such a situation does not permit regulation of or supervision of its contents. This shows a rather ambivalent position with regard to the legislation on the one hand and practical solutions on the other. The changes made in syllabi for religious education have done little to improve knowledge and skills for peaceful co-existence because the subject of religious education has a marginal position in Estonian education.

3. QUALITATIVE STUDY WITH STUDENTS

So far I have covered the topics that give background information for empirical studies. I have discussed methodology and methods used for the research together with contextual and historical factors influencing religious education in Estonia. I have given the rationale for my methodology in section 1.3.1. The mixed methods approach used for empirical studies gave me the opportunity to fine-tune the methods of data collection. Also reasons for using written interviews for a qualitative study about young people views were presented in section 1.3.2. If the emphasis in section 1 was on **why** I used certain methods, then here I focus on describing **how** I used them, and describe the questionnaire, more technical details of the empirical methods and characteristics of the sample of my study. This section is based on two articles written about the qualitative study done in the framework of the REDCo Project: *Meeting Diversity – Students' Perspectives in Estonia* (Schihalejev, 2008b) and *Kohtumine endast erinevaga – õpilaste arusaam* [Meeting difference – students' perspectives] (Schihalejev, 2008a).

3.1 Key information in an empirical study

3.1.1 Questionnaire

My main research question was about the hindrances and potential for developing tolerance towards religious diversity in the context of the school. To answer this central question it was necessary to understand the positions of young people. I first investigated students' own attitudes towards and their expectations and experiences of religion and religious diversity by the means of a qualitative research study. Its main aim was to gain a clearer insight into the role of religion in the lives and schooling of young people. I was interested in the vocabulary used and attitudes held by young people when they speak about religion, the role students themselves give to religion in their personal life and in human relations in general, and where they meet religious diversity and how they value it. I also paid attention to the question of religious education at school and what expectations students have of the subject.

Semi-structured oral interviews with students worked as a pilot phase for the development of the written questionnaire. As described in 1.3.2, written questionnaires were adapted to the language used by young people after oral interviews. A final questionnaire consisting of eight open questions was standardised for all eight countries to make the results comparable. The questions addressed the domains of the individual, societal and educational significance of religion and were, accordingly, grouped under three themes: personal relevance of religion; religion in society and relations; and religion at school (Appendices 1–2).

The first block of questions dealt with religion at the personal level. Question one asked about students' associations with the terms 'religion' and 'God'. I tried to establish the importance of and attitudes towards religion in their personal lives, aiming to distinguish the associations students have with these words. Question two asked about the sources of information through which they learned about religion and what kind of information they get through these sources.

The second block of questions focused on the social dimension of religion and on questions of dialogue and conflict. Question three was concerned with whether young people talk about religion, what they value in such discussion and on which occasions it happens. If they do not speak about religion, what are the reasons for this? Question four asked about the experiences students have of religion, both problematic and positive ones, things they value and see as important. Do they see a different worldview as frightening or interesting? Question five asked about reasons whether or not people of different religious backgrounds can live peacefully together and why.

The last block of questions dealt with religion at school. Question six asked students to imagine that they could decide on policies at school and asked if they would allow religion to appear at school and why. Question seven was interested in topics which students would like to study about religion at school. The final questions enquired whether the teachers could be religious and how the studies about religion should be organised.

The questionnaire was completed by 73 students from three schools. Next I will give information about the selected schools and the rationale for choosing these.

3.1.2 Sample and the procedure

As was described in section 2.1.1, Estonia is comprised mainly of two bigger ethnic groups. The religious distribution as well as socio-economic status of people from different parts of Estonia is uneven. To get a variety of opinions I decided to include a school from a rural area and others from towns. The schools in Estonia have adopted very different forms of religious education, as described in section 2.1.2. The qualitative study was carried out in three schools which differ in their geographical, demographical, linguistic[9] and religious background and also in the organisation of religious education. Only municipal

---

9   There were 470 Estonian-medium schools and 118 Russian-medium municipal schools in the year of the study (data according to EHIS, available at: https://eh-jas.hm.ee/avalik/oas/Otsing.uix accessed 10.06.2006).

schools, run by local authorities, were chosen. For reasons of anonymity, capital letters A, B, C are used to designate schools in this section.

School A is a rural school in Southern Estonia, dating back to the 17th century. It is situated in a homogeneously Estonian-speaking area. A Lutheran church plays a remarkable role in the life of the local community. The building of the new school, that meets the requirements of a basic school, was largely organised and initiated by a local pastor in the 1990s. Due to this initiative and good relations with the pastor, religious education has been part of the curriculum for 13 years already. Religious education aims at introducing basic Bible stories, teaching an understanding of Lutheran cultural background and, in the 8th grade, teaching about different confessions of Christianity and world religions represented in Estonia. Although it is an optional subject, almost all students take it from grades 1 to 8. The students in grade 9 do not have religious education during the final year of their studies but they will have studied it before.

The respondents were from grades 8 (10 students) and 9 (15 students); all the students have had religious education experience during their studies at School A. The questionnaire was answered by students on November 20, 2006. The questionnaire was available on the internet (http://www.eformular.com/ olgasch/redco.html). Students were offered the possibility of completing it on paper, if it was more convenient, but nobody chose this option. Students from the 9th grade gave the longest and most elaborated answers in comparison to all other groups. It is worth mentioning that, shortly before the study, respondents had visited a Muslim community group, a Jewish community and school, and a Catholic monastery in Tallinn. Many of their answers were influenced by these experiences.

School B is a Russian-medium school situated in a predominantly Russian-speaking industrial town in Northern Estonia. The school has a unique history of sharing the same building with a religious Orthodox school for several years. Most of the students in the Orthodox school were from religious families; some children had been accepted from ordinary schools, where they were not succeeding (having learning or behaviour problems). Religious education took the form of confessional studies, including basic Orthodox teachings and participation in the liturgy. The school has now been closed for economic reasons; the students continued their studies at School 2, where religious education is not taught.

All 20 respondents were from grade 9, a few of them had been students in the Orthodox school for several years, but most of them had no previous personal experience of religious education. The students answered the questions on December 6, 2006 during their final lesson. The answers were mainly rather brief but with some exceptions that were both personal in tone and extensive in coverage.

School C is a relatively new school, dating back to 1991. It is located in a suburb of a Western Estonian town. The students mainly belong to working and middle class families. As it was established during the period of religious revival, religious education was introduced into the new school. The first headmaster appointed a teacher of religious education and set up a compulsory course of religious education in the 10th grade dealing with world religions. Although the school has no connection with any church, the teachers of religious education have been Baptists, but the content of the religious education has been inter-religious.

The respondents from the 9th grade (17 students) had never studied religious education; grade 10 (11 students) had studied religious education for almost three months at the time the questionnaire was administered. The questionnaire was delivered on November 24, 2006. In this case the answers differed greatly according to the grades the students were in, especially regarding attitudes towards religious education.

I will present students' responses using a code, which includes an identifier of gender, worldview and experience of religious education. The questionnaires are decoded in the text below according to the code key introduced in Table 2. For example 'f-nr-02-A+' labels a girl from the School A, grade 8 with no religious affiliation, who studies religious education. As it is impossible to know if a student took part in religious school in School B, a question mark is used.

Table 2. Codes for quotations

Gender	Worldview	Number – school & grade	School & Religious education
f/m	at/ch/pr/nr/or/ur	01–73	A+/B?/C-/C+
f= female **m**= male	**at**= atheist **ch**= not specified Christian **pr**= protestant, Lutheran **nr**= no religious affiliation **or**= Orthodox **ur**= undefined religion, destiny	nr 01–10 = School A, grade 8 nr 11–25 = School A, grade 9 nr 26–45 = School B, grade 9 nr 46–62 = School C, grade 9 nr 63–73 = School C, grade 10	**A+** = School A, have studied RE for 8 years **B?**= School B, mostly no RE or in some cases Orthodox RE **C-** = School C, grade 9, no RE **C+** = School C, grade 10, have studied RE for 3 months

The profile of the sample by gender and immigration background is similar to that of the whole population. There were 39 boys and 34 girls in the sample. The mother tongue profile is also similar to that of the overall population. Students with an immigrant background are all from School B, most of them

(17 from 20) having family roots outside Estonia (with one or more parents born outside Estonia). 6 respondents (8%) do not have Estonian citizenship, but only 2 (3%) being born elsewhere.

The specified worldview corresponds for the most part to the data of the Census from year 2000 (Table 3). Worldview was difficult to define for Estonian students – 42 out of 73 could not define their worldview. Since, according to the poll of 2000, the younger generation in Estonia relates to religion less than the older generation does, the worldviews of 15–19 years olds are presented in the table. It is worthwhile pointing out that Russian-speaking students were more eager to identify with a specific tradition – 11 out of 20 students regarded themselves as Orthodox. The higher percentage identifying with the Orthodox tradition in comparison with the rest of the age group could result from the peculiarities of the school with its former connections to the Orthodox Church, and also to the higher percentage of Orthodox in the towns (Hansen, 2002, 121).

Table 3. The structure of sample and of the population: worldview

Religion	Sample age 14–17 N 73	%		Total in Estonia age 15–19 N 103 772	%
Atheist	6	8		5 978	6
Christian	5	7		1 742	2
Lutheran	2	3		5 278	5
Orthodox	11	15		8 756	8
Religion	6	8		223	0,2
Destiny	1	1			
Nothing concrete	42	58	No affiliation	37 505	36
			Not defined	44 291	43

Source: Statistics Estonia, http://pub.stat.ee (accessed 10.06.2007)

3.1.3 Quantity and quality of data

Before conducting the study permission from parents and students was requested. All the students in selected schools and classes were asked to answer the questionnaire. Later the answers of those, who were outside the age group (17 years old), were dropped. In School C, grade 10, part of the class filled in the form while others were busy with the lesson. In School A, in grade 8, a teacher was present at the beginning of the interview, but left after ten minutes. In School B the teacher was always present, but stayed far enough away not to see the answers given. In other classes no teacher was in attendance at any time during the interview. In all classes, throughout the time students were completing questionnaires, I was present to answer possible questions from the students. The length of the answers was rather short and depended partly on the school. In School B the average length was 119 words, in School A 174 and in School C 126 words. The longest answers in the School A group could result from the use of computers. No answers were given for six questions from School B and six questions from School C. Sometimes one-word answers were given for questions that demanded longer answers: 14 questions in School B, five in School A and two in School C. The most difficult (not answered or answered with just "*Do not have*") was the 4th question regarding personal experiences of religion.

3.2 Presentation of results

3.2.1 Personal views on religion

3.2.1.1 Associations with words 'religion' and 'God'

The main distinction for answers to the questions about associations with the words 'religion' and 'God', was between words related to church and tradition on the one hand and non specific, often rather critical expressions, on the other. More Christian-coloured words were used for 'God' than for 'religion'.

Even if the available data do not permit quantification, certain patterns of answers caught my attention. Most of the terms related to a Christian background, especially when describing God. They were used both by the students from a Christian denomination and by students without any specific worldview. Russian speaking students listed more words and the words were often church-related. Two respondents could not find any meanings for the words given. Estonians found fewer words, mainly general words (e.g. 'belief'). Only the Estonians named world religions and religious education.

Students without any specific worldview used fewer words and their vocabulary was mostly distant and more general in nature: belief (it could be just a word or a longer expression, e.g. "*belief in something or somebody*"), or religious convictions, ideology, traditions, customs, rituals, society and some world religions were also mentioned (Judaism, Buddhism, Islam). The distant attitude was expressed by relating religion and God only to the past, e.g. referring to "*world history*", or to other people.

> "*By God we mean that personality who is in heaven and who is regarded as creator of all but I personally can't say if god has created universe or not.*" (m-nr-13-A+)

An attitude of distance was also expressed describing religion as *"fabricated"* by man, being nonsense, e.g. *"[God is] a nonexistent ideal who is worshipped"* (m-nr-55-C-), or mentioning other negative connotations of religion: *"Religions and all the bad things that have been done in the name of religion"* (m-nr-50-C-).

The students who regarded themselves as Lutheran, Orthodox or as other Christians used more personal and Christianity-related words in their associations. The personal and Christian-coloured words were ecclesiastical and religious artefacts (mentioned mostly by Russian-speaking respondents): icon, cross, Christ, church, Bible, blessed water; activities such as baptizing, pilgrimage, and making the sign of the cross; there were also such concepts as sin, angels, paradise, creed, Ten Commandments and forgiveness. Admiring epithets and properties were ascribed to God: creator, almighty, helping, benevolent, understanding, the most important, most honourable, infallible, caring, source of faith, etc. Personal attitudes were shown by using adjectives or words for religion such as: aspiration towards pure and right, spiritual, hope, truth and goodness, holy, love and help. Also the statement of personal belief and attachment were represented here, such as *"[Religion associates with] the religion that I confess"* (f-nr-23-A+). Usage of a personal pronoun (I, we, our, my) instead of indirect speech showed there was also a certain amount of personal commitment.

"[God is] somebody who is immortal and rules us from above." (m-ur-73-C+)

Some students asked for help in answering the question, because they did not understand the meaning of the word 'religion'. The confusion was mirrored in the frequent short answers from students without any religious affiliation and without experience of religious education.

One can conclude that even if the majority of the students did not regard themselves as Christians, the words used for religion and God were mostly derived from Christian tradition. The students who thought of themselves as Christians used more Christian and personal words and expressions, while others may have had difficulty in understanding the words and used more distant and general words and also indirect speech.

3.2.1.2 Importance of religion

When they were asked about its importance students accorded religion remarkably low significance. Only nine respondents said that religion had an important place in their lives, and some stressed how small its importance was in their life. One third of the respondents declared that there was no place in their lives for religion at all, but totally negative attitudes towards religion were not typical.

Nevertheless, short answers to that question, e.g. *"religion is important"* or *"not important"*, appeared to be very ambiguous. Not all the students gave further explanations of their attitudes. It was difficult to assess the importance of religion, especially when given just a short evaluation, e.g. the answer *"It is not very important"* could mean 'not at all important' or 'quite important'. For example, a girl who stated that religion had little importance in her life, reported all the activities she did, including teaching smaller children in Sunday school.

> *"Religion is **a little bit** important for me because I go sometimes to church with mother, we have religious education at school, I go to bible group and teach small children in Sunday school. And I rarely read the bible as it happens." (My emphasis)* (f-pr-07-A+)

No importance for religion. One third of the students expressed clearly that religion was not important for them at all, they do not believe, are not interested, don't regard it as something necessary for them or they are indifferent towards religion. The reason for the declared low importance could be that the students often regard religion as confessing some specific religion or belonging to some particular religious community.

> *"Religion doesn't mean for me personally anything as I don't belong to any religion."* (f-nr-08-A+)

As was mentioned above, some students had difficulty in understanding the word; others had no experience with religion at all or they confessed that they had little knowledge about it. A few answers expressed not only low relevance of religion, but also very negative attitudes towards believers.

> *"I am an atheist and don't believe in God. I think that a person believing in God is stupid and naive. Religion – it is just snatching money from people."* (m-at-26-B?)

The importance of religion among the respondents was in accordance with their specified worldview – Christians regarded it as more important and students without any worldview as less important. The importance of religion was introduced by three main fields: the importance of religion in coping with life, the importance in orientation to tradition, and the search for truth (with or without faith in God).

The importance of religion in coping with life. Religion was viewed as important even by some students who did not regard themselves as committed to some religion. Religion, more specifically knowledge about different religions, was seen as an important factor in understanding different opinions and nurturing their tolerance even if their own disbelief was mentioned. This factor was mentioned only by students who had studied religious education.

> *"Religion is important, to know how people from different countries act in a situation and what is holy for them. By knowing religion I get to know how to act with other nations, [and how to behave in order] not to offend them."* (f-nr-14-A+)

On a more personal level, students presumed that religion helps them to cope with difficulties and has special importance in critical times. Also it was seen as a tool to unite society and counter negative human characteristics. Even a boy, who described himself as an atheist, confessed that he sought help from religion at times of difficulty.

> *"Religion is not very important to me but sometimes I must seek for help from there as well."* (m-at-69-C+)

In some cases answers mirrored personal and an almost intimate confession of faith, as was stated by an Orthodox girl.

> *"For me God is very important! And I like my religion; I believe in God and he helps me."* (f-or-34-B?)

The importance of religion in orientation to tradition. Only a few students related their religion directly to tradition; mostly they were representatives of the Orthodox tradition. They stated the religious traditions they followed, as well as referring to their own baptism. Orientation to a tradition could be explained in more general terms – in valuing tradition *"what comes from ancient times"* or ceremonies belonging to some concrete religious tradition.

> *"If someone dies he could be buried religiously, a gravestone would be erected according to the religion."* (m-or-35-B?)

The importance of religion in the search for truth was the most often mentioned among all the reasons. The quest for truth was used as an argument to consider at both ends of the spectrum – the low or high importance of religion in one's personal life. The students who tried to give grounds for the low or no importance of religion for them, argued mostly that they did not believe or they were not able to believe in God. Such forms of reasoning could be seen as a search for the truth. However, importance of religion was seen as the need to believe in something or as a means to access the truth.

"For me the truth is important in the world and if it is accessible by religion then it is very important." (f-ur-67-C+)

Answers to the question about the importance of religion supported greatly the surmises of the previous section – religion is recognized as not a very important factor in the lives of young people. At the same time, religion by its function is seen primarily as a personal choice or personal matter, not a societal force. Students' responses concerning the importance or meaninglessness of religion are given mostly in personal terms in relation to truth claims or as a means to cope with the difficulties of life, and not in terms of belonging to a group or tradition.

3.2.1.3 Sources of knowledge

From the responses the main sources of information can be seen as belief-nurturing on the one hand and non-confessional on the other. Belief-nurturing, namely Christian, sources are connected to the family (in some cases including relatives outside the immediate family circle), and places of worship, Sunday school, and the Bible. All the other sources (school, media, friends, literature, newspapers, TV, travelling) can be regarded as non-confessional and mostly giving information about different world religions. For students with a Christian worldview the main source of information was family and church, while school and other sources were important for children without a Christian background. A clear difference occurred between Russian-speaking and Estonian-speaking students, the former having primarily belief-nurturing and the latter having non-confessional sources, especially if they had experienced religious education.

The most frequent context for encounter with religion was school, especially for Estonians. The second in importance was family, especially for Russian-speaking respondents. Also media were important, and church or other places of worship were named by some respondents. Friends were mentioned rarely, this corresponding to answers for the third question. Literature, the Bible and travelling were also mentioned in answers.

An interesting division was apparent between Estonian and Russian-speaking students: almost all Russian-speaking students named family and relatives; friends were mentioned twice, media, church and school just once. At the same time only exceptional Estonian-speaking students mentioned family as a source of information, while school was important for the majority of Estonian-speaking students. It could be that the school's importance as a source was partly due to the fact that religious education is taught in those Estonian-speaking schools where the survey was conducted. In an Estonian class, where religious education is not taught, only half the students mentioned school as their source; in other classes the same answer was given by almost everyone.

For nearly half of the Estonian-speaking students, school was the only source of information about religion. In conclusion, school has enormous importance for Estonian students as a source of information about religion, a role played by family for Russian-speaking students.

If one looks at the answers concerning the content of information provided, it is remarkable that for the most part no specific experiences were mentioned. One third of students responded in very general terms: 'many things', 'nothing' or 'can't remember'. The answers of others were also general and too short to enable any elaborate conclusions to be drawn from them. Students mentioned things they had learned. There was information about Christianity and information about different world religions and general topics related to religion.

The Christian-oriented group of answers contains information about God (that He can help or He exists), about church, Bible stories, pilgrimages, baptism and Christmas – all of these were grouped under Christian content of information. The second group contained other information about history, different world religions and customs, about different gods, why religions are needed, religious education, religious violence, and broadening one's mind.

Mostly the content reflected the source of information – from belief-nurturing sources students received Christian-related information, while from other sources more general topics and world religions were mentioned. As mentioned above, Russian-speaking students identified family, particularly grandmothers, fathers or mothers, as their primary source of information. The information they received introduced them to their faith tradition.

> *"My father told me who is God. And he gave me a Bible to read; I read the Bible and got to know who God is."* (m-or-42-B?)
> *"My mother told Bible stories about Jesus and we had lot of Bibles at home already when I was a small child."* (m-or-28-B?)

Even if the source of information and the content was 'belief-nurturing', the information was not always integrated into respondents' worldviews. They might not agree with an inherited tradition or beliefs.

> *"Before I thought that God indeed exists but now I don't think so, I am sure he doesn't exist. If he existed he would not have taken away from me three dear people in three years when I was still three years old."* (f-nr-37-B?)

The 'non-confessional' sources of information were especially important for getting information about other religions and general topics. For Estonians who have had no religious education, information about religion was associated mainly with history, and often had no place in contemporary life.

> *"Mainly in history, which countries and during what time religions **had** existed."* (My emphasis) (m-nr-49-C-)

The students with religious education experience and with school as their primary source of information mainly named world religions and different religious customs; they also mentioned that learning about religions had broadened their understanding of people and the world.

> *"That beside Christianity there are many other religions and customs."*
> (m-at-69-C+)

The information from other sources besides family and school was source-specific. Specific information from the media was not remembered, but negative effects of religion, such as wars and extremists, were mentioned.

> *"The media reflect every day how somebody explodes himself somewhere far away, how the people from some religion are killed."* (m-nr-13-A+)

The information acquired from a church was related to the traditions and teaching of that particular church. Examples included mention of Jesus or God, what is celebrated during Christmas and what is baptism. The most integrated and personal knowledge is expressed when giving information introduced by the family.

> *"It was said to me that God sees everything and punishes us for bad deeds. But the most important thing was that God exists at all."* (m-ch-30-B?)
> *"My granny is a believer and she has taken me with her when I was a little. I was so young and I don't remember anything special, but I know that it was sung and I played with dolls."* (f-nr-56-C-)

The information students get from different sources is heavily source-specific. Homes provide students with information about the religious views and traditions of the family, while school provides more general information. The ability to be tolerant and have 'insider' views of other religions different from their own was mentioned only by students who had experienced religious education on a regular basis.

3.2.1.4 Summary

A current analysis shows that understanding of the meaning of the word 'religion' by Estonian students is mostly abstract and impersonal. Many students were puzzled by the meaning of the word 'religion' and their answers reflected their distance from the concept. More than this – it proved difficult for Estonian students to define their religious affiliation. This was reflected in many answers. Russian-speaking students were more open about their personal attitudes and they also demonstrated their familiarity with the religious tradition they belonged to, though some confusion about religion and its meaning could be observed here too. For example, an atheist looks to religion for help in difficult times or the person without any religious affiliation refers to "*my own religion*". Such answers show that the meaning of, and the attitudes towards religion are fluid; they are in the process of formation and not fixed for students.

Gender played no significant role in answers to either general questions or to those regarding personal views on religion. Some minor differences arose when students identified their religious affiliation – girls were more likely than boys to declare themselves to be without any particular worldview. The declared importance of religion was the same for girls as for boys.

The word 'religion' had associations with different religions, especially for Estonian-speaking respondents, while 'God' had an association mostly with Christianity, even for those students without any religious affiliation. At the same time, the personal importance of religion was considered to be low. Responses from students show that they indicated the role of religion in their personal lives as little as possible. Being religious is not 'cool' and does not belong to the codes of youth culture. It can be concluded that even if the majority of students did not regard themselves as believers, the words used to describe religion and God were related mostly to Christianity. The students, who related themselves to a Christian tradition in speaking about religion and God, used more Christian terminology, personal words and statements, while others used more distant and general vocabulary and syntax.

Two main sources for religious information were named by students: school and family. For Russian-speaking students, family was the most important source of information and that information was mostly related to Christianity. Very few Estonian-speaking students have religious backgrounds or can get information about world religions at home; the primary source of information for them was school, which introduced some knowledge about different religions. If the students had no religious education experience and no religious background at home, their information was limited to history and examples of the negative influence of religions. If they had religious education experience, the picture was more differentiated, and positive as well negative examples were used.

It is important to highlight the school's role as a source of information on religious issues for the children with non-Christian backgrounds. The majority of students had the school as the main, and many of them as the only, source of information about religion. For students with a religious background the school also played a very important role, filling a gap of knowledge about different religions. The role of the school in this cannot be sporadic and should not be underestimated. In order to get balanced information, including about other worldviews beside one's own, it seems to be important to have religious education at school although, as demonstrated later, students without any experience of religious education did not agree with it.

3.2.2 The social dimension of religion

3.2.2.1 Religion as a topic of conversation with peers

As presented above, religion was not valued as an important issue in general. This is mirrored in answers to the question concerning religion as a topic of conversation with friends. Less than a quarter of respondents answered that they spoke with friends on religious topics at least sometimes. In general, the attitude could be described by the following quotation.

> *"Sometimes yes, sometimes not, it depends on the topic. But mostly not."*
> (m-or-42-B?)

The reasons for not speaking. There were four main reasons given for not speaking about religion with one's friends – not interested; not believing; having too little knowledge about it; and religion being a too personal topic to discuss openly.

The most frequently mentioned reason was disinterest. Some students expressed their astonishment that religion could be a topic to speak about with friends – they declared that they had not come across it or saw no reason to talk about it. Others stated that they had other topics to speak about or that talking about religion was boring for them or it was not popular among their friends.

> *"As it is not important for us. Every person has arranged his own priorities and religion is one of the last ones for me."* (m-nr-50-C-)
> *"We have more clever things to do."* (m-nr-01-A+)

The second group of reasons was related to either their own or their friends' lack of belief or just feeling they did not want to talk on these issues. Unfortunately several students did not explain the reasons why they did not discuss religion, if the main reason was similar to 'not interested' or if there was anything to do with a feeling of shame or a wish to avoid quarrels.

> *"No. Because my friends don't believe in God and we have other topics [to talk about]."* (f-nr-40-B?)
> *"It seems silly to speak about it aloud, in public."* (f-or-33-B?)

They usually talked about more casual issues and topics connected to everyday life. Some mentioned that they did not have knowledge, or were not able to speak about it. Some students declared that religion was too complicated or a philosophical subject.

> *"We don't speak because it is about serious things, but on these topics we speak rarely."* (m-or-45-B?)
>
> *"I don't know, maybe it is a rather difficult topic and there is no one to speak with about it or just afraid. I don't know."* (f-ch-03-A+)

The last of the reasons, used mainly by the Russian-speaking sample, was seeing religious topics as being too sensitive and personal a matter to discuss with friends. The students confessed that neither they nor their friends were the kind of people who could be trusted in speaking about intimate things. For some students with a religious background the topic was seen as too personal a matter. Some were rather restricted and said that they were ashamed to speak about religion aloud in public. Others were afraid of quarrels that could arise because of disagreements on religious topics.

> *"We don't have mutual understanding."* (m-ch-31-B?)

The reasons to speak. No specific occasions were identified for speaking about religion; the topic arose occasionally; one could be "*in such a mood*" or could hear something fascinating and out of the ordinary.

> *"These topics come when we are hanging around, if there is a corresponding mood."* (m-or-27-B?)
>
> *"We speak if it comes up or if we have heard something new and interesting."* (f-at-65-C+)

Those who spoke about religion rarely named concrete topics of discussion. The topic spoken about could relate to looking for an answer to an existential question, thinking about death and afterlife or sharing one's own doubts with friends.

> *"There have been occasions when doubts arise over his existence, are we right?"* (m-ch-44-B?)
>
> *"If it is spoken that there is no God, then questions arise, or when it is spoken that they don't believe in God."* (f-or-34-B?)

The impetus for discussion could also be encountering a view different from one's own regarding understanding of the world, different opinions, traditions and customs. Some had tried to understand why religion is needed or to sympathise with a different worldview in everyday life, or to reflect after a certain topic was discussed in religious education. Only Muslims were occasionally mentioned specifically; mostly students argued in general terms.

> *"We have talked but seldom. We have discussed why they have such customs and why they act so and why we are so different..."* (f-nr-19-A+)

For some students religion only came up as a topic while telling jokes about religions or religious people. Another reason mentioned for speaking about religion was religious violence as presented in the media.

> *"If we accidentally do speak, then maybe again it's about cruel acts carried out."* (m-nr-51-C-)

It is very difficult to identify what were the factors which led to speaking or not speaking about religion. When looking at the responses of students with or without religious backgrounds, in general terms (speak – do not speak), it seems this did not have much of an effect on the results. If one compares the topicality of religion to the importance of religion, it is mostly those who did not recognise religion as an important issue for them or saw religion mainly as part of a tradition who did not talk about religion. The more religion was connected with truth claims and coping with life, the more a student talked about it with friends. The other factor could be the age of respondents. Only one 14 year-old respondent said that he spoke with friends about religion, while half of the 15 year-olds, among students who had studied religious education for many years, included religion as a topic of discussion.

The differences in answers come up again if we look at reasons given for not speaking about religion. Students with religious backgrounds referred to religion as too personal a matter and to the unbelief of their friends, while the dominant group with no religious affiliation did not use these categories. However, the students with no religious affiliation still spoke about religious topics and tried to understand diversity particularly if he or she attended religious education. But not all the students who attended religious education reported that they spoke about religion in their everyday lives.

3.2.2.2 Experiences of religion

For many of the students it was not an easy task to name some experiences of religion. Almost one third of the students said they did not have any experiences of religion; some did not answer the question at all or gave very general answers, stating only that experiences were positive or negative, and giving no hint at all of abstract or more concrete examples. There were an equal number of good and bad experiences mentioned; only a few students offered both a negative and a positive example. Some answers and examples were neutral in their nature or it was difficult to decide if the respondent regarded it as a negative or positive experience.

Experiences with religious people, representing a different worldview from one's own. Most of the examples given were about meeting a religious person. Students pointed out that they had noticed the different behaviours or customs of some people, for example not celebrating birthdays. Diversity was noticed in baptism, wedding or funeral ceremonies, and also historical studies about Egypt and its ancient religion were mentioned.

An experience meeting a religion or worldview different from one's own was regarded negatively mostly when it was connected with proselytising. In such instances, believers were regarded as boring and sometimes even as frightening. Jehovah's Witnesses were mentioned in particular.

> *"Some are going from apartment to apartment and sound off about their faith, it makes me crazy (Jehovah's)."* (m-ch-30-B?)
>
> *"People who have different religion speak about totally other things that don't interest me. That is why it is uncomfortable to be with them. A good experience is when someone says something interesting about his religion."* (f-nr-02-A+)

The difference in lifestyle and also in understanding of life could be challenging or frightening. The lifestyle of religious people could be seen as negative: explosions caused by Muslims, an unpleasant neighbour, or boring lives were mentioned.

> *"These people are somehow so different and they must follow the things they have in religion and they can't live their own lives."* (m-nr-21-A+)

From history, the fact of Nazis killing Jews was mentioned as a negative example. Some students thought that religion was a ridiculous *"product of the human brain"*; it was only for weak, even mentally disordered people.

> *"It seems to me that people come to a religion to benefit (themselves) and because of lack of moral support, so I think that they are morally weak people."* (f-nr-41-B?)

Encountering difference was sometimes seen as a positive, enriching and interesting experience. In most cases it was seen as an exciting and challenging event by students who had studied religious education. They saw religion as providing a possibility for practising tolerance. Many students from School A referred to an excursion and meeting different representatives of diverse faiths as *"cool"* and interesting. Also students with religious education experience from another school named interesting experiences while travelling or living abroad; or visiting a beautiful church.

> *"My experiences have been very good. I was living in Canada, where I got to know Muslims and Hindus and learned a lot of new things."* (f-at-65-C+)

Experiences with one's own religion were mentioned by some Lutherans and mostly by Orthodox respondents, whose answers revealed personal stories, attachment or pain felt in connection with religion. Experiences with their own religion were predominantly seen as positive. Only a bad dream and funerals were mentioned as negative examples. Good experiences of religion were associated with meeting a kind and helpful person, living a pure life (usually a church-related person), and respecting or lending a hand to other people.

> *"People I see in a church are very kind and spiritually mature. They always help, give advice."* (f-or-33-B?)

Personal religious experiences were brought out as positive examples: a baptism, answered prayer and participation in a service. Negative examples in the field of personal experiences included an unanswered prayer, funerals and a bad dream.

> *"Once I had a dream about God. I didn't tell it to anybody. The dream was rather terrifying and made me want to cry. I have never communicated with religious people but I believe in God. In our apartment there is a pouf with icons and sometimes if I feel really bad I share my problems with it and I feel that they disappear."* (m-or-28-B?)

Some answers reflected the fact that students did not know whether their friends were religious or not and this was interpreted as a positive example. Particularly interesting is that, when tolerance was not asked about directly, not having experience with any religion was seen as positive, and not being religious was described as a precondition for good relations.

> *"We don't particularly have people with a certain religion. We all get on well."* (m-nr-54-C-)

Taking into account that some students did not answer the question (there were fewer unanswered questions in School B, where children had a more religious background), and that many claimed not to have any experience of religion, the data showed that positive experiences of contact with religion related to family. In a comparison between three Estonian-speaking groups of students (with eight years, a few months and no experience of religious education respectively) it emerged that the more they had experienced religious education the more they found positive examples as well as negative ones. Russian-speaking respondents without a religious background predominantly stressed the negative impact of religion, as did Estonian-speaking students without a religious background or religious education experience.

From the students' answers they appeared rarely to meet or to acknowledge religion in their everyday life. Meeting a different worldview from one's own was largely seen as an unpleasant, boring or frightening experience. While religious self-identification helped students to see the positive influence of their own religion, the chance to study religious education enabled them to recognise religion in everyday life and to see meeting difference as a positive or enriching experience.

3.2.2.3 Religious pluralism

Although their experiences of religion were neither the best nor the most common occurrence among students, most of them did not see religion as a reason to separate people. Students' views on the possibility for peaceful co-existence of different religions were not uniform, but most agreed that it was possible where there was mutual respect: half of the students thought it was possible, a quarter that it was impossible, while almost a quarter saw both possibilities and some could not say.

The arguments put forward for the impossibility of peaceful co-existence, if they existed at all, were short and general. Many times it was stated that it was not possible, without any further explanation. The sceptical arguments could be subdivided into two main types. The first group of reasons covered potential for wars and abiding quarrels at home, while the second raised the issue of people imposing their views upon others.

In their answers it appeared that the respondents did not like conflicts or did not want religion to be a source of disagreements. The main reason brought forward as to why it is impossible to live peacefully together, was the quarrelling and constant arguing about religion that might result.

> *"I know my acquaintances, who have different religions and a husband says to his wife to go to his church but she doesn't want to and says that she goes to her church and they have constant quarrels, arguing and scandals."* (f-or-34-b?)

Probably in these cases co-existence was understood in terms of family life, not so much in terms of society. Occasionally it was evident but for the most part it was not possible to distinguish whether they were speaking in terms of family or society. In addition to general remarks about constant arguing and the uncomfortable atmosphere, some personal examples were introduced about relatives, friends or themselves. If the difficulty of co-existence was understood at the societal level, the arguments were general statements about bad relationships or disagreements. In some cases examples from history were presented – crusades and religious wars in particular. Both, personal and historical views are present in the following quotation.

"No, because I, who almost believe, argue very much with people who believe the same and if the religions are even different, it would be a catastrophe because they would argue and even fight about whose god(s) are the right one(s). We know already about crusades from history." (f-ur-67-C+)

The second reason was similar – palming off your worldview on a spouse. The reason for having this as an argument could be one's own experience and feeling uncomfortable, when annoyed in this way – a fact frequently mentioned in students' experiences with a religion different from their own.

One reason given for the impossibility of peaceful co-existence was exceptional: a boy without any religious affiliation mentioned religious reasons for the impossibility of living together.

"They can't because they would be afraid of each other and would be afraid that an evil spirit comes and makes their life a hell." (m-nr-50-C-)

Arguments for the possibility of living together varied from societal to individual ones. This time the arguments and examples tended to be more personal; concrete examples from society and students' own experiences were used. Those who stressed the societal dimension were able to mention two different faith communities living peacefully together in their neighbourhood: Orthodox and Lutherans, Christians and Jews, Buddhists and Mormons. Respondents understood that in reality a society was very seldom totally homogeneous.

"In the town there are two churches; an Orthodox and a synagogue. Some go to one and comply with their customs, others to the other." (m-or-45-B?)

At a more personal level, some students had some acquaintance with families including representatives from different religions and they knew them to be happily married nevertheless.

"Yes, because for example nowadays people making up a family often have a different creed but at the same time they have happy families and a good marriage." (f-nr-41-B?)

For many students it was difficult to imagine that religion could be something to get passionate about or make into a problem. As religion was not important for them and they did not talk about religious topics, it was hard to believe that somebody could be bothered to create conflicts over religious matters. A common argument was that religion could not interfere with relationships because nobody cares.

"Yes they can, why should anyone bother if some representative of another belief lives next to you?" (f-nr-51-C-)

If the respondent saw **both possibilities**, saying that representatives of different religions might live together given certain preconditions, the main prerequisites for co-existence were respect for a different worldview and customs, and people possessing mutual tolerance and love. In addition, good will was mentioned as an important precondition. Although, the extreme and external demonstrations of belief were not regarded as a good precondition for peaceful co-existence, respondents did not make generalisations about all representatives of a religion.

> *"Yes they can if they respect each other's religion, but if they don't, then I think it is not advisable. Because, let us suppose that neighbours were a Muslim and a Christian. I have a feeling that Muslims don't tolerate other believers very much because they have only one god and they don't acknowledge other gods. And if another believer lives in this neighbourhood, then I don't think that anything good will come out of it. Although it could turn out to be a wrong opinion because not all Muslims are so crazy, too. So, broadly speaking, they can indeed."* (f-ch-03-A+)

If religion was seen as a secondary factor, sometimes other more important factors were named, in addition to religious affiliation, for making it possible to live together despite differences. These were personal qualities, having friends from different religions, keeping religion a private matter, and shared interests and activities.

> *"They can. Because beside a creed there are a lot of other things what can unite people. For example, I don't believe in God but my friend does but I am not against it, we go together for training."* (m-at-26-B?)
> *"I think they can indeed. Why shouldn't they? I think that representatives of different religions can get along completely well. It is more up to characters. But if you will thrust your faith unto your neighbours, then problems can arise indeed."* (m-nr-12-A+)

Comparing the answers of different groups of respondents, it would appear that regarding oneself as a person with religious affiliation or a person without any affiliation, did not make any difference to whether or not peaceful co-existence of different religions was seen to be possible. Nevertheless, the argument that religion was too marginal to cause any troubles or disagreements was mostly used by students without any particular worldview and mostly, too, by students who had not experienced religious education. It seems that the impact of religious education is not straightforward – it does not make one think that peaceful co-existence is the only possible outcome. Youngsters with experience of religious education saw the problem of peaceful co-existence as more complex, using more unassertive expressions such as "*might be possible*" and gave other preconditions beside religious ones. The students who claimed not to have any experience of religion were the most sceptical about the possibility of living together peacefully, even more so than those who declared that they had had a bad experience of religion. However, to speak about relations or even a cause-effect connection between these parameters on the basis of a qualitative study would be too premature.

3.2.2.4 Summary

Religion was not very important at a personal level. Neither was it seen as very important at a group level or in the relations the students have with others. It seems that the secular framework discourages the expression of worldview differences. Another reason could be that students long for harmony and a peaceful life and that a strategy to avoid conflict is to avoid the topic and conversations on these issues. The students spoke slightly more frequently about religious topics if they had a religious background or they had experienced religious education. Students with a religious background declared more positive experiences of religion. As the negative number was the same for students with and without religious affiliation, one can suggest that religiousness did not make them blind to negative aspects of religion. Students without religious affiliation declared less experience of religion,, but the more students had learned about religions, even without any personal religious background, the more they seemed to have an eye for positive examples and an inclination to speak about them.

Although the importance of religion did not depend on gender, girls did name more positive experiences of religion and less negative ones. Also, religion was more often a topic of conversation for girls than for boys. But the differences were insignificant; no generalisations could be made on this point. Boys almost always understood the question of living together on a societal level, while girls justified their positions with examples from the lives of families where representatives of different religions lived together peacefully or where there was tension and altercation. Girls from School B especially responded in this way.

For the most part religion was seen as neither a factor of conflict, since it was not considered to be important, nor an opportunity for dialogue. Instead it was seen as something boring or annoying but not as a source of discord. In speaking about the possibility of peaceful co-existence students usually did not use personal examples but remained reserved and impersonal. Religious background did not have much effect on their attitudes toward peaceful co-existence, but did make reasons more personal, while experience of religious education made their way of thinking more complex and multi-faceted.

Probably due to the higher religiousness of the Russian-speaking population they had more experiences of religion. Also they were slightly more sceptical about the possibility of living together with a person of a different religion.

3.2.3 Education about religion in school

3.2.3.1 General attitude towards religious education in school

When reading the answers of students regarding religion in education one must keep in mind emotive discussions against religious education in the Estonian media in recent years, but not in the Russian media. Mostly attitudes towards religion in schools are focused on the question of religious education. The attitudes mirrored in the media regarding religious education are usually not based on personal experience, as most of people in Estonia have not had any experience of the subject. In the case of the REDCo project, the sample included both students without experience of religious education and also a minority group in Estonia of students with personal experience of religious education.

If asked about the possible place of religion at school students saw it only in terms of the subject religious education. In the sample, the answers were clearly placed in three groups – equal numbers of those who were opposed and those who were in favour, plus a group who thought it should be a voluntary subject. In the following section I will consider the students' arguments more closely.

Reasons against religious education could be grouped into three main sets: seeing religious education as a confessional subject, an overloaded timetable, and dissonance with the aims of the curriculum and its scientific approach.

1. Many students without any experience of religious education or with experience of a confessional Orthodox school, regarded religious education as a confessional subject, its purpose being to teach students to believe. In the view of these students such a subject cannot have any place in school, because they could not imagine it in a secular school with children from different religious, and especially non-religious, backgrounds.

> *"No. Why should it be? I don't believe in God!"* (f-nr-37-B?)
> *"No. Because there are students with different confessions at school."* (m-or-29-B?)

Usually this confessional approach interpretation of religious education is joined with the comment that such a subject could be taught at school but it should be voluntary for the student. Students proposed, that those who want such (confessional) instruction could attend some studies organised by faith communities and special religious schools or look for other sources of information – books or the internet. Religion was also seen as a private matter.

"No. Religion – it is a private matter. If you wish – study, if not – don't. There is no need to force people." (f-nr-40-B?)

2. In Estonia it is common knowledge that the students' timetable is overloaded. The students know this from their own experience, so their point concerning that question is well justified. Sometimes they also stated that the subject was not really interesting for them.

"There are too many lessons and tests already at school, so an additional subject (religion) would overload students who are not interested in that topic." (f-nr-52-C-)

3. Religion was also seen as contradictory to all the other subjects and the aims of school to promote a scientific worldview. Again, special institutions offering religious education were named by Orthodox students. Religion was considered not to fit into the school system; even the low academic attainment of former students from a religious school is mentioned.

"No. It is just another surplus lesson and even more children from the ecclesiastical school have poor academic achievement." (m-at-26-B?)

Although religious literacy was not explicitly regarded as contradictory to schooling, some students found that there were more urgent skills to be learned.

"No. Because you must teach children professions, not religion nowadays. You can study religion yourself if you want to." (f-or-33-B?)

Reasons given for religious education are three-fold: the interest of the topic, its relevance to everyday life, and moral-religious reasons were taken into account. I will look at each of these in more detail.

1. Most of the students in favour of religious education regarded it as an interesting, even exciting topic. Some students gave hints about things they would be interested in or would like to learn: basic information about different religions, Bible stories and parables, discussions about books and films. Engaging with religion was regarded as something that broadens one's worldview and helps the learner to understand the world.

"Yes, because everyone should know basic rules about different religions. So one can better understand the world." (m-at-72-C+)
"Yes, I have a feeling that religion is exciting. There are many interesting stories in the Bible that make you think. I love parables. I think that more of such films as "The da Vinci Code" must be produced." (m-or-28-B?)

2. One of the students came up after filling in the questionnaire and asked for advice on how he should behave in a Muslim country. He was going to a Mus-

lim country soon with a sports team and felt uninformed. Some answers mirrored the same concern – religious education should be available in the school, as it is needed when one visits a foreign country, both in terms of learning appropriate behaviour and avoiding offence to others, and in terms of understanding the culture.

> *"Certainly should be. As it educates and is useful for us. If you are going to another culture you would know something about it."* (f-nr-70-C+)

3. Also religious and moral explanations were put forward. When religious education was seen as a confessional subject, then it was regarded as a means to introduce God and religious worldviews to unbelievers. It was hoped that such a subject would improve students' morality, even save young people from spoiling their lives. When religious education was viewed as a non-confessional subject it was considered to be a tool to nurture tolerance and to make students more sensitive towards other religions.

> *"Yes, it should. Because you shouldn't take another's belief just like "we are the important ones and they are nobody" and it would be good indeed if we knew more about other religions."* (f-nr-16-A+)
> *"Yes, I think so, because studying different religions nurtures tolerance."* (f-nr-67-C+)
> *"Yes because children must know who God is and what the religious world is."* (m-or-42-B?)

There was also a group of students who suggested that religious education could be a **voluntary subject,** organised only for those who needed it. This group was distributed equally among those who had studied a religious education and others who had not. The rationale brought forward reflected the same range of views as that put forward against religious education – understanding religious education as a confessional subject or an overloaded timetable; but the most common explanation was lack of interest. Only in one case were tensions with families' religious convictions mentioned.

> *"It [religious education] should be [part of the school life]. But it should be voluntary because maybe somebody doesn't want to study it; that puts him off or disturbs his family somehow. In our school it is voluntary but you can opt out only if you submit a letter with the signature of a parent." (m-nr-13-A+)*
> *"I really don't know. But at the same time I think if there are believers in a school somewhere, then why not?"* (f-nr-56-C-)

It is possible to discern a very strong connection between the school and students' attitudes towards religion at school: most students of School B (a school teaching predominantly in Russian) dismissed the idea of any form of religion at school; only two saw it as necessary and one thought it could be accepted under certain conditions. Two respondents from School B, who thought it possible to have religion at school, had a religious background (and so had perhaps attended a religious school). In other schools, students were more positive about religious education. So, could it been concluded that Russian-speaking students did not want religious education while Estonian-speaking students did? If we look at the data not from a socio-demographical perspective but in connection with students' experience of having religious education or not, the picture comes clearer. The students did not want religion at school if they did not have it at school (School B and School C grade 9) and they saw it as needed, or at least as a possible subject, if they had experienced it (School A, School C grade 10). In School C, in the class with no religious education, half of the students did not want any form of religious education. By contrast, in one class that did have religious education the resolute 'No' was used in only two cases and not at all in the other class.

There was a higher degree of agreement in support of religious education in School C grade 9, where students did not have religious education, than in School B. However, even if this was a higher proportion than in School B, it was remarkably *lower* than in the grades which did have religious education (grades 10-12). The more positive attitude towards religious education in comparison with School B could have been influenced by the students who had studied RE at upper levels as was clearly stated in one of the answers.

> *"In my opinion there should be religious education at our school. My friend has it at school and it is known to be interesting."* (m-nr-54-C-)

3.2.3.2 Proposed contents of religious education

Although a proportion of students stated that religion should not be part of studies at school, only a few refused to give a list of topics the school must cover, if the subject about religion were to be introduced. The answers were focused on the content of religious education, not on its form. Only four students gave some hints about possible aims and methods used in religious education such as *"organize discussions on these topics"* (m-or-27-B?), *"to understand motives of people from different religions"* (m-ur-63-C+), *"what is expected after life, how we should live"* (m-or-35-B?). Mostly students named more concrete topics related to facts, representing a very knowledge-based orientation. This is not surprising, as school education in Estonia is very information-centred in general. It would be difficult for a student to imagine or even understand another approach (see also section 5). The topics presented lay between learning about one's own religion and learning about other religions; also, generic topics concerning religion were included rather than any particular religion.

Some students named more abstract topics concerning religion as a phenomenon – what is religion? Why do people need it? What would happen if you
joined a religious group? Are there any grounds for religion? These questions
were mentioned by students both with and without a religious background, and
both with and without experience of religious education. The students who had
declared their Christian background introduced some existential topics: Does
God exist? How can we live good lives? What will happen after death? At the
same time some students (mostly those with experience of religious education)
mentioned the importance of tolerance and understanding a different worldview,
irrespective of their own religious affiliation. One might have assumed that
individual religious affiliation would add a more personal approach and passion
to the explanation, but usually this was not the case. The following two examples are typical, the first from a student with a religious affiliation and the
second, presenting a more elaborated argument for tolerance, from one without.

> *"[Students should learn] how to behave with representatives of these religions,
> to learn about these religions and to explore the background of religion of your
> own country."* (f-ur-67-C+)
> *"1. That there are particular customs in every country; 2. They should be re-
> spected; 3. Religion is not forced upon believers but a free choice and it is re-
> garded as necessary. He [a believer?] has a belief in something and he has
> someone to talk to if he hasn't anyone else (god)."* (f-nr-19-A+)

The most interesting and relevant topic for students, especially Estonians, was
learning about the religion of others. They wanted to know how religions began,
what their traditions, customs and rules are; what they teach their followers
(beliefs, gods and creation stories); what they celebrate (festivals, customs and
rituals). Also some students found it worthwhile to learn how different religions
are constituted in their history and culture (sacred history and religious persons;
church architecture, scriptures and symbols of religions, pilgrimages, sacred
things and beings). Usually no specific religion was stated; they wanted to learn
about different religions, large and small ones, different beliefs – generally to
know some interesting facts concerning the religious world.

> *"About beliefs of different countries, their customs and why these customs/rules
> have been made."* (f-nr-02-A+)

A completely different conception of the content of religious studies was that of
religious education as introducing a student (in)to the Christian tradition. The
respondents, who were mostly students from School B, covered topics regarding
history of the church (including biographies of saints, the history of Jerusalem),
teachings of the church (Bible, knowledge about Old and New Testaments,
about Jesus, the Ten Commandments, creeds, understanding of God and after-

life), living as a Christian (prayer, how to live: not smoking, drinking, lying, killing, and stealing; how to behave at church).

When the answers from different schools are contrasted, the distinctiveness of School B is obvious. Almost half of the students saw Christianity as the only content of religious education, while the other half saw it as a legitimate topic alongside learning about other religions. Only two respondents from School B did not mention Christianity at all. Probably the Orthodox school's influence in School B has shaped their understanding of religious education. At another extreme is the 9th grade of School C, seeing different religions as appropriate content in 14 answers out of 15. In all Estonian schools and classes Christianity alone was mentioned just twice, while only religions and general topics were mentioned in four answers out of five. In classes with experience of religious education, Christianity was identified as one of the topics for study, but not the only one, by a quarter of the students. This shows that the Estonian-speaking students who attend religious education feel more relaxed about studying Christianity and are not afraid of being indoctrinated through studying it.

The answers to the question about the place of religion at school were compared with responses concerning the content of world religions. It might have been expected that if a student wished to learn about different religions instead of one, they would see it more as a subject to be studied by all students. However this assumption could not be verified; in fact, students tended to regard religious education as an optional subject if they also considered that different religions should be studied.

3.2.3.3 Does the teacher have the right to be religious?

There were an equal number of those who thought that a teacher must believe in order to be able to teach religion from a background of personal experience and deeper understanding of religion, and those who saw believing as a disadvantage, because of the fear of indoctrination and of partiality. The third group of students, equal in number with previous two, had a neutral position not seeing the teacher's religious commitment or lack of it as an issue at all.

The reasons against a religious teacher. One third of all respondents would prefer a non-religious person to teach about religion. The main concerns were fear of indoctrination, even brainwashing of students or choosing topics telling about only one religion, usually different from the students' worldview, as could be seen from the answers to other questions. This fear was never supported by any concrete examples of attempts by any teacher to indoctrinate, but was rather abstract and was probably influenced by public discussions or general prejudices about the eagerness of believers to intervene into people's privacy.

"No, they should not. They should be impartial. If a teacher belongs to one religion, she/he would concentrate more on the religion she/he belongs to." (f-nr-70-C+)

Even some students from a school with religious education gave this as a reason, although their teacher is a committed Christian. In an oral interview I asked if there had been any examples of the teacher indoctrinating students. The were extremely surprised and expressed the view that they had not even known that their teacher was religious at all: *"No, she is totally normal!"*

Also some students were afraid that a teacher, whose worldview they did not share, could not be impartial when assessing their achievements, and it would also be rather difficult to have a discussion with such a person. These students, who took the view that it is better for a teacher not to believe, argued that otherwise the teacher would brainwash students or would not tell them about anything other than their own religion.

Being religious was regarded as a bad model for students, not appropriate for, and contradicting the worldview of the majority of students'. In a less extreme form the view was expressed that such a teacher would not be understood by students (mostly without religious affiliation) or that students could feel uncomfortable.

> *"They shouldn't. Then I could not behave, certainly they would have some sessions of moral lecturing. You never know if you act well or badly."* (f-nr-57-C-)

Why should a teacher believe? Those who argued that a teacher must be a believer said that he or she would have a deeper understanding, either of the subject or of God.
> *"Should be, how else? An unbeliever would not know so much as a believer."* (f-nr-40-B?)

Students in favour of a religious teacher valued the greater interest such a person would have in the subject; they could have fascinating stories from their own experiences to tell rather than presenting only distant and cold facts. Some arguments were constructed from their own (positive) preconceptions about believers – they would be more empathetic and understand students better, without having "*teachers' pets*". As the unbelievers tended to regard a religious person as a bad example, similarly the students with religious affiliation wanted the teacher to set a positive example for students.

> *"They should [believe] so they can set a good example for students."* (m-ch-44-B?)
> *"Could be, then they would assess all children equally, they would not have favourites."* (m-ur-63-C+)

The third group said that **it is not important if a teacher is religious or not**, the teacher could represent some particular religion, but it would not be a necessary precondition for a teacher to have a personal attachment to some religion. Most students did not explain why it was not important, but for others it seemed that the knowledge and pedagogical skills of the teacher were more important than being religious. As with arguments against having a religious teacher, here also the need for impartiality was stressed – it was said that a teacher could be a believer so long as (s)he did not force students into faith, present material or lead discussions with bias and did not try to indoctrinate his/her students. The professionalism of the teacher was seen as more important than religious affiliation.

> *"There is no difference, if she/he teaches the subject well, then a teacher could be even a Satanist."* (m-at-61-C-)

The responses of Estonian students did not differ between the schools – only a few wanted a teacher to be religious, others answered equally *"can be"* and *"must not be"*. There were more students from the class without religious education who saw the religiosity of the teacher as a serious threat to their views about religion, if compared with students who had religious education. But negative attitudes towards a religious teacher could be due to the negative connotation of a religious person in general (see section 3.2.2.2 "Experiences of religion") associated with an irresistible urge to indoctrinate students into their own religion. Students from School B differed remarkably in their attitudes: three students out of four would prefer a religious teacher, while in Estonian schools religiosity was seen rather as a disadvantage for a teacher. The reason could be that it was made clear in the Russian questionnaire that the question was specifically about a teacher of religious education, while in the Estonian version this should have been understood from the context and it is possible that some students mistakenly related the question to a teacher in general. The second and more influential reason could be that Russian-speaking students saw religious education as more confessional than Estonian-speaking students did (see the previous section "Proposed contents for religious education").

In analyses of responses regarding students' attitudes to the suggested content of religious education, it became obvious that if a student saw the content of the studies as being only Christian, they unanimously expected a teacher to be a Christian. The less they expected Christianity to be the content, the less happy they were with the idea of a religious person teaching at school. Only three respondents out of 38, who did not mention any Christian topic as relevant for school, wanted a teacher to be a believer. For others it was considered to be a disadvantage or not important.

In conclusion, it can be said that in the case against a religious teacher there were two main arguments unfolding – the fear of being indoctrinated and feeling uncomfortable with a different worldview. Religious affiliation was justified in the students' view in cases of confessional religious education or by greater competence in religious issues brought by a committed person.

3.2.3.4 Religious education

The question about the organisational model of religious education seemed inappropriate for some students, who emphasised that there was no need for any model of religious education; a few others did not answer the question or could not decide what they preferred. Others tried to answer the question even if they had responded before that they did not want any religious education.

One third of the students preferred to have common religious education lessons for all students **together**, regardless of their worldview. There were three main arguments used in support of studying together. The most frequently given reason was the benefit of shared knowledge about different worldviews. Religious education classes should not be separated along the lines of different worldviews, as the knowledge one acquires is worthwhile for everyone.

> *"All students [should study] all religions, to learn about other cultures, a person is not alone in the world."* (f-ur-67-C+)

Somehow similar but yet different were arguments about the possibility of sharing one's worldview with others and the necessity of building up a common understanding. Both were striving to find common ground but the means suggested for achieving this goal were diametrically different. The sharing of one's own views and opinions would fulfil the desire to know more about each other's convictions and at the same time to remain committed to one's own opinions.

> *"They should have common education as they would know more about each other's faith; certainly one should not influence others to change their belief."* (f-nr-14-A+)

In some cases the building up of a common understanding was believed to be achievable through shared knowledge and uniform understanding.

> *"All the students should have [religious education together]. For example all would understand the same thing even-handedly."* (m-ur-73-C+)

The third mentioned reason was that it would be easier to organize religious education in a joint group; a subject organised in separate groups would be difficult to accomplish.

One third of students were in favour of studying religion in **separated groups** according to students' worldviews and they gave two main reasons for their choice. First of all they found it important to remain faithful to one's belief. It was felt as most comfortable and understandable to study one's own religion taught by a teacher who shares your religion and with students of the same background, in order to keep your own religion.

> *"No, nobody must be interested in a different religion but should study his/her own."* (m-or-28-B?)

It seems that these students wanted to avoid quarrels and controversies in such a sensitive subject as religion, so they saw the best solution as to separate different worldviews from each other.

> *"It must be separated, because quarrels might arise between representatives of different religions."* (f-nr-41-B?)

The division of students into groups, not only by religious affiliation but also by interest in the subject, was also deemed possible. Remarkably only ten students cited the **voluntary** form of religious education, which is demanded by present Estonian law, as their choice.

> *"I think that those who want to study religion should have it. But for those who do not want to study it, there is no need to study it as it does not interest them and they would not participate in it anyway."* (f-nr-52-C-)

The major differences emerged when schools were compared. Students from School B never mentioned the possibility of a subject 'for those who are interested' and they preferred clearly to learn about religion in groups. Again, it corresponded to their view on confessional religious education. Students in all the classes with religious education also did not see religious education as a voluntary subject (only one student from each class having religious education chose that option) and were more in favour of the form they were taught by – all students together, seeing religious education as needed for minimising tensions between different groups in class. At the same time, Estonian respondents, who had no personal experience of religious education, were those who mostly suggested the option of a voluntary subject as currently stipulated by Estonian law.

In conclusion, all groups were looking for ways that were appropriate to their worldview and experiences, and for types of religious education that would avoid tensions between students. The Russian-speaking students were more in favour of a confessional subject to confirm their Orthodox identity, students who had experience of religious education preferred a subject shared by all and those without experience of religious education preferred the subject be an extra option for others, if it was provided at all.

3.2.3.5 Summary

The most significant differences in students' answers occurred in relation to their more or less personal experience of religious education. There were three main groups regarding attitudes towards religious education – students who had personally experienced religious education and were in favour of the subject; students who saw it as a voluntary subject for interested students; and those who saw it as a confessional subject for believers. Opinions about religious education depended most of all on the experience they had or did not have of religious education and to some extent on their vision of what it should be.

In general, the desired content of studies about religion was connected to giving information about different religions for the Estonian sample and about one's own religion for the sample of School B. The answers of Russian-speaking students differed from all given in Estonian classes. Russian-speaking students were strongly against religious education and (or because?) they saw it as a confessional subject. This confessional understanding emerged when they described its aims and contents. Christianity should constitute the major part of it and it should introduce a student to the religion to which he or she belongs culturally. Also a teacher was seen as preferably being a religious person in order to understand the subject. This reflects the Orthodox approach, that religion is first of all lived and celebrated – so devotion is a precondition for understanding religion. The preference for a confessional approach to religious education could be rooted in the history of a particular school or in the need for affirmation of ethnic identity while living in Estonia. The last hypothesis is supported by different studies conducted on the identity of Russians in Estonia, but could be called into question by the notion that most students were against religious education.

Estonian students without any experience of religious education would not choose to study religious education themselves and recommended that lessons should be organised for other students interested in such matters. Even if the subject was seen as optional, it should be non-confessional, dealing (almost without exception) with different world religions and being taught by a strictly objective teacher. For the teacher the 'not believing' worldview is seen as normal (even normative), while a Christian or theistic worldview is seen as biased and wrong. The desire for a voluntary form of religious education and the declared need for knowledge about different religions went hand in hand.

The students with experience of religious education held a position that religious education supports their understanding of the people around them and makes them culturally educated. They wanted to study world religions but also to know about Christianity and to be able to understand the history and culture of Estonia and Europe. They wished for neutrality, but tended to be more pliant – they saw the need for certain preconditions in order to allow for, or even appreciate, the religiosity of a teacher.

The responses about the form of religious education were compared to the answers on the desired content of religious education. One might assume that the more the content dealt with different religions the less it would be seen as a voluntary subject. However, just the opposite was found in the sample; most of the voluntary cases came from the group wishing to learn about different religions. If the desired content was predominantly Christian, then more than half of the respondents wanted to study it in different groups and not as a voluntary subject. Only a minority of students specified the voluntary form of religious education, which is currently demanded by Estonian law, as their choice. The reason could be that the form of religious education required by law was not practised in any of the schools represented and they just could not come up with such an option. Significantly, none of the students with a particular worldview wanted to have voluntary religious education; they either wanted to study it all together or in groups.

Some gender differences emerged in the answers. The girls were rather more enthusiastic about having religious education than boys. At the same time, boys were more resolute regarding the teacher being religious – boys used the stronger wording, "*must be*" or "*must not be*", as compared with the girls "*could be*", a believer. Girls were slightly more interested in studying religious education together, while boys wanted more to stay in groups. There was a similar goal in both cases – to have harmonious relations, but different means to reach this were expressed. Boys argued for separation in order to avoid conflicts on religious matters, while girls instead preferred joint studies in order to share with others one's own experiences and common knowledge.

The students' opinions about the form and content of religious education reflected the situation at their particular schools – mostly they were satisfied with the way things were, no matter what was current practice. If they had not experienced religious education up to now, they preferred not to have it in future either and if they had it now, then they were very happy in general terms to continue with it. For students it was difficult to imagine forms of school religious education that they had not experienced. This did not mean that if the options were given they would not consider them. Even if attitudes regarding religious education were different, the reasons given evinced clearly fear of being indoctrinated and fear of quarrels activated by religious education. These arguments were supported by discussions in society but never by their own experiences in school.

3.3 Reflections and conclusions

3.3.1 Religion – perceptions

Religion did not have a very visible role in the lives and contexts of the young people and was often viewed as so personal and confidential that students hardly spoke about it.

There was a rather sharp difference regarding the meaning of religion for Estonian and Russian-speaking students. Estonian-speaking students were much more distant towards religion than Russian-speaking young people. Family played a crucial role in the religiousness of Russian-speaking students by introducing them to their (mostly Orthodox) tradition. The importance of family for the Russian-speaking population has been pointed out by different surveys made in Estonia comparing ethnic and religious backgrounds (for example, Liiman, 2001). Also Masso and Vihalemm (2004) in their identity research have pointed out the bigger influence of the family in identity-formation among Russian-speaking youngsters. But the influence of the family cannot be taken as automatic and enforced obedience by the children, but rather as valued and internalised belief. In their answers students from School B showed personal attachment to religion, while talking about their experiences of religion.

From the responses in the current study religion appears to have a minor role in the view of Estonian-speaking students – they seldom regard themselves as belonging to any religious tradition, they have few experiences of religion and they almost never speak about religion with their peers. Even religious students who do speak about religion are more likely to discuss religion with like-minded people. Thus religious education has great importance in creating a safe environment and in teaching skills of dialogue about and among representatives of different religious and secular worldviews.

The religion which students know most about is Christianity, as it is introduced in school lessons or in the homes of the few religiously affiliated families. It is difficult for students to make choices based on such a small amount of knowledge about religion as they have. Also other surveys conducted about religiosity in Estonia report the low importance of religion to Estonian respondents. The proportion of people who cannot define their religious affiliation or worldview is very high (65–75%) according to different surveys made in Estonia (Statistical Office of Estonia, 2002; Liiman, 2001; Halman et al., 2005 etc). As presented in section 2.1.1, the low importance of religion also includes beliefs and values in addition to (not) belonging (European Commission, 2005; Rüütel & Tiit, 2005).

The reasons are manifold – they go back to atheistic propaganda conducted in Estonia, as well as to the fact that children usually have neither a religious upbringing at home nor religious education at school. Kilemit and Nõmmik conducted a research study (2002) regarding the understanding of the word 'religion' by Estonian adults and found it to be a very confusing issue among respondents; it seemed to be too abstract and impersonal. Are the students inclined to untraditional, New Age movements, as could be suggested by the results of Euro barometer survey, when 54% of the Estonian sample said they believed in 'some sort of spirit or life force' (European Commission, 2005)? Nothing in the answers of students for this study alluded to their interest in or acquaintance with this kind of view. The oral interviews gave the impression that the students lack knowledge about religions and that makes it difficult for them to specify their religious or unreligious affiliation. For example, a girl without any religious affiliation gave an account in her interview of her own relation to religion.

> *"In that sense that... I mean certainly there is somebody somewhere. I don't deny that it is so. And I respect people who believe, it is their personal choice ... But in such a way that I myself, I don't go to church. But I would like to be permitted to be baptised and be confirmed. I would like that. Why? Actually because I have an idée fixe that I want to get married at a church in a white dress and so on. And maybe I am not a confirmed atheist; I do believe in God ... Maybe I don't believe in that Christ's crucifixion, in such a strict way, but in God generally I believe. Somebody helps indeed."* (Oral interview 2, female, no affiliation)

Lea Altnurme has pointed out that although people in Estonia may have religious experiences, they are often unable to express them (2006, 306).

Kaisa-Kattri Niit in her research (2002) about social axioms held by university students in Estonia found that, even if students scored very low in religiosity, they demonstrated openness towards difference. This was probably true for the students in universities but it could not be said of the 14–16 year old students surveyed at the time. Even if students held very optimistic positions regarding the possibility of different religions living peacefully together, this did not show their positive attitudes towards religion. Mostly religion was seen as neither a factor of conflict nor an area for dialogue. It was not considered that it could be taken seriously enough to inspire conflicts in society. More often religion was seen as something annoying and boring, rather than as a focus of discord.

3.3.2 Potentials of school

It is difficult to speak about any religious denomination in Estonia as a majority group (see 2.1.1). Not just a single denomination or religion, but the whole 'religious community' constitutes only a minority in Estonia. Moreover, Kilemit and Nõmmik (2002) found that the word 'believer' has strong negative connotation for Estonians. This sheds some light on one of the reasons why students do not like to speak about their religious convictions. That could also explain the hesitation of female respondents to attach themselves to some religion. The religious person can end up as an outcast, as demonstrated in an oral interview:

> *"For example at school ... there was a boy, I don't even remember from what religion he was, I don't know it even. He was kept at a distance – he had his own friends who believed the same way. Because we didn't believe we didn't communicate with him. Maybe we thought that we don't have anything to talk with him or so."* (Oral interview 2, female, no affiliation)

In the situation where families do not support the religious literacy of students, the school has a crucial role in supporting children's ability to make informed choices on matters of religion, giving information about different religions and enhancing readiness for mutual understanding and respect. There is a strong need for a balanced approach to religion, showing the positive effects, not just the dangers already known from other school subjects and the media.

The sociologist Aune Valk in her introduction to an anthology about differences of Estonians in comparison to other nations says:

> *"In the multicultural world it is possible to value differences and not to be afraid of them for a person who knows who he is and who are the others. Uncertainty and ignorance about oneself and fear in front of otherness often go hand in hand and are some of the main reasons for incipient ethnic conflicts."* (Valk, 2002a, 11–12)

Most likely this is equally true for religious differences and clashes; fear in front of the 'other' could be lessened by increasing familiarity with different religions. This can shed light on reasons why the students with no experience of religion scored least of all in believing in the peaceful co-existence of different worldviews, even less than those students who only referred to negative experiences of religion.

The introduction of religious education has had strong opposition in the media and in educational circles in Estonia (see section 2.2.1). Mostly the people who are against it have had no personal experience of religious education. In the survey, students' way of looking at the place religion in school depends on their actual experiences. Students who have not experienced religious education are afraid of brainwashing and quarrels activated by the subject. Some of the students, even if they appreciate religious education, hesitate to choose the subject. In an oral interview a boy gave reasons why he thought students did not choose an optional religious education:

> *"No, I do not know, some students are embarrassed certainly if religious education is a voluntary subject. I do not know how it could be solved in Estonia so*

that there wouldn't be any mocking and so on. Certainly it was problematic in former classes. That the children [who choose the subject] would be ridiculed as believers and so on. They want ... they do not want to be different from others and are afraid of being out of the circle of friends, of company. They are afraid of being different." (Oral interview 4, male, protestant)

A similar bias and suspicious attitude to religious people can be traced in the view that the teacher's secular non-religious worldview is seen as normative and neutral, while a Christian or theistic worldview is considered to be biased and wrong.

3.3.3 Religious education: changing attitudes

Does religious education have the potential to change attitudes in order to increase tolerance? In addition to ethnic differences, experience of religious education seemed to be the most important factor; comparisons of the answers by classes were often most fruitful in finding differences and patterns. What were the characteristics of the students, who had experienced religious education compared to those who had not? First of all, they noticed or at least expressed that they had noticed the influences of religion in their surroundings and in the lives of people around them more than did students without any religious education experience. Also they demonstrated more complex ideas about religion and religious people, and were able to give examples of religion's appearance in contemporary life. They found differences to be interesting and fascinating, while students without religious education showed their impatience with approaches different from their own. Those, who had religious education, talked about religious issues and noticed the positive influences of different religions and religious people. Religious education made them curious and also gave them the skills to talk on religious matters. Certainly, this could only be a hypothesis and without having a quantitative survey any far reaching conclusions would be inappropriate.

The complexity of thinking occurred most obviously in argument about the possibility of peaceful co-existence. Students who had experienced religious education refused more than others to give simple answers, giving other preconditions to be fulfilled besides being religious. Also, when asked about the religiosity of the teacher, they brought other factors into consideration before they gave the last word pro or contra.

The main distinction occurred in answers regarding religious education where my findings correspond with those made in the study by Saar Poll (Saar, 2005). Although all the sample schools of my study with religious education practised joint studies for all, the students from these schools were almost unanimously in favour of joint religious education dealing with world religions.

The need for peaceful co-existence was appreciated in many answers. Students had developed many different solutions to avoid conflicts on religious terms: some did not speak about religious topics to avoid being hurt by the remarks of peers; others wanted religion to be studied in separate groups so that disagreements would not be aired; others yearned for an opportunity to share their own views and opinions in a safe environment, and to build up a common understanding instead of segregation. Religious education does not facilitate tolerance and mutual understanding *per se* but it has great potential, provided that the fears and expectations of students are taken seriously, and that the possibility is provided for sharing opinions or to meet representatives from different religions and speak to them.

The main results according to the actors voiced during the fieldwork were as follows:

1. Mostly religion was seen not as a factor of conflict as it was not considered to be important, nor as a dialogue. Religion tended to be seen more as something annoying and boring, not as an apple of discord. Nevertheless, the 'not believing' worldview was seen as normative and neutral, while a Christian or theistic worldview was considered biased and wrong.

2. The primary source of information about different worldviews was the school. The way of looking at the place religion could have at school depends on the experiences students had. Students who had not experienced religious education were afraid of brainwashing and quarrels actuated by religious education. The students who had experienced religious education were more open to speak on religious issues and to see positive sides of religions and religious people.

3. The views of Russian-speaking students and Estonian-speaking students differed greatly. Whereas Russian-speaking students tended to have a more intimate relationship to religion – it was a key factor in their identity – Estonians were more secularised but also more in favour of studies about different religions.

4. QUANTITATIVE STUDY WITH STUDENTS

Data with more generalisability were needed in order to answer my central research question more fully.[10] Although the qualitative study has a value of its own, a complementary quantitative study was also needed. Thus, on the basis of results and quotations from the qualitative interviews completed in the various REDCo countries, a quantitative study was designed by the quantitative study subgroup of which I was a member. We aimed to look for the spread of views and to test some of the hypotheses of the qualitative study in a bigger sample (the procedure is described in detail in Friederici, 2009, 18–19). The main research question of the quantitative study was: 'What role can religion in education play concerning the way students perceive religious diversity?' There were three sub-questions for the quantitative study: What role does religion have in students' lives? How do students consider the impact of religions on human relations and society? How do students see religion in school and the impact of religion in education? The procedure for the development of the questionnaire with two steps of pre-test is discussed in 1.3.2 "Views of students: quantitative study". The sample and results of the Estonian quantitative study are presented below. The triangulation of the results of the qualitative and quantitative studies is discussed in section 6.

Some attitudes held in Estonia with regard to religion are well illustrated by the fact that the special award in 2008 for advertising Estonia went to a team of young people who presented Estonia as the most a-religious country. The advertisement which was meant to introduce Estonia for foreigners used a verse from John Lennon's song "Imagine" – "*Nothing to kill or die for and no religion too*" (Engelbrecht, 2008), stressing that Estonia is a peaceful secular country without religion which could cause conflicts. How far are such attitudes spread among teenagers and what other possibilities, if any, do they see for religion in their daily life, in society and at school? Also I wanted to investigate the attitudes of young people towards religious diversity and which strategies they prefer in meeting a person with a different worldview from their own. In the following section I describe the procedure for data collection, and also give arguments for the choice of and description of the sample. I then present the results of the quantitative study.

---

10 This chapter is based on the article *Options beside 'and no Religion too' – Perspectives of Estonian Youth* (Schihalejev, 2009e).

4.1 Key information about the quantitative study

There were three main research questions for the quantitative study, as described in section 1.3.2. The first section in the questionnaire (q. 1–36) dealt with the questions of how students see religion in school and the impact of religion in education. It included questions about their own experiences with religion at school (q. 1–12 and 20–25), the rights of religious people that they accept at school (q. 13–19) and what they expect of the types and outcomes of religious education at school (q. 26–31 and 32–36).

In addition to the question about their own and their parents' affiliation (dealt with at the end, in q. 122–127 to avoid putting respondents off answering the other questions), the second section (q. 37–61) also investigated the role religion has in students' lives. It consisted of questions about the importance of religion (q.37), what students believe in (q. 38), how often they practise their religion (q.39–44) and from where they get information about religion (q. 45–51). It also included the range of attitudes about religion (q. 52–61, 86, 92, 95, 96). The impact of religion on students' daily life was also touched upon in the third section of the questionnaire, with questions concerning the people they speak with about religion (q. 62–67), and the different contexts in which students might experience heterogeneity (q. 68–77).

The third section (q. 62–112) consisted of questions and statements about the general impact of religions on human relations and society, as reasons to speak about religion or not (q. 87–97), statements about the societal dimension of religion (q. 78–86 and 103–112), and the strategies students prefer to use in meeting a different worldview (q. 98–102).

Questions used to test our hypothesis about differences in tolerance and openness to dialogue related to religious attitude, and encounters with religious diversity at school and in everyday life, were scattered throughout the questionnaire and discussed in section 4.3.1.

The questionnaires in English, Estonian and Russian are presented in Appendices 3–5.

4.1.1 Description of the sample

Although the Estonian sample for the REDCo quantitative survey was purposive and not directly representative, it was still designed to be educationally significant and rational. The goal was to have a bigger sample than the minimum of 400 demanded by the REDCo agreement. One thousand, two hundred and eight (1208) students in Estonia between 14 and 16 years of age completed the questionnaire. As a result of the procedure of including all the parallel classes in schools, the gender balance was satisfactory (48% males, 51% females).

There was some statistical data available about the 14–16 years old population, so I tried in sampling to reflect the diversity and heterogeneity of the Estonian population, with no major groups left out. The main criteria for selecting schools were geographical location, type of school, and model of religious education. Given the difficulty of obtaining permission to conduct a survey about religion in schools, I had to have a flexible procedure for replacing a school if permission was denied. Below are the descriptions of the criteria used and the selection procedure.

1) **Geographical location; urban and rural schools**. Although Estonia is small, its regions differ in the composition of people, with diverse migration and ethnic backgrounds, religious affiliations and socio-economic indicators. Uneven distribution of ethnic and religious composition of the population is discussed in section 2.1.1. The incorporation of different areas increased the likelihood of having a sample with a varied ethnic and religious background.

In order to compare different factors I concentrated on three geographically different regions and added some schools from locations of interest. 1) The Northern region of Estonia is an industrial area, and many immigrants live there. I also chose schools from Tallinn, the wealthiest region in Estonia, and from its surroundings. I added a school from Narva, a town in North-Eastern Estonia, with more Russians and immigrants living there, and a larger percentage of Orthodox, and also people having lower economic status. 2) The Western region is represented by schools from Pärnu county, with a moderate number of people with a migration background and average income; in addition I included a school from an island, a remote area with almost no immigrants. 3) The Southern region is a rural area, and most of its residents are of lower income. I selected schools from Viljandi, Põlva and Tartu counties, with an exceptional region of Old Believers[11]. In this region there is also a university town, Tartu. I tried to find contrasting schools in each region (for example, a school in a city centre, another in the suburbs, and another in a rural area).

---

11 The Old Believers (Russian: *старове́ры* or *старообря́дцы*) separated from the Russian Orthodox church after 1666-1667 as a protest against introduced church reforms and continue liturgical practices which the Russian Orthodox Church maintained before the implementation of these reforms. The first Old Believers arrived in Estonia in the late 17th century, escaping from the persecution of the Russian government. Nowadays, there are almost 15 thousand Old Believers by birth living mostly in eastern Estonia; they comprise an ethnic minority, clearly distinguishable from other Russians in Estonia due to their unique traditions and religion. (Ponomariova & The Society of Old Believer Culture and Development, 2003) According to the Statistical office there was a much smaller number of Old Believers living in Estonia in 2000, about 2500 people.

2) **Type of school**. According to the homepage of the Estonian Ministry of Education and Research a fifth of students went to a basic school[12], which is usually smaller in terms of the number of students attending; four-fifths went to secondary schools in the year of the study. The sample reflects the distribution of students according to school type (Table 4).

Table 4: Distribution of types of school in Estonia in general and in the sample

	Schools in Estonia	Schools in the sample	Students in Estonia	Students in the sample
Basic	223	6	30 000 (20%)	236 (20%)
Upper secondary	232	15	123 000 (80%)	992 (80%)
Municipal	490	19	147 000 (95%)	1070 (89%)
Private	33	2	4 400 (3%)	138 (11%)
State	32	0	3 600 (2%)	0

Sources: http://www.hm.ee and http://www.ehis.ee/ (accessed 16.09.2007)

There are only a few private schools in Estonia and some state schools (usually for students with special needs), while most schools are run by the municipality (Table 4). I included six basic schools and 15 upper secondary schools; 19 municipal and two private schools, including a religious school. I excluded schools for students with special needs. One of the private schools is confessional, although only slightly more students with a religious affiliation than average attend it. Another private school is not religious; the parents pay tuition fees and mostly have higher socio-economic status.

The language of instruction was one of the indicators in choosing the schools. In addition to the REDCo qualitative survey about the views of young people on religion (see section 3), many recent studies have revealed differences between schools with Estonian and Russian languages of instruction (e.g. Ruus et al., 2007; Veisson et al., 2007; Toots et al., 2004). Ethnic Estonians make up two thirds of the Estonian population; more than a quarter of the Estonian population consists of Russians (Table 5); the percentage of ethnic Estonians among children of school age (aged 7–16) has increased to 77–78% (Lauristin, 2008, 46). Like its population, schools in Estonia differ also by the language of instruction – there were 369 Estonian-medium schools, 83 Russian-medium schools[13] (18 of which use both Estonian and Russian languages for studies) and three English-medium schools (Estonian Ministry of Education and Research, http://www.hm.ee (accessed 16.04.2008)).

---

12 A basic school gives education until the end of compulsory education, when children are 16-17 in age. An upper secondary school in Estonia usually has classes for children 7-19 years of age.

13 It is difficult to say how many Estonians and how many Russians are there, as some Russians and students from other countries go to Estonian schools, although most Russians, Ukrainians and Belorussians go to Russian schools.

Table 5: Ethnicity of Estonian population and of the sample

	Estonia, ethnicity	The sample, language spoken at home
Estonians	921 062 (69%)	956 (80%)
Russians	344 280 (26%)	230 (19%)
Others	77 067 (5%)	7

Source: Statistics Estonia, http://pub.stat.ee (accessed 10.06.2007)

It is difficult to determine the ethnicity of the sample, as this question was not asked, but language used at home was asked about instead. In the sample, 956 spoke Estonian at home, 230 Russian, four English, one Swedish, one Finnish, one Italian and fifteen did not answer the question. All the students who did not answer the question were from Russian-medium schools. A bigger number of Russian-medium schools would have increased the variety of ethnic background, but it was difficult to obtain agreement from Russian-medium schools (of the 36 Russian-medium schools invited to participate, only four agreed), even though I used a Russian language questionnaire in these schools.

3) **Religious education and its model**. There are no figures for the number of students in Estonia who study religious education; probably it is under 1%. It did not make sense to incorporate so few students. In the sample I included schools which had never had religious education (8) and those which had religious education this year (7) or had religious education in the school curriculum, but without the subject being available to students aged 14–16 years (6). In a school which offered religious education some classes would take the subject and others not; some students would have chosen the subject and others not. In the year of my study 1078 students in the sample did not study religious education and 130 did study it. An additional 162 had studied religious education for at least one year during their studies at school. The students differed also by length of study of religious education. The inclusion of schools where religious education is not taught, where religious education is taught only in primary classes, or where religious education is taught recently or is incorporated into the whole school life, enabled the exploration of the views of students who had experienced different educational models concerning living in a pluralistic society.

4) **The religious background of students**. With regard to religious background I had only the data from a poll of people 15 years and older conducted in 2000 (Table 6). In order to include most religious groups I looked for Russian-speaking Orthodox students in Tallinn and Narva, Old Believers in special areas in eastern Estonia, Estonian speaking Orthodox students in South-Eastern Estonia, and Catholic students and students with other religious backgrounds in two schools with an open Catholic ethos[14].

---

14 There are slightly more students with (different kinds of) religious affiliation (19% in schools with a Catholic ethos, and 15% in other schools). Not only Catholic parents, but

Table 6: Religious affiliation of Estonian population 15 and older, of the age 15–19 and of the sample.

	Total population age 15 and older	Total number in Estonia age 15–19	Sample
	Total 1 121 600	**Total 103 772**	**Total 1 208**
Not defined[15]	730 845 (65%)	82 019 (79%)	1021 (84%)
Orthodox	143 554 (13%)	8 756 (8%)	52 (4%)
Lutheran	152 237 (14%)	5 278 (5%)	12 (1%)
Atheist	68 547 (6%)	5 978 (6%)	5 (less than1%)
Other Christians	24 137 (2%)	1 742 (2%)	74 (6%)
Other religions	3 882 (Less than 1%)	235 (Less than 1%)	44 (4%)

Source: Statistics Estonia, http://pub.stat.ee (accessed 16.04.2008)

The number of students who did not define their religious affiliation is higher than expected from the national figures, while the number of religiously affiliated students is lower. The religiosity of the younger generation is known to be lower than in the overall population, as has been seen in comparison of the overall population of 15–19 year olds in Table 6. Another factor was the fact that there were no options added to the question about their religious affiliation (q. 126); this probably increased the number of those who did not answer the question, or who answered 'no' or did not distinguish different denominations (as in answers such as 'Christian' or 'religion').

The procedure of selection schools and classes for the research

The selection of schools consisted of three steps; each criterion was counter checked. In the first step were included schools where extended fieldwork had been conducted in religious education lessons, and qualitative research about students' views on religion had been undertaken as part of the REDCo Project. Then I found schools without religious education, but with similar characteristics to the sample criteria, or the classes from the same school who had no religious education. In the second step I listed the schools which have integrated religious education in the basic school and found their 'twins' as in the first step. In the third step I acquired a balanced sample by adding schools with the criteria missing from the current sample list.

As specified in the research questions, I surveyed the students who were 14–16 years old; most of them in grades 8–10. I focused on grade 9, the end of basic and compulsory schooling in the selected schools. In schools where there were fewer than 50 students in grade 9, I asked students from grade 8 to fill out

---

also those with other religious affiliations choose these schools for their children, as there is no school with their own religious or confessional ethos.

15 The respondents who said that they do not have religious affiliation could not define it or refused to answer the question.

113

the questionnaires. The grades who studied religious education were included in the sample, if students were 14–16 years of age.

Altogether, 71 letters were sent to schools and 21 replied positively. In my sample I dropped all the responses from students who were younger than 14 (19 students) or older than 16 years old (141), leaving 1208 respondents aged 14–16. The desired and actual samples are presented in Appendix 6.

Reflection on the sample. The sample accurately represents the religious, geographical and socio-economic distribution of Estonian students. The higher number of students who have studied religious education enables comparison of subgroups, but this can influence the reported attitudes of the whole sample.

4.1.2 General procedure of the fieldwork and comments of students

The fieldwork was carried out by me and two university students in seven schools, and by teachers in 14 schools who agreed to collaborate from December 2007 to March 2008. The field guide with an introductory text was developed for those who conducted the survey in the schools in order to guarantee a similar procedure in all schools. The questionnaire was completed during a school lesson, according to the field guide. The questionnaire took 10 to 39 minutes to complete.

Some students (263) wrote comments on the last page of the questionnaire, explaining their choices (74) or evaluating the questionnaire. There were 42 critical or negative comments, for example "*I have got a headache from your tests! Please, do not do such tests anymore, please!*" (EST505) and 14 positive ones, for example "*I hope that this questionnaire helps to make life more peaceful and better!*" (EST551). The attitudes to the questionnaire mirrored the range of opinions, from some positive ones who found that it specially helped religious students to feel better, to many negative reactions complaining about the length and irrelevance of the questionnaire. In answering the questions, students without a specific religious background had trouble with many questions. Other students complained that it was impossible to say yes or no, or to agree or disagree with some statements. To make a decision would require binary thinking, where simple answers could be interpreted in too many ways. Many students (126) wrote about their own belief or disbelief at the end of the questionnaire. The attitudes ranged from very negative "*All believers should be cremated!*" (EST583) or "*In my view religion is totally foolish and it has led people to death for totally nonsensical reasons. But I do not have pity on them, if they are so stupid.*" (EST99) to religious ones "*Jesus is my father, my creator and my keeper. I believe in him and you can believe too, then he comes and helps!*" (EST163). Students expressed also their attitude to religious education, from a view that it is a waste of time (e.g. *"Religion is codswallop, we do not need it as a separate subject at all*!!!" (EST318)) to very positive attitudes that it is an important tool for becoming more tolerant (e.g. *"Different religions are interesting and younger students should be also taught about religion"* (EST289)).

4.2 General presentation of the results

In the following I present the responses that the students in Estonia gave on the REDCo questionnaire. The sections of this section are structured to match the research questions. In all the sections a common structure was used: the groups were compared on their experience of religious education, religious affiliation, and language. First data description is presented in blocks of different subtopics, then the data is summarised and data interpretation is presented. Although differences according to gender were discussed in my article on the quantitative research (Schihalejev, 2009e), their detailed presentation is left out here as the gender differences are not within the focus of my main research question. Nevertheless, I do think that gender differences are important to consider in education and some important points illuminate the results, so they will be reported in the summaries of every paragraph and in the sections of interpretation.

I was primarily concerned with the impact of school, so I was interested in how different experiences with religious education have influenced students' attitudes. Here I distinguish four groups. The first group, 'no RE', consists of those who have never studied religious education (734 students). The second group, 'integrated RE', are those who do not have a separate subject of religious education but the school has integrated it into the curriculum; students may attend religious services, or may have a chaplain at school (207 students). The third group, 'RE long ago', are those who studied religious education a long time ago, usually as a voluntary subject in primary classes with content oriented to Bible stories and Christian festivals, but dealing also with students' values (83 students). The fourth group, 'RE recently', consists of those who have studied religious education during the previous or current year, with content focused on world religions (159 students), some of them have studied the subject for eight years. Some of the students studied religious education in a school where it was optional and others were in schools where religion is taught as a compulsory subject. From those who studied religious education in primary classes, 31 chose to study it themselves and 44 were from classes which had common studies for all. Most of the students who had studied religious education recently had it as a subject for all students (150) and only a few (9) chose it according to their own interest. This can affect their motivation but it can also be an important factor in the way they felt when studying.

One may assume that religious affiliation can influence attitudes about religion and religious plurality. It was difficult to group students according to religion, because there were too few representatives of each religion or denomination. I took the answer to the question 'Do you have a certain religion or worldview?' as the point of departure: does a student identify himself or herself as belonging to any religious tradition? The students who had a non-religious worldview, such as atheism or agnosticism were grouped with those without any worldview, as the number was too small to group them separately. In the section I refer to these different groups accordingly as 'affiliated' and 'non-affiliated', keeping in mind that the data do not show their religious beliefs or religious participation. In addition, if questions in the questionnaire are closely related to the research hypothesis, then the dependent variables of tolerance (q. 55, 76, 77, 83, 103–106) and readiness for dialogue (q. 34, 78, 87–97, 98–102) were checked against the independent variables, including religious affiliation (q. 126, 127); how important students think religion is (q. 37); and what they believe in (q. 38).

The qualitative survey showed astonishing differences between the religiosity and attitudes towards religious education of Russian- and Estonian-speaking students. The groups here were divided by the language of questionnaire that the students used. For brevity, I will refer to the students who filled in the Russian questionnaire as 'Russians' and those who filled in the Estonian questionnaire as 'Estonians', although I do not exactly know their ethnicity and some students who speak English, Swedish or Finnish at home, are also included as 'Estonians'.

Data analysis was done with SPSS, using ANOVA and chi-square analyses. Only results with probability less than 0.001 are discussed. The measure of effect size (Φ) was calculated additionally to take into account sample size and strength of the relationship. As there were many results with $0.1<\Phi<0.15$, only $\Phi<0.15$ are discussed as significant; where there were small differences in the answers of different groups with $0.12<\Phi<0.15$, but the small differences were supported by a recurrent pattern of similar statements, these are presented. In the interest of comprehensibility for non-specialists in statistics, if significant $\Phi<0.1$, it is regarded as weak; if $0.1<\Phi<0.3$, it is modest and if $0.3<\Phi<0.5$ it is regarded as moderate – the bigger it is, the more significant is the difference between the compared groups.

The most interesting and telling results are illustrated by figures. The means are presented on a scale where the bigger numbers show higher agreement, higher frequency and higher importance to make the figures more intelligible.

4.2.1 What role has religion in students' life and in their surroundings?

4.2.1.1 Data description

In this section I will look at the relevance of religion to students and the role religion plays in their contacts with peers. As described in section 4.1.2, almost 85% of respondents did not write about their religious affiliation (q.126–127). Christians were most numerous among students with a religious affiliation (11%) and few students (4%) were from other religions or wrote the general term 'religion' as the specification of their worldview.

The number of students who did not specify their religious affiliation was higher among 'Estonians' (88%) than 'Russians' (68%). In addition, Russian-speaking students identified their denomination (usually Orthodox) more than 'Estonians'. Those Estonians who claimed to have a religious affiliation tended to say that they were Christians without distinguishing denominations.

Religious belief and practice

In this section I worked with questions 37–44. The low importance of religion, on average, in students' life was apparent in almost all questions of this block. Answers to the question about the importance of religion inclined heavily towards a low value of religion for respondents, where a very small importance of religion was declared by more than half of students and only 5% of students claimed that religion was very important for them.

This evaluation is consistent with the content of the beliefs and practices they perform (or do not perform). Every fifth student believes in God, while every third respondent does not believe in God or any kind of spirit or life force. All the graphs of answers for religious activities inclined very heavily towards 'never': three of four students never pray (mean $\bar{x}=1.55$[16]), almost the same number never read sacred texts ($\bar{x}=1.54$), and over half of respondents never attend religious events ($\bar{x}=1.61$). Thinking about the meaning of life ($\bar{x}=3.1$) or about religion ($\bar{x}=2.44$) scored higher – only every fifth student never thinks about religion and only every tenth never about the meaning of life. Thinking about the meaning of life was the most practised from the all activities in the list, with a 'flat' distribution of answers.

Studies of religion. There are no significant differences according to their religious education with regard to students' or their parents' religious affiliation, what the students believe or how important religion is to them. The distribution of 'affiliated' and 'non-affiliated' among students with different models of religious education was similar. Nevertheless, some answers about how often

---

16 Means on the scale: 5 – about every day, 4 – about every week, 3 – about once a month, 2 – less than once a month, 1 – never.

students participated in religious activities differed modestly. Those who have studied religious education thought more frequently about religion, even if they studied it long ago (Φ=0.215). The students who have studied religious education recently tended to think more frequently about the meaning of life. The students who learned religious education 'long ago' used least of all the option 'never' in answers for the frequency of such religious activities as 'visit religious events' (Φ=0.208), 'pray', and 'think about the meaning of life'.

Religious affiliation. 'Affiliated' students regarded religion as moderately more important (Φ=0.469) and believed in God more than the 'non-affiliated' (Φ=0.414). 'Affiliated' students practised religious activities more than 'non-affiliated', but they were also more likely to think 'about the meaning of life' (Φ=0.253). The smallest difference was in using the internet to obtain information about religion (Φ=0.273); the biggest difference was in frequency of praying (Φ=0.487). A closer look at this in combination with ethnic background is presented below.

Chart 3: Importance of religion (q. 37) by language (means)[17]

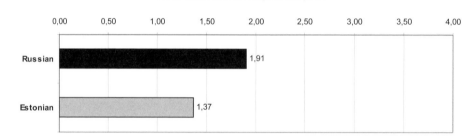

Language. When the two ethnic groups are compared, one must have in mind that there were remarkably more 'religiously affiliated' among the 'Russians' than among the 'Estonians' (36% and 12% accordingly). Many but not all answers of the 'Russians' are therefore similar to the subgroup of 'Estonian affiliated students'. How has the higher proportion of religious affiliated students among 'Russians' influenced their attitudes? 'Russians' not only belonged to, but also valued religion as more important (Φ=0.207; Chart 3). Significant differences were found with regard to the contents of belief (Φ=0.371; Chart 4): more 'Russians' than 'Estonians' believed in the existence of God, while more 'Estonians' than 'Russians' claimed to believe in nothing.

---

17 Means on the scale from 0 – absolutely not imortant up to 4 – very important.

118

Chart 4: Statements of belief (q. 38) by language (%)

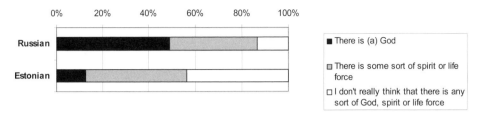

The most interesting distinctions in frequencies of religious practices were found when groups are compared by language and religion. Every fourth Russian-speaking 'non-affiliated' student claimed that religion is important or very important, while only every tenth Estonian 'non-affiliated' student did so. 'Estonian affiliated students' found religion to be very important or important in 61% of cases, 'Russian affiliated students' in 50%. This corresponds well to other statements of the two groups, including believing in God, and participation in different religious activities. Prayer is practised among 'Russians' more frequently; even some 'Russian 'non-affiliated' pray every day (7%), but 'Estonian religious affiliated students' more frequently pray on a regular basis than 'Russian religious affiliated students' (Chart 5).

Chart 5: Frequencies of religious practices (q. 42, 43) by religion and language (%)

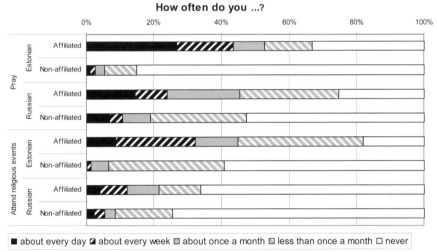

Religious affiliation for 'Estonian' respondents could be clearly identified by the higher percentage of those praying if they have religious affiliation (63%), or never if they do not have religious affiliation (85%). In contrast, 'Estonians' attended religious services more than 'Russians' (Chart 5): 66% of Russian

119

respondents **with** religious affiliation never attend religious events, while the number of Estonians **without** religious affiliation who do not attend religious services is 59%. If one looks at regular attendances (at last once a month, to exclude those who happen to go once a year or have been some years ago to funerals), there are still similar numbers for 'Estonians' who have religious affiliation (42%); the corresponding number for regular attendance for 'affiliated Russians' is 22%. For those without religious affiliation regular participation in religious events is about the same for both groups.

Sources of information

In this section I worked with questions 45–51. For the sample as a whole, family was seen as the most important source of information about religion followed by school.

The distribution of positions on the importance of different sources of information followed a normal curve, with a small tendency to 'not important' in all answers except family, where the answers were distributed almost evenly, and 'faith community', where the most frequent answer was 'not important at all'. I will now consider the effect of differences in experience and environment.

Studies of religion. The students who studied religious education recently valued school as the most important source of information about religion; the difference between different groups was the most significant for school (Φ=0.248). They also used the media and in internet more than the others to get information about religion (Φ=0.16; Chart 6).

Chart 6: Sources of information about religion (q. 45–51) by model of religious education (means)[18]

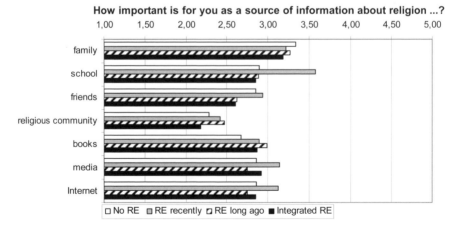

How important is for you as a source of information about religion ...?

---

18 Means on the scale: 5 – very important, 4 – important, 3 – a little bit important, 2 – not important, 1 – not important at all.

Religious affiliation. There were some significant differences for sources of information between 'affiliated' and 'non-affiliated' students: religious community ($\Phi=0.36$), family ($\Phi=0.253$), books ($\Phi=0.217$) and friends ($\Phi=0.156$) were more important for the 'affiliated' students. Other sources were also more important for the 'affiliated', but without significant differences. The most important informants for the 'affiliated' are family ($\bar{x}=3.98$), books ($\bar{x}=3.35$) and friends ($\bar{x}=3.24$); while family ($\bar{x}=3.18$), school ($\bar{x}=2.96$) and media ($\bar{x}=2.9$) were important for the 'non-affiliated'.

Language. 'Russians' valued all the sources more highly than 'Estonians'. The most significant differences were for family ($\Phi=0.278$) and friends ($\Phi=0.229$). 'Russians' tended to consider family and friends as the most important sources of information about religion, while for 'Estonians' family and school are the most important. In addition differences in opinions about the internet ($\Phi=0.18$) and media ($\Phi=0.171$) were modestly significant; 'Russians' were more likely to regard the internet as 'very important' and Estonians more likely to have intermediate opinions about the media. It may be somewhat surprising that faith community did not play any distinctive role for 'Russians' as a source of information, but if one takes into account that religious events were rarely attended by 'Russians', this finding makes sense.

Attitudes towards religion

In this section I worked with questions 52–61, 86, 92, 95, and 96. More general statements, such as 'religion is important in our history' and 'it is possible to be a religious person without belonging to a particular faith community', but also 'respecting other people' were more agreed with than statements of personal commitment and of religion influencing one's life. Although religion was not seen as very important by students, almost half of them disagreed and only every fifth student agreed with the statement that religion is nonsense.

Most of the students agreed that religion is a private matter and that religion is inherited from the family. For other statements the distribution was flat; respondents did not have a common opinion. Every third student (30–40%) used the option 'neither agree nor disagree' for almost all the answers in this group. I will now consider the effect of different experiences and influences on viewpoints.

Studies of religion. Four statements in the group of attitudes towards religion had modestly significant differences in responses related to students' experience of religious education. The students who had studied religious education, or whose school has integrated it into the curriculum, were more likely to agree with the statements 'Religion is important in our history' ($\Phi=0.193$) and 'I respect other people who believe' ($\Phi=0.168$) and to disagree that religion is nonsense ($\Phi=156$; Chart 7). The statement that religion is nonsense was mostly agreed with by students without any experience of religious education (mean

$\bar{x}=3.21^{19}$, while for others $\bar{x}=3.52–3.5$). Interesting is the fact that those who studied religious education long ago agreed more strongly with the last statement than did students of any other group; also they were more likely to think that religion is inherited from the family ($\Phi=0.175$).

Those who did not study religious education agreed more that they do not know about religion ($\Phi=0.166$); and they were also less interested in talking about religion ($\Phi=0.154$). None of the other answers showed significant differences.

Religious affiliation. The 'affiliated' agreed moderately more with most of the statements in this section, either in regard to their own belief ('Religion is important to me because I love God' ($\Phi=0.47$, $\Phi=0.317$)) or the beliefs of others ('I respect other people who believe' ($\Phi=0.366$)). If different variables of religiosity are compared, then the statement 'I respect other …' was most agreed with by those who valued religion as very important ($\bar{x}=4.37$) and students who declared their religious affiliation ($\bar{x}=4.13$); least agreement was shown by those who considered religion as absolutely not important ($\bar{x}=2.59$) and did not believe in god or any spirit ($\bar{x}=2.89$).

Chart 7: Attitudes towards religion (q. 55, 56, 58) by model of religious education (%)

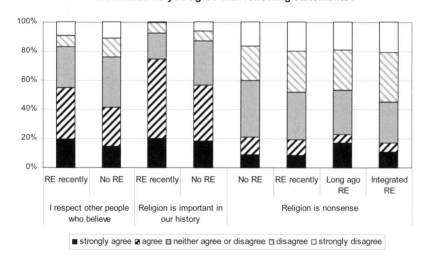

The 'affiliated' also disagreed more strongly with the negative statement 'Religion is nonsense' ($\Phi=0.317$). There were only three exceptions in this block, where differences were insignificant: readiness to change one's mind, doubts about God and 'you can be a religious person without belonging to a particular faith community', which were equally supported by both groups (Chart 8).

---

19 Henceforward, if not listed otherwise, means on the scale: 5 – strongly agree, 4 – agree, 3 – neither agree or disagree, 2 – disagree, 1 – strongly disagree.

Chart 8: Attitudes towards religion (q. 55, 56, 54, 59, 60) by religious affiliation (%)

How much do you agree with following statements?

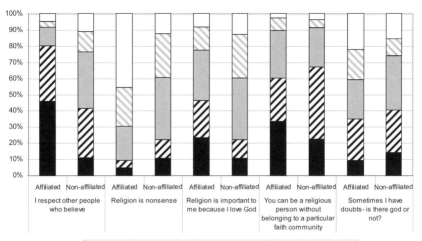

■ strongly agree □ agree ▨ neither agree or disagree □ disagree □ strongly disagree

A strong bipolarity among the 'affiliated', despite no differences of means compared to 'non-affiliated', can be observed for two statements: 'religion is something one inherits from one's family' and 'religion is a private matter', where the 'affiliated' either 'strongly agreed' or 'strongly disagreed' with these statements, while others used more middle options. There were modestly significant differences in answers to the statements 'I don't know much about religion and thus I can't have an opinion' ($\Phi=0.30$) and 'Religion does not interest us ....' ($\Phi=0.287$), where the 'affiliated' disagreed more with the statements than the 'non-affiliated'.

Language. 'Russians' agreed modestly more with statements that they love God ($\Phi=0.287$), religion determines their life ($\Phi=0.194$), less significantly with other statements about the positive impact of religion on their life, but also in these cases they were remarkably more likely to use the option 'agree strongly'. 'Russians' were more likely to disagree with the statement that religion is open to change ($\Phi=0.208$). The statement of the social impact of religion 'religion is important in our history' was more likely to be disagreed with by 'Russians' than by 'Estonians' ($\Phi=0.182$). 'Estonians' were more likely to accept that a person could be religious without belonging to any religious community ($\Phi=0.182$).

Although more 'Russians' than 'Estonians' agreed that religion belongs to the private sphere ($\Phi=0.213$), 'Estonians' agreed that religion is inherited from the family, while 'Russians' were more divergent – both were likely to strongly agree and even more to disagree with this statement ($\Phi=0.213$). 'Estonians' were more likely to think that they know too little about religion, so could not have an opinion about it ($\Phi=0.177$).

Talking about religion – with whom?

In this section I worked with questions 62–67. Overall, students hardly spoke about religion with anybody or at all. The most popular option for all the answers of this group was 'never'. It is obvious that students rarely discussed religion – all the means were less than 2.[20] Those least spoken with were 'other students at school' and 'religious leaders'. Four students out of five spoke about religion with their family members, friends and classmates less than once a month or never; they were most likely to discuss religion with a teacher – about every fourth spoke with a teacher about religion at least once a month. Again I present the effect of different influences on views about these questions.

Studies of religion. There were no differences in some cases – talking about religion with religious leaders, other students at school, and family. There were moderately significant differences for those who had studied religious education recently if compared to all other groups in talking more frequently about religion with teachers ($\Phi=0.46$; Chart 9), classmates ($\Phi=0.34$) and some differences in talking with friends ($\Phi=0.158$).

Religious affiliation. Although the 'affiliated' talked more about religion, they rarely talked about it at school. The significant differences occurred only outside of school – students talked more often with family members ($\Phi=0.312$), friends ($\Phi=0.26$) and religious leaders ($\Phi=0.34$).

Language. Even though 'Russians' valued family and friends as sources of information about religion, the reported frequency in talking about religion with them was almost the same as among 'Estonians'. Significant differences existed with regard to talking with teachers ($\Phi=0.161$) and classmates ($\Phi=0.136$) – 'Estonians' were more likely to talk with them on a regular basis, the 'Russians' more likely never; instead 'Russians' were a little more likely to talk with religious leaders about religion regularly ($\Phi=0.15$).

---

20 Means on the scale: 5 – about every day, 4 – about every week, 3 – about once a month, 2 – less than once a month, 1 – never.

124

Chart 9: Talking about religion (q. 62, 64, 66) by model of religious education (%)

How often do you talk about about religion with ...?

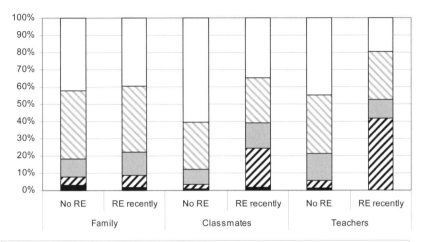

Contacts with different religions

In this section I worked with questions 68–79. If one takes into consideration the low importance of religion, it is not surprising that more than half of the students did not know their friends' or classmates' views of religion, or even if their classmates belonged to any religion. Every fourth student believed that there were no students at their class belonging to (another) religion. The data, according to the religious affiliation students stated themselves, show that 10% of students studied in classes where none of the students had a religious affiliation. 35% of students did not socialise with students of a different religious background outside of school, and 28% said that they communicated only with the similarly minded at school. From the comments given in response to the question it seems that religion is not a factor in friendships.

Studies of religion. In two aspects, students who had experienced integrated religious education differed from the others. They were more likely to believe that their views on religion were different from their parents' ($\Phi=0.153$). They shared the view with those who had studied religious education long ago, that in school they do socialise with students having a different religious background ($\Phi=0.148$).

Religious affiliation. For the group of questions on how much students associated with people of different religious backgrounds, the biggest difference between the 'affiliated' and 'non-affiliated' was that the 'non-affiliated' were less likely to know about the religion of their friends, classmates or family members and parents, whereas the 'affiliated' tended to mention that they had friends (Φ=0.179), classmates and family members of different religions, and they associated with them in their spare time (Φ=0.149) and at school (Chart 10). However, there was no significant difference between the 'affiliated' and 'non-affiliated' as to whether they **preferred** to socialise with peers of the same religion as themselves at school and in their spare time. Surprisingly, the less students valued religion, the more they preferred to go with similarly minded (i.e. non-religious) people at school and in their spare time. The same was true of students who did not believe in God or any spirit. There were no significant differences according to religious background for the question about whether friends and classmates shared their views (Chart 10).

Chart 10: Contacts with other religions (q. 69, 70, 72, 74, 75) by religious affiliation (%)

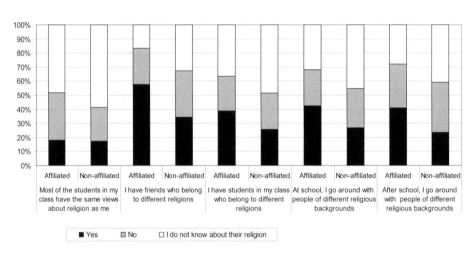

Language. The most striking difference between 'Russians and 'Estonians' was that 'Russians' were less likely to know about their parents' religion and to have parents of a different religious background (Φ=0.199). In addition, they were less likely to know their parents' views on religion and they believed that their parents thought about religion differently from themselves (Φ=0.161). The results contradict the answers given at the end of the questionnaire, where students had to report the religion their parents belong to. The differences on religious diversity in the family were not so significant in these later questions and 'Estonians' tended to use the option that they did not know their parents' religion more frequently.

Summary of results occurring in different groups

Religion was not considered important by most of the respondents. They saw religion as more important in history than in their own life. Family and school played the most important role in providing information about religion.

The personal relevance of religion did not seem to be directly correlated to the form of religious education. There were no differences in terms of belonging or belief in God between the groups who had experienced different models of religious education. Students who had studied religious education believed more in 'some sort of spirit or life force' and were less likely to hold atheistic views or, conversely, to believe in God. Also the variables of personal relevance of religion (e.g. 'Religion determines my whole life', 'Religion is important because I love God', 'Religion helps me to cope with difficulties') did not distinguish groups according to their different experiences with religious education studies. Still, some minor changes in the importance of religion, thinking about religion and thinking about the meaning of life were detected: students with experience of religious education avoided the more negative extreme positions. Also, students who had experienced any of the forms of religious education (religious education in primary school, religious education in secondary school, integrated religious education) valued religion as a societal and historical phenomenon more highly and acknowledged the need for mutual respect more than those who did not have such studies. The students with religious education experience tended more to be ready to change their views about religion and to think that a person can be religious without belonging to any religious community.

In conclusion, religious education did not make students more religious but they did change values – religion was not regarded as something to be afraid of or regarded as 'a stupid relic from past', but as an at least acceptable choice for some people. The attitudes of those who had experienced religious education in primary classes were somewhat contradictory. On one hand, these students said that they attended religious services and prayed more frequently. At the same time they saw religion as nonsense and saw religion as a source of conflict more than other groups did.

The students who had studied religious education recently used and valued more knowledge-based sources (school, books) in finding information about religion. Their interest in and readiness to talk about religion with people of different backgrounds was higher than among those who did not have special religious education. In addition, students who studied religious education valued tolerance more highly, and also they more often saw differences as not only normal but also as an interesting part of life.

Students with a religious background were much more positive not only about religion but also about differences in general. They saw religion and all the sources as more important than their peers without a religious affiliation.

They spoke more frequently about religion, but did so mainly with like-minded groups – family members, friends and religious leaders. Probably more surprising were the findings that the 'affiliated' and 'non-affiliated' had equal doubts about existence of God, were equally ready to change their minds and thought that it was possible to be a believer without belonging to any religious community, with neither preferring the company of peers of the same religious background in school nor in their spare time. The 'affiliated' were more aware of the religious background of their fellows. They spoke more frequently about religion in the family and with friends. They did not exchange ideas on religious issues with people of different religious background, such as for example classmates, but neither did the non-affiliated students.

Language proved to be a very important factor in the way religion was understood. 'Russians' believed in the existence of God regardless of their religious affiliation, while for 'Estonians' belief in God tended to be determined by their religious affiliation. 'Russians' valued more 'individual' practice such as prayer; and family and friends as sources of information about religion. They valued religion more as a moral guide and help in life; they were also less ready to change their mind on religious issues. The opposite was the case for statements about the social impact of religion, taking part in religious events, religion being important in history, valuing the school as a source of information and a place to talk about religion; all were more valued by 'Estonians'.

Some patterns in answers according to gender could be also found. But the results were sometimes contradictory. More girls than boys declared their religious (e.g. Christian, Buddhist, Taoist etc.) and non-religious (e.g. atheist, agnostic) affiliation; boys preferred more not to state any view. Although the means for the importance of religion showed that girls regarded religion as more important (45% of females regarded religion as absolutely not important or as not important, while 60% of males did so), the positive extreme of the scale ('very important') did not show any gender differences. In the content of belief boys held more atheistic views, while girls preferred more to believe in 'some sort of spirit or life force'. This option was probably felt as less 'extreme' in comparison to believing in God or holding atheistic views. Girls tended more to be ready to change their views about religion than boys did and were more cautious in seeing religion as nonsense. At the same time many other variables showed no gender differences ('Religion determines my whole life', 'Religion is important because I love God', 'A person can be religious without belonging …', 'Religion is inherited from family' or 'Religion it is a private matter'; also almost the same value was given to friends, religious communities, media and the internet as sources of information about religion). Although girls showed more positive attitudes towards religion, the frequency of religious practice did not differ from that of boys: for most of these activities boys stated more extreme positions ('every day' and 'never') more frequently than girls, but girls prayed a little more frequently. Girls were more positive about school, books and family as the sources of information about religion.

4.2.1.2 Data interpretation

Most of the students in Estonia saw religion as a historical or distant phenomenon, probably relevant for somebody else, but not for them personally. Religion was not a topic to discuss. Most of the students were not hostile to religion but they saw it as a distant or very private matter, not to be shown openly in any way.

In contrast to some public concerns in Estonia that religious education would convert students to Christianity, it was impossible to find any evidence of this. Even those who studied Bible stories in primary classes did not believe in God more than others, although they tended to be less atheistic and to believe more in 'some sort of spirit'. Such a spiritual dimension could be detected in their slightly more frequent attendance at religious services and praying, and more often thinking about the meaning of life or about religion. The students who had studied religious education recently showed more readiness to start a conversation with people of different backgrounds and valued differences more highly. Probably the knowledge they have about different religions, and skills they acquire, lessened their prejudices about religious issues and their fear in relation to difference. The idea that a more tolerant family background may influence the views of students who studied religious education seems weak, because the most tolerant views were held by those students who studied religious education recently and happened to study at schools where all or almost all students from corresponding classes studied religious education. In addition, the 'natural control group' of students from the same school, but from different classes who had not yet studied religious education, showed less tolerant views.

Students' religious background was most influential in the personal dimension of religion, as was expected, but it did not affect doubts about the existence of God. As was demonstrated in section 4.2.1.1, in the Estonian case, the religious affiliation of young people is closely related to one's beliefs and practices (see page 117 and Chart 5 on page 119). As most students did not have any religious affiliation (see table 6 on page 113), and religion was one of the lowest priorities among Estonian students in both REDCo quantitative and qualitative studies and in some other studies conducted among students (e.g. Rüütel & Tiit, 2005) and on bigoted attitudes towards religious people in Estonia (Kilemit & Nõmmik, 2002; Valk, 2007b, 171–173), we can reasonably assume that those students who, in spite of the anti-religious climate, admitted that they had a particular religion, did themselves have some degree of personal commitment to religion. The wish to belittle one's religion was evident also from the qualitative study (see the first example on page 76).

Although students with a religious affiliation were more aware of their friends' religious background, they did not choose their friends on that basis. They talked about religion and valued people with a similar religious background to theirs, while avoiding controversial topics in segregated groups. This shows their wish to be taken seriously and they achieved this by avoiding topics which could exclude them from their peers.

It can be concluded that, with regard to gender, girls tended to use more polite and mild expressions for their attitudes toward religion and boys were more resolute in their opinions, but the gender differences in religiosity were not very big. Probably there are no clear gender roles with regard to religion in Estonia; girls are not expected to be more religious, and it was impossible to distinguish specifically 'girlish' or 'boyish' ways to think about religion. The bigger importance of religion for girls could be caused by girls' preference not to take extreme positions, but to use 'middle of the road' options instead, since this pattern was also followed in their answers to other questions.

Although the difference in responses of the 'affiliated' and 'non-affiliated' was significant, there was a whole group of statements where distinctions between ethnicities proved to be even more significant. The content of belief was based more on ethnicity than on the religious affiliation of 'Russians'. The beliefs and religious practices of 'Estonians' seemed to be more affected by their religious affiliation or lack thereof. 'Russians' tended to see religion as a part of their identity, often regardless of their religious affiliation. They saw religion as private and individual, not related to social life. In this respect it is surprising that 'Estonians' were more likely to accept that a person could be religious without belonging to any religious community. One explanation could be that 'Russians' felt more attached to believing in God, while 'Estonians' believed in some sort of spirit or life force, where religious tradition did not play such an important a role.

Another surprising tendency was that 'Estonians' were more likely to believe that religion was inherited from the family while 'Russians' believed that they did not share beliefs with their parents. Probably this could be explained by confrontation between adolescents and their parents. Among the 'Russians' it is worthwhile to disagree about religion in order to find out one's own, intimate and individual belief, while for 'Estonians' this issue is just a theoretical question about 'other' people who probably inherited their beliefs from their family.

4.2.2 How do students see the impact of religion in a society?

4.2.2.1 Data description

Religion in a society

In this section I worked with questions 82–85. About half of the students did not take a stand on negative or hostile statements about religion or religious people. The majority of the students disagreed that 'religion is source of aggression' and that 'without religion the world would be a better place', but many did agree with such statements. The means were respectively 2.6 and 2.8.

Chart 11: Religion in a society (q. 83, 85) by religious affiliation and model of religious education (%)

To what extent do you agree with the following statements your peers have made?

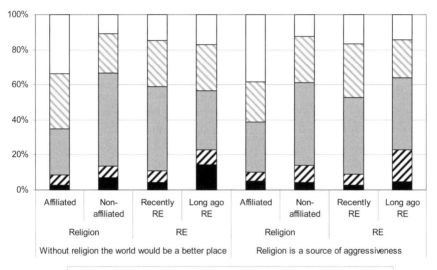

Studies of religion. The students who studied religious education long ago differed most remarkably in all their answers in this section. They agreed with those who had experienced integrated religious education more than the others that religion was a source of aggression (Φ=0.16; Chart 11). Although the other differences were not so significant, they were still remarkable as such views occured in some other 'intolerant' statements – those who had studied religious education long ago agreed more than the others that the world would be a better place without religion and that religious people were less tolerant. These paradoxical results are discussed in section 4.2.2.2.

The students who had never studied religious education were less interested than all other groups in the views of their best friend about religion ($\bar{x}$=3.11 if compared to those who studied religious education long ago $\bar{x}$=3.56 or recently $\bar{x}$=3.44).

Religious affiliation. The 'affiliated' disagreed modestly more than others with the hostile statements that religion was a source of aggression (Φ=0.267) and the world would be better without it (Φ=0.287) or religious people were less tolerant (Φ=0.195; Chart 11). The answers of students were compared also by different independent variables, including religious affiliation, how important they thought religion was or what they believed in. The differences are quite remarkable, especially with regard to the importance of religion. 'Without religion the world would be a better place' was less agreed with by those for whom religion was very important ($\bar{x}$=1.75), who had a religious affiliation ($\bar{x}$=2.09) and who believed in God ($\bar{x}$=2.13), most agreed by those for whom religion was not important at all ($\bar{x}$=3.21) or who had no religious affiliation ($\bar{x}$=3.18). The students who valued religion were more likely to be curious about their fellows' views on religion than students for whom religion had no relevance in their lives (means respectively 3.95 and 2.71).

Talking about religion – why?

In this section I worked with questions 87–97. Despite rarely speaking about religion (see 4.2.1.1 "Talking about religion – with whom?") students were not so negative about its effects. Equal distribution characterised most of the answers in this group. Most of all students agreed that talking about religion is interesting because of different opinions ($\bar{x}$=3.5). In addition they agreed slightly more with the statement that they knew too little about religion to be able to talk about it ($\bar{x}$=3.2) and it did not interest them ($\bar{x}$=3.2). The most disagreed with statements were that it was embarrassing to talk about ($\bar{x}$=2.4) and that they talk about 'how stupid religion' is ($\bar{x}$=2.6).

Studies of religion. Those who did not study religious education differed from all other students in many answers from this group. They agreed more that they did not know about religion (Φ=0.166) and, with those who had studied religious education long ago, that it was embarrassing to talk about religion (Φ=0.162; Chart 12). The same pattern occurred with interest as with knowledge – those who had not studied it, were also less interested in different opinions (Φ=0.151). Although there is a weak significance, it is still remarkable that students, who had studied religious education long ago agreed that they talked about the stupidity and cruelty of religion. Again the implications of this are discussed in section 4.2.2.2.

Chart 12: Reasons to talk about religion (q. 91, 90) by model of religious education, language and religious affiliation (%)

To what extent do you agree that talking about religion ...?

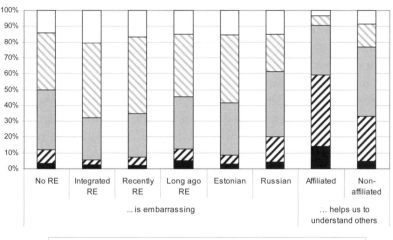

Religious affiliation. All the positive attitudes towards the values of talking about religion were supported significantly more by the 'affiliated', without any exception. The statements 'it helps us to understand others' (Φ=0.221; Chart 12) and 'it helps to shape my own views' (Φ=0.221) were the most distinctive among the positive statements. Some negative statements showed even bigger differences (e.g. 'I do not know about religion…' (Φ=0.300) and 'religion does not interest us ….' (Φ=0.287)).

There were no significant differences between groups about the statement that it is embarrassing to talk about religion. The very strongly negative statement '… how stupid religion is…' showed only small differences – the percentage of those strongly agreeing with the statement was the same across groups. More significant differences could be found if the variable of how important religion is is taken into account (some examples of means for 'religion is very important' *vs.* 'not important at all' are given in brackets): talking about religion is interesting because of different views people hold ($\bar{x}$=4.03 *vs.* $\bar{x}$=2.97), it helps to shape one's own views ($\bar{x}$=3.78 *vs.* $\bar{x}$=2.49), it helps one to understand others ($\bar{x}$=3.88 *vs.* $\bar{x}$=2.56). All the statements followed the same pattern: the statements were more agreed with the more the person valued the importance of religion for himself or herself.

Language. Four statements showed modestly significant distinctions. 'Russians' were more likely to agree or to agree strongly that it was embarrassing to talk about religion (Φ=0.194; Chart 12). Although 'Estonians' were more likely to think that religion is a boring topic or that they know less about religion, so cannot have an opinion (Φ=0.177), they were more likely to agree that different opinions make talking about religion interesting (Φ=0.158) and helped to build peaceful relations (Φ=0.154).

Meeting a different opinion – how?

In this section I worked with questions 98–102. The questions about how students would react to a peer with a different religious view showed that students were likely to listen but not to allow the views of others to influence them, and were least likely to try to convince others of their own views.

Studies of religion. There were no significant differences between groups according to their experience with religious education, in the ways they reacted to a peer with different religious views. However, those students without religious education tended more to ignore and convince than discuss and find common ground.

Religious affiliation. The only significant difference was in trying to discuss personal views (Φ=0.165; Chart 13), where the 'affiliated' said that they would more likely use this strategy. More significant differences could be found on the basis of the importance of religion; here the students for whom religion was not important preferred to ignore the topic ($\bar{x}$=4.23 *vs.* 'very important' $\bar{x}$=3.80), while those who valued religion favoured discussion of opinions ($\bar{x}$=4.46 *vs.* 'not important at all' $\bar{x}$=3.23).

Chart 13: Way of reaction to a different view (q. 99, 102) by religious affiliation and language (%)

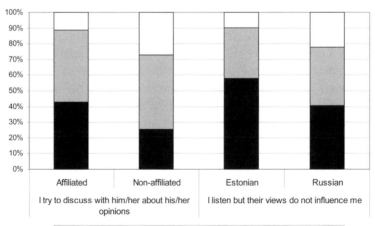

Imagine that a pupil of a different religious faith wants to convince you that his/her religion is the best one. How do you react?

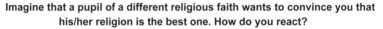

Language. There were no significant differences in responses to this block of questions, except that 'Estonians' were more likely than 'Russians' to listen modestly to a different view but not to be affected by it (Φ=0.169; Chart 13).

People of different worldviews and religions living together

In this section I worked with questions 103–106. The statement that representatives of different religions cannot live together was not responded to by almost half of the students. The questions on the views about differences revealed that students agreed that respect for others' religions would help in coping with differences and disagreements on religious issues. Students in Estonia tended to disagree with the statement that they do not like to live with members of other religions.

Studies of religion. In answer to this group of questions, those without experience of religious education differed from all the other groups. They disagreed more strongly that religious differences lead to conflicts (Φ=0.184). They were almost without exception the only ones who strongly disagreed with this and also with the statement that representatives of strict religions cannot live together (Φ=0.168; Chart 14). In addition they agreed less that respect can help people to live peacefully together (Φ=0.16). In contrast, they were modestly more likely to dislike people from other religions and to want to live separately from them (Φ=0.161).

Chart 14: Views about people of different religions living together (q. 103–106) by model of religious education, religious affiliation and language (%)

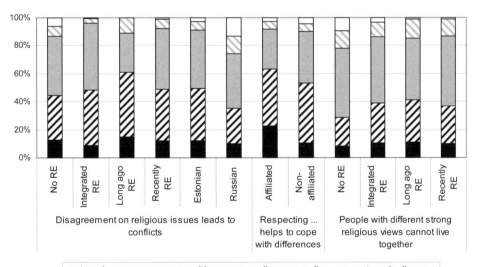

135

Religious affiliation. Students with a religious affiliation tended to have more tolerant attitudes than the 'non-affiliated'. They were modestly more likely to agree that respecting the religion of others helps to cope with differences (Φ=0.143, Chart 14) and to disagree with the view that they did not like people from other religions and did not want to live with them (Φ=0.147). There was no significant difference between the 'affiliated' and 'non-affiliated' for the other two questions.

If different variables are compared, there was more respect for living peacefully together by students who valued religion as very important ($\bar{x}$=3.81), respondents who declared their religious affiliation ($\bar{x}$=3.75) and those believing in a spirit or life force ($\bar{x}$=3.69). Those who found religion as absolutely not important ($\bar{x}$=3.22) and did not believe in God or any spirit ($\bar{x}$=3.37) showed the least agreement. The very strong statement 'I don't like people from other religions and do not want to live together with them' was most agreed with by those for whom religion was not important at all ($\bar{x}$=2.43) and who did not believe in God or a spirit ($\bar{x}$=2.4). It was least of all agreed by students with a religious affiliation ($\bar{x}$=1.98) and for whom religion was important ($\bar{x}$=2.00).

Language. Striking differences in attitudes towards the possibility of living peacefully together appeared between language groups. 'Estonians' agreed modestly more that strict religions cannot live together (Φ=0.268) and that disagreements on religious grounds led to conflicts (Φ=0.215; Chart 14), but they also took the view that respect can help towards peaceful co-existence (Φ=0.216).

How people of different worldviews and religions could live together?

In this section I worked with questions 107–112. Knowledge about different religions was highlighted as the most helpful factor for living peacefully together, whereas keeping religion to oneself and strong regulation by the state were not believed to be as effective in building peace.

Studies of religion. Students with 'no RE' believed less than others that knowledge of religions could help in living peacefully together (Φ=0.192; Chart 15) or that knowing someone personally could help (Φ=0.159).

Religious affiliation. For most questions in this group there were no differences between students with and without a religious background, except religiously affiliated students had stronger opinions about the effects of harsh laws about religion (Chart 15).

Language. There were some significant differences in this block of questions, 'Estonians' being more positive about all ways to improve peace among different religions. 'Estonians' valued knowledge about each other significantly more highly (Φ=0.320; Chart 15), but common activities (Φ=0.275; Chart 15), shared interest (Φ=0.258) and personal relations with representatives of a religion (Φ=0.252) were also more believed to be effective. Less agreed upon was the idea of keeping religion private, a view supported especially by 'Russians' (Φ=0.172). 'Russians' believed also slightly less in state regulations.

Chart 15: Ways for people of different worldviews to live together (q. 108, 112, 110) by model of religious education, language and religious affiliation (%)

There are people from different religions living in every country. What do you think would help them to live together in peace?

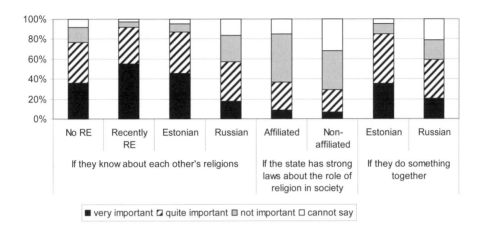

Summary of results according to different groups

Estonian students also showed their distant attitude to religion in this group of questions by saying that the topic did not interest them, they did not know about religion and they had a low opinion regarding any positive outcomes of speaking about religion. Nevertheless, they believed in respect and the possibility of living together with people of different religions. They valued the role of knowledge and did not believe that keeping religion private would foster peaceful co-existence.

As the students attending different forms of religious education did not differ by their religious affiliation, it was interesting to see how they differed in relation to respect. The students who had never studied religious education differed from all other groups in relation to all the statements on respect for religion and differences on religious grounds. Students without religious education agreed less that they have respect for believers. They also believed least of all in the effectiveness of respect in helping to live together peacefully, while those with integrated religious education or recent experience of religious education were more optimistic about this. The statement 'I do not like people from other religions…' was most agreed by students without religious education and least by those with an integrated form of religious education. Students without any experience of religious education were less informed and thought that religion is

137

an embarrassing issue to talk about. Students who had studied religious education saw positive effects of speaking about religion both for themselves and for understanding society. Somewhat unexpected was the finding that students without experience of religious education believed less than the others that religion may cause some conflicts or that people of different religious backgrounds cannot live together; those who studied religious education long ago were most ready to agree with these statements. The students who had learned religious education in primary school were more ready to see religion as a source of aggression. In contrast, students with recent religious education experience were more open to religious differences and were more respectful of religion than those students without such experience.

Religiously affiliated students showed more respect and readiness for dialogue with people of different views about religion. They valued more highly respect, knowledge and personal relations to foster peaceful coexistence between different religious groups.

'Russians' agreed more that it is embarrassing to talk about religion. They also believed more that people of with strong religious views can live together and that people do not come into conflict on religious grounds. At the same time, they were more sceptical about various means to improve relations, including respect and strict laws.

Some of these variables showed differences between genders, while others did not. For example, girls and boys did not differ on seeing religion as a potential source of aggression. Also they were shared a preference for going around with similarly minded peers. Girls and boys were equally puzzled by the questions about whether they had problems in revealing their views about religion at school, and over half of both genders agreed that a student who showed openly his or her religious beliefs could be mocked. Although there were no significant gender differences for the questions about how often respondents spoke with others about religion, the girls were more positive about many outcomes. They were more interested, for example, in what their best friends thought about religion, and they also believed more that talking about religion helps one to understand others, and helps people to live peacefully together. They also felt it was interesting that people have different views, and that this diversity helps to shape one's own views. Boys agreed significantly more that religion is a boring topic and slightly more boys agreed also that they were not interested in religion. Girls proved to be more interested in looking for and finding harmony in their surroundings and between religiously diverse groups; they also valued respect and knowledge about religions more than boys. Boys showed themselves to be more militant – they did not like differences and would ignore them or try to convince others of their own views more than girls would.

4.2.2.2 Data interpretation

The views of students on the role of religion in society contradict their other responses. On the one hand they valued knowledge of different religions in fostering peaceful co-existence and did not believe in keeping religion private. On the other hand, they said that they did not know about religion and were not interested in such knowledge. Perhaps, since religion was not considered to be important to them, they found it difficult to imagine that it could be important enough for people to fight over, or that if conflict did arise they found it difficult to imagine that it could be resolved.

Why were the students with early religious education experience in several answers more hostile to religion? It could be that their understanding of religion has not become sufficiently complex and consistent with other aspects of their development, while, at the same time, they have rejected their childhood understandings. In contrast, students with recent religious education experience were more open to religious differences and respectful of religion than were students without such experience. At the same time it was detected that students without any experience of religious education believed less that religions could cause any conflicts, being less aware of the potential of religion for conflicts or hardly understanding how it (being so marginal) could cause any conflicts.

The more open-minded views on religious diversity of the religiously affiliated students could be due to their minority position. As described above, they were quite well adapted to open-mindedness and they would only benefit from such an attitude, so perhaps they were trying to create the reality they dreamed of by expressing a belief in it.

Why did 'Russians', who were less likely to believe that they would be teased on religious grounds, think that it was embarrassing to talk about religion? This reaction corresponds to their individual approach to religion discussed earlier. Their religion is so private, that it is not considered to be proper to discuss it; religion is seen as having primarily an individual, rather than a societal, dimension. This could explain why they believed less in religions' potential to create conflicts and were more sceptical about different means to improve relations, including respect and strong laws. Religion is believed to be a personal matter, and therefore not a cause of social conflict; for the same reason they felt that there was no need for tolerance in order to improve relations.

4.2.3 How do students see religion in school?

4.2.3.1 Data description

It was easier for students to take a stand on questions about religion in school than about religion in general. The number of students who chose the middle option 'neither agree nor disagree' in the questions about religious education was usually about 30%, which is less than in other blocks of questions.

Evaluation of experiences with studies of religion

In this section I worked with questions 3–12. The statements of interest in and importance of dealing with religion had a normal curve of distribution, with almost equal numbers of students agreeing and disagreeing with the statements. Statements about the positive impact of education on religious issues and on the peaceful and respectful co-existence of people from different religions were more agreed upon. The statements about the usefulness of religion in learning about oneself or in making moral decisions were rejected. The statement about possible quarrels because of such studies was strongly rejected. We can now consider the reactions of the groups of students.

Chart 16: Evaluation of religious education (q. 3–6) by model of religious education (%)

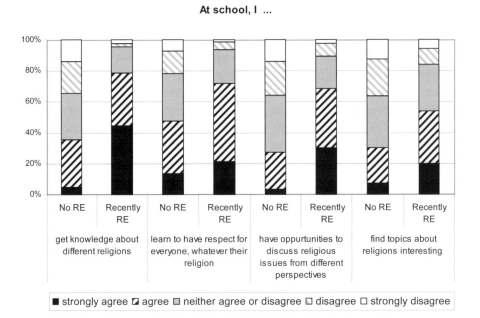

Studies of religion. The students who had studied religious education recently rated their studies about religious issues much higher in all aspects than other groups: they considered more than any other group that they gained knowledge about religion ($\Phi=0.49$; Chart 16), they could look at topics from different perspectives ($\Phi=0.397$), religious education was interesting ($\Phi=0.18$) and they could learn to respect people from different religious backgrounds ($\Phi=0.219$). Together with students who had experienced religious education long ago or had experienced integrated religious education they considered that it is important to deal with religion at school ($\Phi=0.20$) and that it helps in understanding contemporary events ($\Phi=0.17$). Only views on making moral decisions and learning about oneself showed no significant differences between the groups.

Religious affiliation. The 'affiliated' students were more positive in their ratings than the 'non-affiliated in this group of questions almost in every case, but the differences were not as significant as between those who learned religious education recently and those who had not. The only exception in this respect was with regard to the personal impact of these studies, where the 'affiliated' agreed more with the statement that religious education helps them to learn about themselves ($\Phi=0.205$); there were no significant differences in the case of those who had studied religious education or had not. The 'affiliated' diverged modestly from the 'non-affiliated' by their strong agreement with the views that they learn at school to respect other religions ($\Phi=0.198$), that religious topics are interesting for them ($\Phi=0.167$) and that they are important to deal with ($\Phi=0.163$).

Language. 'Russians', modestly more than 'Estonians', agreed strongly that at school they learn to respect everyone ($\Phi=0.27$). All the other statements in this section were agreed with more by 'Estonians'. The statements about the societal dimension were modestly more agreed by Estonians: studies on religious issues help in understanding current events ($\Phi=0.255$), and in living together in peace ($\Phi=0.238$), and it was also considered to be important to learn about different religions ($\Phi=0.228$). More personal evaluations, such as 'learning about religion helps to understand oneself' or 'to make moral decisions', did not show significant distinctions.

Expected outcomes of religious education

In this section I worked with questions 20–25. Students rejected the idea that school provides or should provide religious beliefs. In addition more personal, although not strictly religious aims, such as developing moral values or one's own point of view were less agreed with than other statements. In the students' view religious education should rather help them to understand the world. The most agreed statement was that knowledge about religion helps in understanding history, and the least agreed was that it should support the development of moral values. There were no significant differences according to their experience with religious education.

Chart 17: Outcomes of religious education (q. 24, 25, 21, 22) by religious affiliation and language (%)

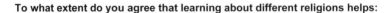

To what extent do you agree that learning about different religions helps:

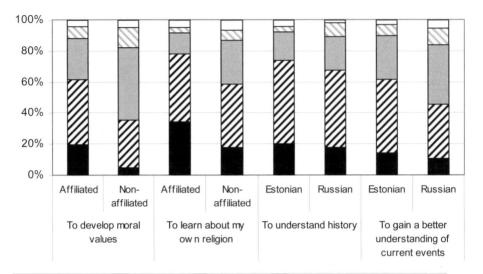

Religious affiliation. The 'affiliated' agreed with all the statements of the block, such as with the personal outcomes of religious education to develop moral values (Φ=0.252; Chart 17), to develop one's point of view (Φ=0.228; Chart 17) and the more interpersonal statement 'to understand others and live peacefully with them' (Φ=0.206) and less markedly in learning about one's own religion (Φ=0.186).

Language. 'Estonians' agreed slightly more that learning about religions helps one to understand history and current events (Chart 17).

Aims for religious education

In this section I worked with questions 32–36. Religious education, in the students' view, should be knowledge-oriented. The students strongly rejected the idea that school should provide religious beliefs for students ($\bar{x}$=2.4). All other aims were more appreciated ($\bar{x}$=3.7–3.5) and 'to get objective knowledge' was the most agreed with.

Studies of religion. Only with regard to confessional aims of religious education did all the students equally disagree with the statement; other statements clearly distinguished students with 'no RE' from other groups. They agreed modestly less that students should be able to talk about religion at school (Φ=0.228; Chart 18) or to learn the importance of religion for dealing with problems in society (Φ=0.213). They were less interested in getting knowledge about religion (Φ=0.195) or in learning to understand what religions teach.

Religious affiliation. The 'affiliated' agreed more with all the aims, but the differences were more significant in responses to personal aims of religious education: to be guided towards religious belief (Φ=0.248; Chart 18), and also to learn what religions teach (Φ=0.175). The 'affiliated' more wanted students to learn to speak about religious issues (Φ=0.159). The difference about learning to speak on religious issues is even more remarkable when those who regard religion as being very important for them are compared to those for whom religion is not important at all (means 4.12 and 2.96). Still, 'be guided towards religious beliefs' was the least valued aim for religious education also among the 'affiliated' ($\bar{x}$=2.91), while 'learn to understand what religions teach' ($\bar{x}$=3.9) and 'get objective knowledge' ($\bar{x}$=3.86) were the most favoured. The 'non-affiliated' valued objective knowledge ($\bar{x}$=3.62) and the importance of religion in society ($\bar{x}$=3.56) more than other aims.

Chart 18: Aims for religious education (q. 34, 36, 35) by model of religious education and religious affiliation (%)

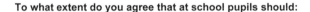

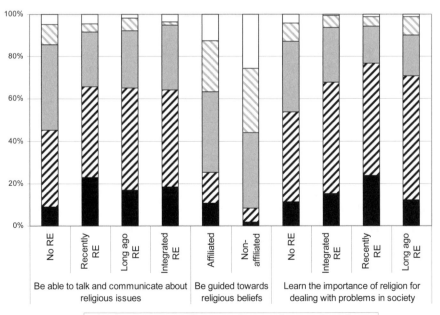

Language. All aims for religious education were more highly valued by 'Estonians', except 'to be guided towards religious belief'. Three answers were modestly different. 'Estonians' valued significantly more that students should learn about the impact of religion on society (Φ=0.24) and that students should be able to talk about religious issues (Φ=0.227). Similarly, 'Estonians' agreed that learning about religions should give knowledge about different world religions (Φ=0.153).

Models of religious education

In this section I worked with questions 26–31. The most agreed statement from the whole questionnaire was that on the voluntary basis of religious education ($\bar{x}$=4.1), where more than half of the students strongly agreed and about one third agreed with the statement. About half of students agreed strongly or agreed that all they needed to know about religion was covered by other subjects. Slightly more students agreed with religious education in groups according to their religious affiliation, if the subject were to be introduced at school. The statement about no place for religion in school was the most confusing for students – half of the respondents could not take a view.

Studies of religion. Only one statement did not reveal significant differences between those with different experiences with religious education: voluntary participation in religious education lessons. Students without religious education experience agreed more than the others that there is no place for religion at school (Φ=0.23). The group with recent experience of religious education diverged modestly from all others in its opinions about religious education. They supported more common religious education (Φ=0.205; Chart 19), they disagreed more with the statement that groups should be separated by religious affiliation (Φ=0.176) and with the statement that religious education is not needed as a separate subject (Φ=0.272; Chart 19). Those who studied religious education long ago had similar positions regarding religious education models to those with no experience of religious education, except favouring more the need for religiously segregated groups in studying religious education.

Religious affiliation. The 'affiliated' valued religious education more highly and rejected the claims that having it as a separate subject was not needed (Φ=0.192; Chart 19) and 'There should be no place for religion in school life' (Φ=0.192). Nevertheless, they opposed more than the 'non-affiliated' the forms of religious education which could cause their segregation, such as optional studies of religious education (Φ=0.215; Chart 19) or studies in confessional groups.

Chart 19: Models of religious education (q. 30, 29, 26) by religious affiliation, model of religious education and language (%)

What is your position regarding different models of religious education in school?

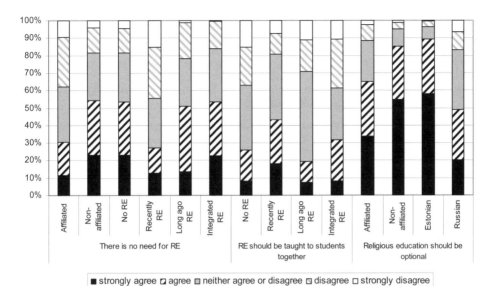

Language. There were no significant differences in opinions about the need for religious education. Significantly, more 'Estonians' strongly agreed that religious education should be optional ($\Phi=0.424$; Chart 19), slightly more also with the need to learn it according to one's own religious background. 'Russians' were more likely to agree with the statement that there should be no place for religion in school ($\Phi=0.18$).

Appearance of religion in school

In this section I worked with questions 13–19. Only two ways for religion to appear in school were more accepted than rejected – allowing the wearing of discreet religious symbols ($\overline{x}=4.1$) and being absent on religious holidays ($\overline{x}=3.4$). More ritualistic and school-oriented demands, such as a special room for praying ($\overline{x}=2.2$) and voluntary services ($\overline{x}=2.2$) were strongly rejected. Surprisingly, a special menu was not seen as acceptable by many respondents ($\overline{x}=2.7$).

Studies of religion. The students who studied religious education long ago or had integrated religious education were slightly more likely to be in favour of several ways religion could appear in school, but especially for the statement about religious services at school, where they agreed more than others with the statement ($\Phi=0.276$, Chart 20); also they supported more the right to be absent from school for religious reasons and to wear visible religious symbols.

145

Religious affiliation. Somewhat surprising was the finding that only two items showed modestly significant differences on the basis of religious affiliation: the right to wear discreet religious symbols (Φ=0.18) and that school should provide facilities for students to pray (Φ=0.17; Chart 20). In other statements, although the 'affiliated' more likely 'strongly agreed', they showed no significant differences in their views if agreements and disagreements are compared.

Chart 20: Appearance of religion in school (q. 19, 18, 14) by model of religious education and religious affiliation (%)

How much do you agree with following statements?

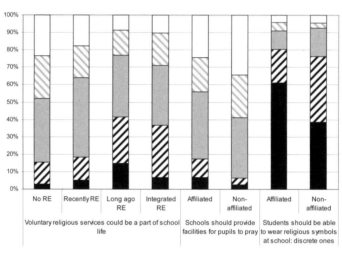

■ strongly agree ▨ agree ▢ neither agree or disagree ▨ disagree ▢ strongly disagree

Language. There were no significant differences for this section of questions; several ways for religion to appear were supported by 'Estonians' a little more than by 'Russians'. 'Estonians' agreed modestly more that students should be able to wear visible religious symbols (Φ=0.156).

Showing views about religion in school

In this section I worked with questions 78, 79, 81 and 82. More students (45%) were interested in the way their best friends think about religion than were not (23%, $\bar{x}$=3.2). At the same time, such an interest was often rather passive – 30% of students agreed and 33% disagreed with the statement that it does not bother them what friends think about religion ($\bar{x}$=3.0). Students were more likely to think that a student who openly shows his/her religious belief risks being mocked ($\bar{x}$=3.4) than to consider that it is problematic for themselves ($\bar{x}$=2.6).

Studies of religion. The group most interested in the views of their friends were the students who studied religious education in primary school (Φ=0.173) and the most disinterested students were those without any form of religious education. Students showed no significant differences about showing their own religious identity at school related to their religious education.

Religious affiliation and language. The 'affiliated' were more likely than the 'non-affiliated' to agree with the personal statements that it is problematic for them to show their religion (Φ=0.207) and that they would like to know about the way their best friend thinks about religion (Φ=0.152), but showed less difference with the general statement that some believers could be teased. For this more general statement, the modestly significant difference was between language-groups, where 'Estonians' agreed more that a student could be teased at school on religious grounds (Φ=0.279).

'Russian' religious affiliated students were most concerned about showing their religious convictions; they were the only ones who saw their own problems as being as bad as the problems of 'a student', while all other groups believed this to be it more a problem for others (Chart 21). 'Estonians', in spite of their lower religious affiliation than 'Russians', were more interested in the way their best friend thinks about religion.

Chart 21: Showing views about religion (q. 81, 80) by language and religious affiliation (%)

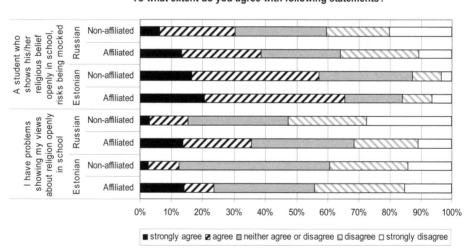

To what extent do you agree with following statements?

■ strongly agree ▨ agree ▫ neither agree or disagree ▫ disagree ▫ strongly disagree

Summary of results according to different groups

The school was not seen as a place to practise religion, nor to be visible; the students also rejected the idea that school provides or should provide religious beliefs. In addition more personal, although not strictly religious aims, such as developing moral values or one's own point of view, were less agreed with than other statements. In the students' view religious education should rather help them to understand the world around them than themselves. The young people, for whom religion seems not to be a part of life, did not see any reason for religion to appear in school or to guarantee rights for students with a religious background; they rather refused these rights, except for wearing discreet religious symbols, which was probably more familiar for them, as some students do wear little religious symbols at school, even without being a member of the particular religion. If students were asked about favourable models of religious education they inclined to choose models familiar to them. The students were usually satisfied with a lack of religious education, or the form of it that they had personally experienced, whatever it was.

Students who had studied religious education, or had religion integrated in a special way into their school life, valued the subject matter more highly and found it to be helpful in understanding society. The students who had studied the subject recently valued objective knowledge, different perspectives, respect for differences and found it to be more interesting than all other students. They rejected, more than others, being segregated by religiously affiliated groups and more likely wanted all students to learn the subject together. The students who had studied religious education a long time ago and not anymore were less satisfied with the education on religious issues they had now and believed that religious education should be taught according to religious affiliation. In addition, students with integrated religious education did not see any need for a separate subject, but they were more aware of the religious rights that a person has than were others.

Students with a religious affiliation did not ask for special rights or facilities for practising their faith at school, except more individually exercised rights such as wearing discreet religious symbols and a room for individual prayer. Religiously affiliated students valued religious education in personal terms, such as making ethical choices and as a point of departure for personal reflection. Although they saw a positive impact of religious education in personal terms and a need for religious education, they were more likely to be against studying it in religiously homogenous groups or as an optional subject. Students without a religious affiliation did not see a problem in revealing their (a-)religious beliefs (although they believed that it could be problematic for some students), while religiously affiliated students saw it as more problematic, both in personal and abstract terms.

'Estonians' were more likely to be in favour of voluntary religious education and about the positive impact of religious education, talking about religion and knowing about its societal dimension, while 'Russians' were against religion at school, including visible religious rights. Especially the similar attitudes to the statement about the right to be excused from school on religious holidays was surprising, as the Orthodox Church of the Moscow Patriarchate has different timings for Easter and Christmas from the official holidays which are according to Lutheran and Catholic traditions. Here 'Russians' took more extreme positions than 'Estonians', but 'agreed' with the statement less than 'Estonians', making for no difference on the mean level of agreement.

Girls and boys were similar in their views about religion in school when the variables were related to confessional and more personal approaches to religion at school (e.g. boys and girls equally disagreed that students should be guided towards religious beliefs, that learning about religion helps to make choices between right and wrong, to develop moral values or one's own point of view). Also some societal effects received similar responses by both genders (e.g. that they received knowledge about religion, they could discuss topics from different perspectives, learning about different religions helped them to understand current events and history and that such studies could create conflicts in class). But many variables about religion in school had more significant differences according to gender. Girls were more positive than boys about studying religious topics at school. The most significant differences emerged in girls' greater agreement that learning about religion is interesting, important and helps people to live in peace. The only significant difference in responses to answers about rights on religious grounds at school was that girls agreed more with the right to wear discreet religious symbols. All other differences were insignificant; boys took more extreme positions ('agree strongly' and 'disagree strongly'), while girls were more reserved.

4.2.3.2 Data interpretation

The school was not seen as a place to practise religion, nor to be visible with regard to religion. On the one hand this showed awareness of institutional limits, seeing a school as a secular body where religion should not have any place. On the other hand, the lack of experiences of such a need also played some role, since religious diversity is not visible in Estonia. Only in schools with integrated religious education, where religion and religious diversity are more visible, were religious rights valued more highly. The support for the *status quo* is seen also in students' general preference for the provision of voluntary religious education or confessional religious education which would exclude most of them from the obligation to take part in the subject. The students were usually satisfied with the form of or lack of religious education they had experienced, whatever it was.

Religious affiliation played the most important role in forming opinions about religion, and a similar pattern could be found here: students differed most significantly in their opinions about religious education, its aims and values, according to their own experience or lack thereof. The students who had studied religion recently valued its impact more highly and appreciated the possibility of learning it. Students with experience of religious education in primary school were more sceptical, perhaps due to the Bible-oriented content of primary religious education.

It is difficult to know how religious students feel at school in Estonia, where they cannot practise their faith openly. As discussed in section 4.2.1 religious affiliation for the respondents in Estonia is related to one's beliefs and practices, having not only nominal affiliation to a religion, but also personal religiosity. According to the answers, students with a religious affiliation were used to keeping religion private. Although they valued the possible benefits of religious education they disagreed with its confessional or optional form. Religiously affiliated students had friends among the 'non-affiliated' and probably did not want to be different from them because of their own religious background or interest in religious issues. Students without religious affiliation were in a 'majority' position; they did not see it as problematic to show their beliefs about religions, while students with religious affiliation did. 'Non-affiliated' students still could see that it was awkward for some other students, although the 'affiliated' saw it as a more urgent problem at the abstract level as well. Probably, in the light of this, religiously affiliated students would like students, themselves as well as the others, to be able to talk about religious issues. One of the influences on their views could be the way religion is dealt in the media and internet forums, where religion and religious people are often severely ridiculed and criticised (Valk, 2006, 175).

With regard to language it must be remembered that there were no Russian schools providing religious education in the sample, although some students had studied it in some other schools in primary classes and also 'Russians' tended to be more religiously affiliated. Their attitudes towards religion, religious practice and content of belief were consistent; their identity as ethnic Russians overcame the effects of their specific religious affiliation. 'Russian' and 'Estonian' respondents diverged in their attitudes about the personal and societal aspects of religion; their answers to the role of religion in school followed an analogous pattern: 'Estonians' agreed more with religious education and other societal statements. Maybe surprising was the difference in attitudes to voluntary religious education. There could be two explanations – that 'Russians' did not want any form of religious education or that the 'Estonian' respondents were more influenced by discussions in the media about the need for voluntary instead of obligatory religious education.

4.3 Conclusions

The main conclusions are presented in the last section of the section. First, the conclusions with regard to the research questions are presented. Second, the answers to the research hypothesis are discussed.

4.3.1 Answering the research questions

What role does religion have in students' life? The role of religion in students' life and in their surroundings is not very visible. Religion belongs more to history and 'others' than to contemporary time and 'oneself' for most students. They do not practise religion, or prefer to do so privately. Religion is often regarded as so confidential that they hardly ever speak about it with anybody or know about the religion of people around them. Students said that they did not choose their friends according to their religious beliefs, but some of them encounter religious diversity in their everyday life or at school. They get some information about religion primarily from family and from school. Religiously affiliated students were more positive about religion, although they had the same doubts and readiness to change their mind as students without a religious affiliation.

Language used by students in their everyday communication proved to be a very important factor in viewing religion. For Russian speaking students religion was part of their identity, often irrespective of their actual religious affiliation.

How do students view the impact of religions on society and relations? Students did not believe in religion's influence, neither in causing conflicts, nor in building peace. They trusted most of all respect as a way to improve harmony. Those who had no experience of religious education at school were less aware of the societal dimension of religion and believed less that religion could cause troubles. The students with no religious education believed more in the risk of being teased on religious grounds. Religiously affiliated students were more positive not only about religion but also about religious differences around them. Religiously affiliated students valued friendship and to avoid conflicts. They preferred mostly to use a code of conduct to keep their religious convictions private.

How do students see religion in school and the impact of religion in education? Although students in Estonia meet religious diversity at school they did not want to study it in a systematic way, organized as special religious education lessons, neither did they see any reason to give special rights to students with a religious affiliation. Their attitudes towards the proper format of religious education mirror their own experience of it, and it is difficult for them to imagine anything beyond their own experience or even more difficult to accept forms of religious education which could cause separation from their group. They did not see school as a place to develop personal views on religious issues; rather they would value learning about religion's historical and societal dimensions.

Students did not see school as a place to develop personal views on religious issues. Rather they took the view that the historical – and societal – dimensions of it, such as tolerance and ability to live in peace with representatives of different religions, should be taught more. There were no tendencies for the studies of religion to make students more religious. However the students who had studied religious education did value tolerance more and saw differences as not only normal but also as an interesting part of life. Those who studied religious education valued school as source of information about religion. They showed more readiness to talk about religion and an interest in talking to people of other religious backgrounds. Also their attitudes towards studies about religions were more positive.

Religious education is specially valued by students with religious backgrounds for whom religious education is an important factor for their identity formation and positive self-esteem. But even by them it is not seen as an introduction to a specific religion but rather as an opportunity for self reflection. They did not want to be segregated on religious grounds, or to study religious education in confessional groups, or as an optional subject. Although they valued the subject, they would rather renounce it than differ from their friends.

Religion is seen by Russian speaking students as a private enterprise, not interrelated to any societally regulated aspect of life, nor as a part of school life in any form.

4.3.2 Reflections in the light of the research hypotheses

1.a Religious students are less tolerant than non-religious students. It is complicated to judge whether religious students are more or less tolerant than non-religious students. First, some indicators for respect were formulated in a way that was easier for religious students to agree with. For example, the statements 'I respect other people who believe' and 'Without religion the world would be a better place' probably have a different meaning for students who believe or belong to some religion since they would be giving statements about people like themselves, while the non-religious respondents would be talking about people different from themselves. Some other statements could be regarded as being more neutral. For example 'I don't like people from other religions and do not want to live together with them' or 'Respecting the religion of others helps in coping with differences' would indicate equally to all respondents that the statement is about 'people who have a different worldview from mine'. Second, there are no criteria for identifying a 'religious' student. For example, is it legitimate to say that a student who has a religious affiliation is 'religious'? To assess this, dependant variables of tolerance were checked against independent ones, including religious affiliation – how important they think religion is or what they believe in.

The most respectful attitudes were held by those who valued religion as very important for themselves, followed by students with a religious affiliation. Nevertheless, one must be cautious not to make too bold statements, as the biggest differences were in statements which were easier to agree with for religious students. Still, the statements about the usefulness of respect and readiness to live together with religiously diverse groups were also significantly more agreed with by the students who held religion as important for them. The differences on views about religion's potential for conflict were small, and these statements were least agreed by students for whom religion was very important or who believed in God. Students who valued religion as very important be-lieved most of all in the effectiveness of respect for living peacefully together. Those who found religion as absolutely not important and did not believe in God or any spirit showed least agreement.

With some restrictions it can concluded that the survey did not support the hypothesis that religious students are less tolerant. Contrarily, the more they thought religion to be important, the more they were ready to tolerate students with a different religion and also to value tolerance in improving relations between different groups.

2.a Students who have encountered religious diversity in education are more tolerant. As the students attending different forms of religious education did not differ by their religious affiliation, it was interesting to see how the students differed in levels of tolerance. A more tolerant family background can be a correlated factor for students who studied religious education long ago or had integrated religious education, as sometimes it was their parents who de-cided on their participation in lessons or that they were going to the particular school. In the case of students who studied religious education recently, it was usually a choice made by their school, so they did not differ in their family background from those without religious education. When the answers to ques-tions about tolerance of these groups are compared, the differences are not so big, but a pervasive pattern occurs in the responses.

The students who had never studied religious education differed from all other groups for all the statements on respect. Students without religious educa-tion disagreed more that they have respect for believers, and they believed also least of all in the effectiveness of respect for living peacefully together. How-ever, those with integrated religious education or recent religious education studies were more optimistic about this. The statement 'I do not like...' was most agreed by students without religious education and least by those with an integrated form of religious education.

Somewhat unexpected was the finding that students without religious education believed less than the others that religion may cause some conflicts or that people of different religious backgrounds cannot live together; those who studied religious education long ago were most ready to believe these statements. It shows that students with no conscious experience of religious diversity at school were less negative or less aware of the potentials of religion for conflicts or hardly understood how it could cause conflicts.

The students who had classmates of different religious backgrounds tended to be more tolerant in their responses than those who did not know about their friends' religion, or who went to religiously homogeneous classes. Even if the results show some differences, the causal relationship is ambiguous. For example, if a student has friends of different backgrounds and holds tolerant views, one can ask – is (s)he tolerant because (s)he has such friends or (s)he has such friends because (s)he is tolerant? Similarly, the 'most intolerant group', those who did not know about the religion of their friends, showed their indifference and somewhat negative attitudes in all questions. Still, students who said that they had classmates of a different religious background had not chosen this situation but had nevertheless more tolerant views than students from homogeneous classes. In my view, if the young people were put into a situation where religious diversity is present and made explicit, they would be forced to develop strategies supporting openness to otherness.

Encountering religious diversity in education can take different forms and have different effects. The trends in the sample suggest that the schools that have integrated religion in their everyday life, making it more visible and less private, support students' readiness for respect and tolerance. The same can be said about providing special studies of religious education, dealing with world religions. The more hostile attitudes of those without any study of religion,, except for dealing with religion in other subjects, can be followed throughout the questionnaire – students without any experience of religious education were holding more negative attitudes to religion in their answers to many questions.

I will explore now the hypothesis of the more active form of tolerance, openness to dialogue, as described in 1.2.

1.b Religious students are less open to dialogue on religious issues than non-religious students. The findings of the present survey refuted the hypothesis that religious people are less open to dialogue. All the statements about readiness for dialogue were agreed significantly more strongly by those who valued the importance of religion for themselves more highly. They wanted to learn to speak about religious issues at school. They were much more curious about others' views and were interested in shaping their own views by listening to and understanding others, and they believed in the positive effects of dialogue on religious issues. They chose discussion instead of ignoring a different worldview. The opposite was true for all the statements about showing no readiness for dialogue (preferring ignoring a person, talking about the stupidity of religion, confessing little knowledge and no interest in talking about religion); these were more agreed by students who regarded religion as not important at all for themselves. Similarly, the less students valued religion, the more they preferred to socialise with like-minded people at school and in their spare time.

The same attitudes showed that when students with and without religious affiliation are compared, the 'affiliated' tended to be more ready for dialogue than the 'non-affiliated'. Students who did not believe in God or any sort of spirit were the least ready for dialogue. However, before one concludes that non-religious students gave answers less open to dialogue, it must be admitted that a person who is attached to some topic is always more ready to speak about it than a person who is not. The most significant difference between students, according to their beliefs on speaking about religion, was interest: non-religious students said that they were not interested in the topic, so all the other statements could be related to their lack of interest.

2.b Students who have encountered religious diversity in education are more open to dialogue on religious issues. The differences related to diverse models of religious education were less significant than in the case of religious affiliation. Nevertheless, there were some significant differences. There were two possible patterns in answers: students with 'no RE' *versus* 'all the others' and 'RE long ago' (in the elementary school) *versus* 'RE recently' (in their current secondary school).

There were two extreme positions, with those with no religious education on one side and students who had experienced religious education (both, recently or long ago) on the other. The students without religious education showed less readiness to have a dialogue on religious issues: they agreed less that 'Students should be able to talk and communicate about religious issues' or 'I like to know what my best friend thinks about religion', that different views would make talking about religion interesting or would help them to understand the world.

Not all the statements were agreed equally by students who had religious education recently and those who had had it long ago. Those, who had religious education long ago believed less than all the others that talking about religion could help one to understand others, but agreed that talking about religion could lead to disagreement, and they were more ready to talk themselves about the cruelties of religion. The most embarrassed to talk were students with no religious education or who had it long ago, while the least embarrassed were students with integrated religious education. The wish to spend time with like-minded people was least felt by students with an integrated form of religious education (about every third student); and the statement was surprisingly most supported by students who had studied religious education in primary school (every second). The more visible role of religion in schools with integrated religious education could ensure that students had to encounter others with different views.

Similarly, the students having classmates of diverse religious backgrounds not only believed that religion could cause problems but also talked about how stupid religion is. This did not prevent them from entering into dialogue on religious issues. Some differences were significant for students from a religiously diverse class, including the following: they were more eager to know about their friends' religious beliefs and found that differences in views made talking about religion interesting. They said that their views could be shaped by such talk and it helped them to understand other people better and what is going on in the world.

Why did students with experience of religious education long ago feel uneasy talking about religion? It is not possible to answer the question on the basis of this survey. Perhaps they had been teased because of their voluntary studies of religious education and the quite hostile attitude in some answers could refer to their self-protective conduct or embarrassment about the childish views they used to hold about religion in primary classes, without having the opportunity to have more advanced approaches to religion in their later studies.

A slight, but pervasive tendency emerged, that those who did not have any form of religious education were less likely to agree with statements about their readiness for dialogue and more likely to agree with hostile statements, while the most interested and dialogical group consisted of students who had recently studied religious education.

Summary. There are more promising models than '… *and no religion too*' in creating peace by mutual understanding and respect built upon an open dialogue and religious literacy. Even if students, who explicitly encountered religious diversity at school, had had some negative experiences with members of different religions, they tended to be more open to dialogue on religious issues. Perhaps it works both ways – on the one hand, if there is a need to have dialogue, one can learn the skills needed for it and become more ready for it. On the other hand, when a person has the skills needed for peaceful dialogue, he or she is more ready to enter into dialogue and sees its benefits. From this perspective, schools should offer students an environment for meeting religious diversity, having dialogue and fostering the necessary skills. Students could profit from it not only as a point of self-reflection but also seeing a more complex picture about religion and acquiring the skills needed in contemporary pluralistic Europe.

5. PROSPECTS FOR AND OBSTACLES TO DIALOGUE IN RELIGIOUS EDUCATION LESSONS

The focus of the third and fourth chapters was on students' views. Now, having obtained their views on religion and religious diversity, and also their hopes and fears with regard to religious education, I will take another perspective. I will still focus on the students but here I will investigate the main potentials and hindrances for dialogue about different worldviews that can be followed in the classroom practices of religious education.[21] I am interested in dialogue as an active and more visible method of expressing one's tolerance, as described in 1.2.1. Answering the central research question involved more than simply interviewing students; indeed, extensive fieldwork in schools, including the observation of classroom interactions *in statu nascendi*, was vital. The present chapter explores the results of fieldwork conducted in schools observing religious education lessons – an as-of-yet unexplored field of investigation in Estonia. Interest in the current subproject stemmed from a desire to explore this question: 'what potential and limitations for dialogue can be identified in students' interactions in the context of religious education classes in Estonia?'

The study was conducted by observing and analysing patterns of classroom interaction. In section 1.3.1 my positioning as a researcher and its impacts on the study were discussed in relation to the subjectivity of such research. A video-ethnographic method of data collection and incident analysis (as described in 1.3.2 'Classroom Interaction') was chosen for the purpose of this study. In section 1.3.2 I analysed the effects of the data collection methods utilised for the study. Following the definition of an 'incident', as described in 1.3.2, I looked for hidden aspects representing the overall structure of interaction and pedagogical context with regard to the dialogue that appeared or was hindered in the classroom interaction. The incidents were identified using a working definition of 'dialogue', as described in the section on terminology (1.2.3). All incidents were gathered into a 'pool of incidents' and then the incidents were transcribed. An example is presented in Appendix 7.

The current chapter consists of three sections. The first provides a rationale for the selection of schools and a contextual description of the schools under study, their ethos, the status of religious education in the schools, and a short portrayal of the religious education teachers and students involved in the study. The second section presents the results of the fieldwork. First it reviews the incidents discovered in schools, demonstrating how the students' readiness and teachers' pedagogical style determine some of the potentials and limitations for

---

21 The present chapter is based on two articles: *Prospects for and obstacles to dialogue in religious education in Estonia* (Schihalejev, 2009f) and *Dialogue in religious education lessons – possibilities and hindrances in the Estonian context* (Schihalejev, 2009c).

dialogue in different contexts. Next it delves deeper into one of the incidents, revealing something of the peculiarities of the particular school as well as some overall structures of the pedagogic tradition and the cultural concepts prevailing in Estonian education. Finally some reflections and concluding remarks are provided.

5.1 Sample: Schools, teachers, and status of religious education

This section will present the arguments behind the selection of the schools under study. Two schools were chosen for the study, both having the most debated and contentious form of religious education in Estonia – namely, that in those schools all students in the class take part in religious education lessons. However, the ethos of the schools, the socio-demographical variables and the approaches of religious education teachers also differed, requiring more complex insight into the classroom interaction patterns in religious education lessons.

Next, the discussion looks more closely at the selected schools, describing their ethos and how they organise religious education, and then a short description of a religious education teacher and of the classes is provided. Pseudonyms are used for schools, teachers, and students.

5.1.1 School C

School C participated also in the qualitative study and a short description of the school is given in section 3.1.2. It is not repeated here, where I will focus on the portrayal of people involved in the study. The school is smaller than other municipal schools in the same town. The children who attend the lower classes are mainly from the surrounding area. At the upper secondary school level, many students attending had not been admitted to other gymnasia in the town but nevertheless wanted to attend one. Religious education is a compulsory subject in the tenth grade at school C, providing a brief overview of world religions.

I visited religious education for two Year 10 classes in November and December 2006. Students participating in the study were aged 16 to 17 years; two thirds were girls, and one third were boys. Two 45-minute lessons were observed, and five lessons were videotaped. Two group interviews with students were conducted after the religious education lessons. Among the students, some had Lutheran or Pentecostal backgrounds, some were atheists, and most had no religion.

The teacher 'Heli' has been a teacher of religious education, Philosophy and Ethics for two years. Several informal talks and one interview were conducted with Heli, who is fond of using different student-orientated teaching methods as she values different learning styles. She believes that the main aim of religious education is to help children to identify their own worldview and to cope with related questions; another aim is that they should become more tolerant towards those with a different worldview.

Heli feels that studying 'about' (see 2.2.3) religions tends to dominate the subject, but hopes to achieve her aims by using role play and asking students to formulate arguments for standpoints different from their own. She tries to find her own teaching style and the methods that work with students with moderate academic and more artistic abilities. A more precise portrait for Heli, as extracted from my article about teachers (Schihalejev, 2009e) is given in Appendix 8.

5.1.2 School D

School D in central Estonia was established at the end of the 19th century. It is one of the best schools in Estonia according to the results of national exams and students' performance in academic competitions and the school is highly selective. Although the subject is voluntary, at the time of the fieldwork all students of humanities – with one exception – still took religious education.

I followed the religious education lessons for a humanities class, with 36 students aged 16 to 17 years old, in January and February 2007 and conducted a group interview with students after one of the lessons. The classroom was arranged as an auditorium with fixed, gradually ascending benches. The setting of the tables supports lectures and teacher-student conversation, but does not support student-student interactions and communication. Three of the video-taped lessons lasted 90 minutes, while the other two lasted 45 minutes. Students provided written feedback about the influence the camera had on the lessons and their behaviour. In addition, at the end of the semester, the students offered comments on the whole religious education course. Some students were Lutheran and some had a Free Church background. Most of the students had no specific religious background.

Most students in grade 10 had not had any religious education before, so the task of the first year of studies was to learn religious vocabulary and the basics of world religions. The teacher of religious education in School D, 'Peter', has been a teacher of religious education and philosophy for more than ten years and is highly valued. In addition to informal talks, two interviews were conducted with him. He sees the aim of religious education as breaking down prejudices towards religion, and demonstrating that religion is worth being regarded as normal. A more precise portrait for Peter, as extracted from my article about teachers (Schihalejev, 2009e) is presented in Appendix 8.

5.2 Presentation of results

5.2.1 Pool of incidents

Using the definition of dialogue as described in 1.2.2, I examined which aspects of dialogue emerged in classroom interactions and under what conditions. On the basis of these analyses incidents were selected for a pool. The incidents are depicted below, according to codes taken from the analysis.

First I analysed the questions that had been raised by teachers and how they influenced the students' contributions in the learning process. Second, I looked for the ways in which the teacher or other students responded to a contribution and the role it played on the interactive level of conversation. All the examples given below are presented to make my arguments more transparent and to give readers the possibility of making their own interpretations. If the written, anonymous feedback of students is used, then the quotations have numbers instead of names. If oral answers are used, then pseudonyms are given.

5.2.1.1 Open and closed questions

I analysed the questions raised by teachers and how they influenced students' contributions to the learning process. After the preliminary analysis, the questions were arranged into three groups. The first group, 'closed questions', required memorised facts to be recalled. There is a clearly distinguishable border between the right and wrong answers. For example: *"How many confessions can you find on this page?"* and *"To which caste did Siddhartha Gautama's father belong?"* If this type of question supports dialogue, the aim would be confrontation. The second group, 'half-open questions', focused on understanding the studied material; they could have more than one right answer, but a border still existed between 'right' and 'wrong' answers. Examples include *"Describe in your own words the meaning of the word 'karma'"* or *"Find a verse in Dhammapada which confirms one of the Four Noble Truths of Buddhism. Can you explain how it confirms it?"* The third group, 'open questions', consisted of questions to which a listener would not be able to say whether or not the answer was correct. Instead, students reflected upon their opinions or preferences or cited examples from their lives. Examples of these questions are *"When would you regard a man to be grown up?"* and *"Which of the books did you like?*" The aim of dialogue, if it emerges, can vary from confrontation to an aspiration to search for common ground.

My first assumption was that more open questions or tasks contribute to an atmosphere in which dialogue can occur, and challenge students to construct their own version of the world and thus make dialogue possible. Could more open ways of asking questions increase students' readiness to take part in discussions?

In **School C**, the analysis of the lessons indicates that the readiness to cooperate and the interest of the students increased when the teacher asked closed questions, expecting memorisation or finding the right answer from worksheets. In particular, when students worked in groups of two to six, they discussed the questions with each other and tried to arrive at a common solution. In addition, some half-open questions that required students to remember the studied material and had more than one possible answer were appreciated by students. For example, a group task on the main concepts of Hinduism in which students had to explain them in everyday language (based on written work on handouts) inspired students. However, whenever the teacher asked an open question about students' opinions or preferences, they seemed puzzled and 'switched off'.

For example, an attempt to discuss an open question in a lesson about holy texts of Hinduism failed. After an overview about the content of sacred texts of Hinduism, the teacher's question "*If you could read one of those texts, which one would you choose, and why?*" did not find any response from students, they either refused to answer or said that they did not have any opinion. In the task of re-wording the main concepts of Hinduism, they started to work actively again. During stimulated recall students explained that the information they had was too superficial and they needed to know more; some exemplification of extracts from different Hindu sacred texts would be necessary in order to make a personal decision.

Only one open question encouraged dialogue: after introducing Siddhartha's birth, the teacher asked students if someone had a special story of his or her birth. A girl from the back row explained how her mother had almost given birth on the street. Other students started showing interest, but still no dialogue took place; the teacher continued with the lesson and the students briefly engaged in side-talk.

In order to take a closer look at an example I selected an incident, 'sketches about Hinduism', from the third lesson in the block about Hinduism in everyday life. Students had been taught the main tenets of Hinduism and then they moved to the role of the religion in daily life. The students created four groups, each of which had to concentrate on one aspect of Hindu life: 'Purpose of life', 'Holy days', 'Prayer', and the 'Four ashramas'. Students read the papers with background information for their sketches. After studying these they prepared drama sketches about what they had learned and they were expected to perform these to the other groups. There was a good distribution of work; almost every student produced something. They could use incense, candles, bells, crayons, articles of clothing, and wigs. Some of the students drew, others thought about the performance. The teacher moved around in order to be available. Students exchanged ideas, asked questions of each other and sometimes of the teacher, and tried to apply the text to what they must perform. There was a friendly atmosphere in the class; students' body language, smiles, and inclinations showed that they were enjoying their work. The classroom was rather noisy.

In the following minutes, four groups presented their drama sketches to the class, but it was difficult to follow what was shown. The room had no raised area and the students performed in a very tiny place in front of the class, so it was impossible to see clearly from the benches at the back. It was difficult to understand everything that was in the sketches without having them read. Only the sketch about prayer was accompanied by an oral presentation in which the students acted out an important part of a Hindu life – puja celebrated at home.

After every group had finished, the teacher asked the students about their impressions.

> Heli: *"Which performance caught your attention the most?"*
> Jane: *"The last one!"*
> Mirjam: *"The last!"*
> Heli: *"What did you understand from it?"*
> Boy Paul: *"Nothing."*
> Several students muttered something that is unintelligible.

Heli explained briefly the contents of the sketches. For the conclusion and personal reflection, she asked what they liked the most and students shouted: *"Everything!"* She tried to get some more precise feedback, but nothing came. The students' interest waned, and their attention turned to other things. Nobody gave any thoughtful explanations.

In **School D** the teacher asked only half-open or open questions, usually not in a personal way but on an intellectual level. There was a certain routine in the class. After Peter asked a question, students had three to five minutes to write down their thoughts, sometimes followed by discussion in pairs. If there was no volunteer to answer the question, the teacher selected students sequentially to answer. Peter subsequently reflected upon the answer so that the student could argue. Usually, no discussion occurred among the students. In addition, the setting of the classroom did not support dialogue among students, as they sat in ascending rows, one behind another, without facing each other.

In an interview, Peter explained that he deliberately avoids personal issues. He argued strongly against encouraging students to talk about their religious experiences and convictions at school. He does not want to make students vulnerable by open talk about their own religious convictions. Nevertheless, he sees the need for personal reflection, as it is crucial for the understanding of the subject (for example, a task to bring out the most important issues from a selected reading). The other possibility is to make them find arguments (for or against, sometimes in line with their own opinion and sometimes regardless of it) about a belief of some religion, such as *"What problems can be created by the idea of a chosen nation?"* and *"Find the reasons why God is not portrayed in Judaism"*.

The students gave their (anonymous) feedback on the course, revealing that discussions were the most valuable part of the lessons. Having open questions in classroom situations was a new experience for them.

> *"The best part of the lessons was discussion, expression of our own opinions and viewpoints. This skill does not appear by itself and it must be practised. Usually students are not given this opportunity; now and again you must follow what the teacher has taught and to write down what is correct for the teacher; but I think that our own views and ideas remain inside us and we are not given the opportunity to express them."* (Student 29)

Students have, for many years, learned by listening to the teacher; they are used to this approach and have mastered it. The new approach seemed difficult and challenging, but very useful to many students.

> *"I have learned to think in religious education lessons. Not that I was unable to do it before but in these lessons I felt mental stimulation and I liked it."* (Student 25)

Both the value of challenging one's own way of thinking and the need to discover one's own views were brought forward. In looking for three components of dialogue, as described in section 1.2.2, deeper understandings of oneself, of others and of the subject, all of them are mentioned by students in their feedback:

> *"I liked that there was an opportunity to think, express your own opinion, argue. And there were no concrete wrong or right answers. The course gave us the opportunity to develop ourselves, broaden our horizon. We could find relations between ourselves and aspects of different religions."* (Student 22)

The students valued not only their own improvements but also had the chance to listen to the opinions of other students. They noted that religious education is the only lesson where they can learn to know each other more:

> *"I liked the structure of lessons, especially where we had to answer the questions. It was not so important for me if I was able to say my opinion to the class but this part of thinking and analysing – it helped to look at things from different*

angles. Listening to others' responses helped also to learn more about class-mates." (Student 19)

The task of reflecting upon their own ideas and exploring different religious concepts was challenging because their knowledge about religions was felt to be too superficial to contribute to an open discussion. Some students reported that they felt bad when they did not have any thoughts but were asked to contribute; others did not regard it as a sufficient reason to avoid discussions.

> "*The teacher's interesting thoughts have made me think often. I had a possibility to think a lot during religious education lessons, although I did not always get good ideas, but you must try hard. There is often a fear that you do not know the topic enough and you can miss the point with your answer, but it is not a sin to make a mistake.*" (Student 1)

Summary

Only a limited amount of dialogue occurs during the lessons, and it is usually restricted to student-teacher conversation on the level of confrontation. Open questions are rare in both schools, also half-open questions were seldom asked in School C; they were usually answered briefly and as though they are closed questions – namely, with only one answer. Theoretically, teachers are aware of the need to use more open questions in order to stimulate an analytical and more personal approach to the subject. In practice, however, the teacher's motivation to use open questions and dialogue between students decreases when open questions consistently fail to elicit a response. Only a very systematic use of open questions, as in School D, proved to be successful and stimulating for students.

More personal contributions and dialogue add to students' understanding and enable them to find common ground, but this is only possible if the atmosphere in a group is believed to be safe enough by students or the teacher. The teacher can create (or avoid) situations and atmospheres in which dialogue is possible. If the teacher believes that sharing religious convictions by students can harm them, the topic is avoided; students can have a distant and more academic perspective. The students appreciate the possibility of expressing their views even though they rarely showed the initiative to volunteer a contribution or engage in dialogue.

5.2.1.2 The teacher's way to respond

Now I will look at two types of feedback given by teachers to students' contributions. The first type is positive feedback, encouraging judgement, such as "*Very good!*" or "*Excellent*". In School C, even if the student gave the wrong answer, the teacher tried to be reassuring; by saying something like "*Your answer is on the right track*" The strategy worked especially well with closed questions but did not contribute to diverse opinions and to improving discussion among the students.

In order to take a closer look I will return to the 'sketches about Hinduism' (described above) and to the feedback given after the performances. Every sketch received warm applause; the teacher agreed with the applause and complimented all of the performances as "*super good*". She asked students to take their seats and commented on the sketches: "*I will start with the last one and briefly describe what they did. They did it very well ...*" While explaining the content of the sketches, she praised the performances. But her evaluation was too general, and it was not clear what exactly she had valued.

The second strategy, which I would call a confrontation – expansion strategy, was used mostly in School D. The teacher developed students' answers by placing them in a wider context or by identifying the strengths of a seemingly simple answer, especially if other students laughed at it.

I will examine this type of response in the incident 'Taoism and Confucianism'. The students had studied these religions and had read some texts from both traditions. At the end of lesson the teacher assigned a task to find weaknesses and strengths of the two traditions.

Leili: "*I would propose that the principles of the religions, Confucianism as well as Taoism, are weak. For example in Taoism the person is valued and the society around him is not as important as the person himself.*"

Peter: "*But what is wrong with this?*"

Leili: "*It brings out many different opinions.*"

Peter: "*But it is even...I would be delighted if there were different opinions in a class.*"

Leili: "*Yes, but if there is a state where there are many different opinions, riots would break out.*"

Peter: "*How is that – do riots arise if there are different opinions and they are allowed to be said, or do the riots arise if there are no different opinions allowed? Yeah, in a word... I used to live in such a state where different opinions were not allowed on conceptual matters, so in some cases you could have a different opinion but in conceptual matters, relating to state affairs, there was no tolerance. And at one point this big state fell apart very quickly. I do not know if it was strength that one could not express a different opinion. But to a certain extent it held it together longer than forbidding it and allowing people to state their opinions. What should I write here?*"

Leili: "*It is a good question. I do not know.*"

Peter: "*As I understood you, you regarded different opinions as a weakness of Taoism? Let us write it here. I would put a question mark here. I don't know, probably here is a difference between different subjects – for example in maths and physics there is no reason to speak about different opinions, let's say in solving an equation. There is one classical solution, even*"

165

if there are several ways to achieve it, but solutions are right or wrong. In the humanities and in religions, I have a feeling that different views are even enriching, giving the approach a certain power. But I may be wrong..."

Miku: *"In Confucianism a strength is that it seeks to create an order and harmony in itself."*

Peter: *"In Confucianism? OK. Harmony – certainly. Harmony is a word that is relatively difficult to see negatively. A negative harmony or weakness as harmony is difficult to see. Order – it is a different kind of word; it is a different kind of word. At a certain moment it could turn into a weakness. But let that rest."*

Peter's elaborations were usually much longer than those of the students. Along with responding expansively, the teacher did not hesitate to dispute an answer by pointing out its limitations, and showing its weak points, especially in the case of more advanced answers.

Some students felt the discussions were too challenging in terms of their own insufficient knowledge of the subject, with the possibility of missing the point since they knew so little yet, combined with a desire to perform well.

> *"Answering the questions in lessons was pretty difficult for me, because my knowledge on some of religions is superficial. We took the subject quickly and concentrated on the most important aspects (unfortunately it is not possible otherwise in such a short time), but I personally like to get a thorough overview before and then to analyse my own and others' thoughts more in depth. At the same time the thinking in lessons was very good."* (Student 7)

Some students reported that they felt bad when they did not have any ideas but were asked to contribute their thoughts. For others, it was unacceptable to have disapproval from the teacher:

> *"I did not like it that teacher always argued against [me], even if the answer was correct."* (Student 8)

Learning through discussion, and gaining experience in expressing themselves was a new experience for the students. It seems that religious education lessons encouraged the students to participate in a way they did not in other classes. However, the quality of facilitation is a key issue in establishing a successful dialogical approach.

In summary, a teacher's way of responding is one of the factors in advancing a dialogical approach in religious education lessons. Positive reinforcement of answers without explanation did not contribute to dialogue, but rather to the feeling that the right and satisfactory answer had already been given. In addition, the teacher's strong role as a facilitator did not encourage students to explore the subject more deeply but to rely on the teacher's arguments or even not to participate in discussions at all.

5.2.1.3 Results and conclusions

Although the two schools were different, some common hindrances to dialogue appeared, exemplifying their wider educational context and in relation to it. The deeper structure of all the incidents showed the learning process in which the teacher is supposed to be central. Estonian education is in a state of transformation – the teacher is expected to have a strong regulative role in transmitting the knowledge and skills that are easily measured by tests. The students are familiar with and good at responding to such teaching methods, as shown by the very high results of the last OECD Programme for International Student Assessment (PISA) test in Estonia (Kitsing, 2008). On the one hand, students are not used to the student-centred approach and have a long-trained habit of listening to the teacher's lecture, and completing a worksheet with a clear and safe border between right and wrong answers. The habit learned during many years in school is how to behave as a student, and this expectation can be an obstacle to a dialogical approach. On the other hand, teachers themselves so far have very limited experience of more student centred approaches. The teacher-centred approach works better with academically talented students but, even so, it does not give space for a more personal form of dialogue – for a shared exploration of thinking and feeling towards deeper levels of understanding - of oneself, the subject and each other.

A teacher's positive reinforcement of answers did not contribute to dialogue among students but rather to the feeling that someone had already given the acceptable right answer. The teacher's strong role as a facilitator did not encourage students to explore a subject but to rely on a teacher's arguments.

However, the data show that there is a wish, both among students and the teachers, for more dialogue in lessons. It is seen as valuable for self-understanding, for mutual understanding, and for understanding the concepts being studied.

5.2.2 Incident: Image of God

Next I will take a closer look at one of the incidents. First I will give a contextual description of the incident, since it is embodied in the whole lesson. A seemingly boring lesson turned into one of the most vivid interactions among the observed lessons. Then I will take a more microscopic look at the thematic and interactive level of the incident and gain different insights on it from the students' and teacher's perspectives.

5.2.2.1 Context of the incident

A selected incident from School D occurred in the second lesson about Judaism; the short transcription of this incident is presented in Appendix 9. Judaism and Christianity are more familiar to students in comparison to other world religions, as they are covered to some extent in history and literature lessons (Danilson, 2007a, 2007b; Jansen-Mann, 2007; Laks, 2007). The first lesson dealt with the notion of monotheism, Holy Scripture, and the Jewish law. The second lesson expanded upon the concepts of the chosen nation and Messiah. The incident occurred at the end of the lesson, when dialogue arose between students and the teacher.

The lesson started with an introduction by the teacher about the contents of the last lesson and topics of the current lesson: 'the belief in a monotheistic God in connection to the concept of a chosen nation'. This was followed by a period for the individual reading of a textbook paragraph, in order to answer the question *"What problems could arise through the idea of the chosen nation?"* As students worked at a different pace, some became bored during the final minutes of the reading task.

Peter asked four different students – all girls – to answer the question. He appreciated all the answers, reformulated, and then expanded them, before placing the presented viewpoints into a broader context and writing short keywords on the blackboard. He also related the answers of the different students to one another. Students took notes and looked down, waiting for the teacher to choose who would be asked next. The teacher asked for volunteers. A girl from the second bench, Rita, referred to the 'superiority' of Jews. The teacher corrected her: *"The Jews believe that they are chosen for suffering. But yes, it is still possible."* He gave an example from everyday life: if one wins the lottery twice, one can feel that *"the rest of the people can buy the tickets but I will win – such a feeling is quick to come"*.

The teacher asked for additional volunteers, but no new answers emerged. He pushed the phenomenon of the chosen nation away from being specifically a Jewish phenomenon. He claimed that something similar can be followed in the desire to be the best nation or to see that a state has a crucial role in world history. He brought the claim back to the concrete level, showing that it is also relevant for Estonians. Peter shared a funny folktale about the competition of languages, in which the Estonian language won second place after Italian with the sentence *"sõida tasa üle silla"* [drive slowly over a bridge]. The students became animated when he told the second story – how Estonians went to Egypt and exclaimed: *"Nii ilus!"* [So beautiful] and so the river got its name *'Niilus'* [Nile]. He also shared a myth about ancient Estonians visiting America; they tasted local fruits that were sweet and called the local people *'maiad'* [sweet-lovers] – Mayas. He concluded that it is possible to see the wish to be important in the history of many nations. He asked if anyone had anything to add, but received no response.

Peter continued by talking about a new subtopic concerning the idea of Messiah, about which students had already read. Students looked in their textbooks to remember what they had read. Peter stressed that it is believed in Judaism that they were chosen for suffering, as is also seen in history – after a short period of independence, they were often captured or deported. Peter explained that the Messiah is believed to be God's messenger, who will establish a kingdom of happiness and justice. He added a short comparison with the Messiah-idea in Christianity. Although the interlude with stories about Estonians cheered students up, their interest soon waned. A boy from the third bench, Juhan, sprawled. He may have been bored or perhaps just sleepy after the lunch break. Some students took notes. Peter assigned the next task: to read the next section in the textbook. Students started reading about Jewish religious life and the synagogue. The students looked tired and were perhaps a bit jaded.

The incident was preceded by noticing a contradiction between the text of the book and a photograph, which the teacher pointed out. According to the textbook, it is prohibited to incorporate images of anything into a synagogue, but some lions were included in the photograph. The students' behaviour seemed to change after the introduction of the contradiction by the teacher, but this only captured their attention for a short while, and soon several of them had become distant. Juhan yawned again,[22] and another student rubbed his face.

Peter wrote the next task on the blackboard: *"Why is God not represented in images in Judaism?"* The teacher tried once more to capture the students' attention by asking them about the proper word for making sculptures. Peter could not find the right word. He criticised himself and then asked students how they call making sculptures – *"Do you model, cut, cast, or what?"* Students laughed and looked refreshed. Peter believed they understood what he meant. He repeated the question, and some students wrote it down.

Incident 'Image'. The full transcription of the incident is provided in Appendix 9. Peter decided to give the task as pair-work, which resulted in a real breakthrough. The lesson had been very teacher centred up to this point; the lecture was alternated only by reading the textbook and a 'teacher asks – student answers' style of conversation.[23] Students changed their relaxed position to sit more erect. They turned to their partners and looked at each other. Many students started speaking at once, while others thought for a while and then commenced exchanging ideas. After a few moments, almost everybody was in-

---

22 In his feedback, Juhan said, *"I was sleepy not because the lesson was boring but I had a short sleep last night"*.

23 In other lessons, he used more varied patterns; he showed extracts from films, the students read extracts from original texts as well as textbooks, and Peter varied the writing of thoughts with small-group discussions.

volved in a discussion; two students alone wrote their notes, as their peers discussed the topic in groups of three. As with every pair-work task in this class, students' interest increased. This is particularly remarkable considering that their attention was decreasing during the previous part of the lesson. Students actively discussed the question for four minutes. Some pairs prepared to answer and started writing notes. The buzz in the class lessened, and Peter started asking students the question. In the next few minutes, the students argued with each other and with the teacher until the lesson ended. This is described more precisely in the next section.

5.2.2.2 Thematic level of the incident

Students were given the task of thinking about the arguments behind the Judaic prohibition of representing God in an image. The first topic was introduced by a boy (Riho), whose argument was based on the authority of the holy texts of Judaism. The teacher categorised the answer as Scripture-centred, very logical, and widely used especially among religious people.

Peter said that, in Judaism, faith must be supported by other logical arguments as well, and asked the second student to respond. A girl (Carola) provided a second reason: fear of making a mistake. Meanwhile, students engaged in a side conversation that not representing God in an image is relevant for Christianity as well.

The next student, Nelly, gave an example of anthropomorphism. The teacher countered with an example from Christianity. Nelly did not agree; she thought that only Christ is represented in imagery. The teacher convinced her with a description of a painting of Michelangelo and icons depicting the Trinity.

Laura introduced a new argument: God is visualized in order to evade contradictions between different perceptions of God.

The subsequent three contributions pointed at the holiness of God, but all three students approached the issue from different standpoints. Maria mentioned that the holiness of God would be undermined if an image were destroyed by enemies of this religion. A more abstract conception of God, without perceptible representation, would not have such danger. Paula indicated the tendency to worship statues or pictures instead of God. Finally, Rita argued for the inner sense of holiness, feeling subordinate in the face of an unimaginable God whose name is not even pronounced.

Figure 2: Thematic level of the incident 'Image'

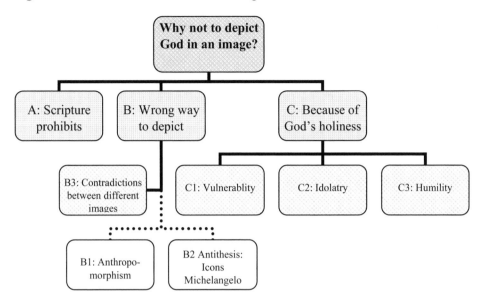

The composition of the thematic level of the incident is very clearly structured, as seen in Figure 2. The next paragraph puts some flesh on the bones of the thematic level. I will look at what hindrances and potentials could be followed at the interaction level of the incident; what is the interaction level for these contributions?

5.2.2.3 Interactive level of the incident

The teacher first asked Riho to contribute (the only boy asked during the lesson), and he answered in a clear, assured voice that the Jewish Scriptures prohibit the construction of images. Some of the students smiled at his answer. Peter expressed surprise at the content of the answer, confirming and appreciating the answer with the longest comment given in this round. The teacher supported the boy's answer very explicitly, showing his admiration for the untraditional answer.

To open the door for further discussion, and stress continuity with more secular justifications, Peter continued with a comment that gave respect to Jewish explanations and showed them as reasonable at the secular level as well, which was understandable for students. His comment further highlighted the value of the first response, and the readiness to listen to more contributions to comprehend such an approach and find common ground with it. Thus, the first contribution established the ground for a dialogue with an imaginable party not present in class – namely, with a Jew.

The teacher asked the next student, a girl from the back (Carola). She answered quietly: "*I think that there is fear of [representing the] image [God] in a wrong way.*" Peter paused, his face expressing that he is puzzled. He repeated the phrase spoken by the girl and asked what the right way to represent God is. Carola looked confused by the remark and answered that nobody knows. The teacher wrote the answer on the blackboard ("*Fear to err*") and asked if anybody else had an example for the kind of misrepresentation they might fear. By writing the statement on the blackboard and asking others for examples, Peter demonstrated his appreciation for the answer and again opened the floor for thinking in the same direction. The girl looked down. The audio recorder catches that, at the same time, another girl (Nelly) and a boy (Karl) from the last bench, were discussing that, in Christianity, God is not represented in imagery either. This activated their thinking; Nelly raised her hand and waited for her turn.

Peter noticed her and asked her to be next. Nelly volunteered, not with the discussion she had with Karl, but with an example of anthropomorphising God:

> "*For example if...they would humanise God, but at the same time God should be something higher, something else and if they describe Him as an ordinary human being...*"

The teacher wrote 'anthropomorphise' on the blackboard and a loud whispering arose from the class: "*But if they would make an image of a frog?*" The remark contributed to easing the atmosphere. Nelly smiled at this remark; she did not feel attacked. The teacher did not react to the remark, but concentrated on Nelly's answer, for the first time clearly objecting to the answer.

> "*But what a suggestion! – Later, let's take Christianity arising from Judaism. And here God is in the image. Let's take Michelangelo ...*"

Nelly was one of the most outspoken students in religious education classes, providing interesting and reasoned contributions. The teacher took a chance to go beyond merely supporting her answer to challenge it. One girl (Laura) in front raised her hand very high. The dialogue with Nelly was not yet finished, so Laura had to wait for a while. Nelly interrupted the teacher's performance very assertively, without waiting for approval to interfere:

> "*But, may I, may I, may I? Is it God's image in Christianity? There is only Jesus Christ's image everywhere!*"

This is the topic she had previously been discussing with her desk-mate. She did not agree with what the teacher was saying.

> Peter continued: "*Let's take Michelangelo...I even have it with me...*"
> Nelly murmured: "*Those artists are just a different topic...*"
> Karl, sitting next to her, whispered: "*He did not hear you...*"

Nelly smiled, put her hand to her mouth as if shouting for a moment, but then listened to the teacher's reply. The teacher wanted to show Michelangelo's 'Creation' on an overhead projector; the screen did not roll down at first but finally he succeeded. He pointed out that the depicted figure is not Christ, but God the Creator. He also gave other examples of illustrating God on icons. Nelly watched him carefully, holding a pen in her mouth. She was convinced by the explanation and did not want to say anything more.

Peter called on Laura, who was still raising her hand. She did not follow the last discussion, but introduced a new explanation: to avoid contradictions and different perceptions of God. Peter repeated the answer, wrote it on the black-board without any comment, and asked for more ideas. Laura smiled.

The next student the teacher called on, Maria, proposed that they would be afraid that images could be destroyed by enemies of Judaism. Peter repeated the answer and wrote "*Bad sign*".

Paula raised her hand, and the teacher called on her. She had been active in other lessons; in this lesson, she spoke for the first time, saying that there is a danger that rather than worshipping God, people may worship the statue in-stead. Peter reinforced her reply by saying that this is often used as an argument against depicting God.

Peter asked for the last contribution. A girl from the second bench, Rita – who often volunteers contributions – spoke out for the second time in this lesson about the holiness of God for Jews. She also drew a parallel about not uttering the name of God since it was too holy.

5.2.2.4 Students' perspective

In the group interview with stimulated recall, three girls and two boys partici-pated; students had the chance to comment on the lesson and how they felt.

Peter often repeated the contributions of students, putting them into a wider context, appreciating them at some level or questioning their logic at another level. His own turns tended to be longer than those of the students. When asked how students felt when Peter paraphrased their contributions and whether he understood them correctly, the students replied that they mostly appreciated how he led the conversations.

> Nelly: "*Sometimes we say a thought and the teacher helps to accomplish it and brings in sides which we were not aware of. He brings our contributions to a level higher than we thought. (...) I think that you present a halfway thought, and then he develops it further.... If it is not exactly the same, what I said about it, I always say that I thought differently. There is nothing wrong that we understand differently. Indeed he likes it that we think differently.*"

Nelly was the girl whom the teacher confronted most often in the lesson. She found it to be a useful and challenging way to learn about her own ideas and develop them further. She was not shy in expressing her disagreements, being very aware of the fact that the teacher liked it. She had no fear of entering into a discussion, but perceived it as a safe and even expected way to participate in the lesson. In the light of her answer, it was surprising that students so rarely argued with the teacher and each other. Learning through discussions – expressing their own views – was often a new experience for them. It seems that the religious education lesson gave them the possibility to participate in a lesson in a way they could not very much in other lessons.

> Paul: "*He certainly communicates with us better than some other teachers do. He pays respect to us, giving us the possibility to state our opinions.*"

The students also commented on the atmosphere of the lesson and teaching-learning methods used. They appreciated that the lessons did not concentrate on simply learning facts, but rather on understanding deeper structures and ways of thinking in different religions. They found that they benefitted from it much more than through simply learning to repeat facts by heart.

> Laura: "*Yes, we discuss more, we do not learn, for example, how the Buddhist monks are called, or merely discrete facts.*"
> Gerda: "*It is more important to get a sense of a religion, to form your opinion, then you understand it more – rather than what the Buddhist monks are called.*"
> Laura: "*It helps us to think, to consider ourselves. But it is certainly more difficult than learning things by heart.*"

With regard to the interaction level, and to the ways Peter gave feedback, students believed that he sometimes encouraged them by approval but usually challenged them as well by pointing out weak points in their arguments. In addition, while looking at the videotaped material, Laura noticed one student's facial expression: smiling when initially approved and then more sorrowful when critiqued. However, in her comments, she stated that the teacher never only referred to weaknesses.

> Laura: "*In the beginning the teacher said that, yes, many would agree with you, then Lisa shone completely. But then the teacher stated that [it was true] in some respects, but not completely. It is fun to look, how her lips turn down ((smiles))…*"
> Gerda: "*To be honest it is quite a bad feeling when it is said that your thought is completely wrong.*"
> Laura: "*In that respect it is rather good that he always mentions something good and something bad, never only that your answer is totally wrong.*"

The feeling of being supported by the teacher's comments, even when a student could not produce a response – was expressed also by Gerda:

"In one lesson where I said that I did not have any idea what to answer, he said, 'yes, it is very difficult to find an answer to that question; it is a very complicated issue'. So you do not feel a complete fool."

Many students were surprised by their own appreciation of the lesson; they had some hesitations before attending religious education classes and might never have thought that they would enjoy the subject, but they did.

Summary
Students are able to be challenged and to appreciate being confronted by dialogue if it is done systematically and in a respectful manner. Even in a context where no representatives of a certain religion are present, dialogue and respect can be built up by encouraging students to enter the logic of the religion and relating it to their own lives. During the stimulated recall, students' contributions were longer and students talked not only to me, but also discussed issues with each other. This suggests that the way they speak in the course of a lesson is determined by what they are used to in relation to the role of a student. Thus, the dialogical approach has significant potential for success if the concept of 'being a student' is changed.

5.2.2.5 The teacher's perspective

Peter teaches three religious education courses at the gymnasium level. The first deals with world religions, the second concentrates on phenomenological and philosophical issues, and the third explores the Estonian religious landscape. Peter's aim for the first religious education course is learning about basic information about religions.

Peter: *"It is the same as learning the alphabet in the mother tongue – learning certain concepts. The first acquaintance with these topics [occurs] in order to acquire a certain small or minimal amount of knowledge on the basis of which one can make some generalisations. Or to go further, that a student could make intentional choices."*

In light of this comment, it was interesting to note that he gave so much time in his lessons for analysis and discussion. He explained that students understand and remember things better if they have to *use* information. Another important outcome he wanted to achieve was that students should realise that religion is not only a historical phenomenon, but is also relevant in contemporary times. His aim was to support students' religious and worldview development, not to form it.

I asked Peter to comment on the way he responds to students. He said that he tries to put their answers into a wider context or to force them to take another step towards more complex understanding. He agreed with the students that this skill is not overly stressed at school.

> Peter: *"I have a feeling that the wider school system works often [within a pattern of] a question, an answer, a question, an answer, a question, an answer. But that the same answer creates actually three new questions and that the answer is interpretable in three, four different ways... I have a feeling that it is a weakness of our school system that this is not dealt with."*

He admitted that discussions evolve differently in different classes; some classes prefer to think more in depth and to do some written essays instead.

Summary

The current approach to education is concerned more with knowledge than personal development, which restricts students' religious convictions to the personal level. The content-orientated aims of religious education can contribute to better understanding of the phenomenon under study, but only indirectly to the understanding of oneself and others. Dialogue is often hindered by students' limited knowledge of religion; thus, the teacher feels trapped both by the short period of time provided in the limited number of lessons available (from 35-70 hours maximum) and students' superficial knowledge – if it exists at all – about major religions. As students are not used to a dialogical approach, the teacher takes a strong regulative and role-modelling position to teach them new habits in learning through participating in open discussions about complicated issues.

5.3 Reflections and conclusions

5.3.1 Hindrances

Habit of teaching and learning. The schools, teachers, and students all revealed problematic points that varied in different schools. Yet the deeper structure of the incidents could be summarised as policy incidents, indicating a pattern of learning process by which the teacher had or was supposed to have a central role. Religious education cannot be seen in a vacuum; it belongs to the wider educational context and can be understood only in relation to it. Students are not used to the student-centred approach. The habit of being a student, learned during many years, can be seen as a hindrance to dialogue in the classroom situation. The teachers' strong role as facilitators tended not to encourage students to explore a subject, but rather to rely on teachers' arguments or not to participate in discussions at all.

Aims. The current approach of education is concerned more with knowledge than personal development and restricts students' religious convictions to the personal level. The content-orientated aims of religious education can contribute best to a deeper understanding of the phenomenon under study, but only indirectly to the understanding of oneself and others. Only a limited amount of dialogue takes place during lessons; usually dialogue is restricted to student-teacher conversations on the level of debate. An approach to study that aims to know facts contributes to a situation in which students feel that only closed questions are appropriate; and even open questions are answered briefly and in a way that one would expect closed questions to be answered.

5.3.2 Potentials

Teaching-learning methods improving dialogue. Dialogue in the search for common ground can be fostered by work in groups or pairs, where the aim is to achieve a common goal. Commonly solved tasks have the potential to contribute to promoting understanding of one another, to require dialogue with mutual understanding, and to enable a understanding of the problem. As evident in the schools which were studied, some students withdrew from open dialogue in the classroom situation, while using dialogue as an instructional method gave some privilege to students with better linguistic and academic skills. The potential in this case is in using a variety of methods to explore the subject in combination with dialogue.

Interest in peers' views. Students are usually interested in the views of their classmates, which can be used to improve motivation and develop a deeper and more comprehensive understanding of a phenomenon. Resources for diverse backgrounds and understandings present in class are worth drawing out first before a teacher intervenes with his or her own contribution.

Systematic introductions of dialogical approach. Both students and teachers desire more dialogue in lessons, but they do not always succeed in the experience. Dialogue is seen as a valuable tool for understanding oneself, others, and the concepts being studied. Students are willing to be challenged by dialogue if it is facilitated systematically and sensitively. If the student recognises that security is available and trust has been built up, he or she may risk entering into conflict or vulnerable areas rather than avoiding them or utilising other ways to deal with them. Students' readiness to participate in an open dialogue during stimulated recall suggests that their contributions in the course of a lesson are determined by the way in which they are used to behaving as students. In this way, a dialogical approach has the potential to succeed provided that the concept of 'being a student' is changed; however, a lack of competences and experiences inhibit doing this successfully.

5.3.3 Dialogical approaches and their adaptability to the Estonian situation

There are several examples of implementing dialogical approaches to religious education in different countries. Some of them follow the example of inter faith dialogue and try to adapt it for the purposes of classroom practice (e.g. Sterkens, 2001 from a Dutch perspective; Schweizer & Boschki, 2004 from a German perspective). An inter faith dialogue could hardly be applied in an Estonian secular context, where the great majority of students do not adhere to any religious or secular community. It is problematic to regard even children who do adhere to some religious tradition as representatives of these religions as they are rarely aware of the teachings of the tradition they belong to, and their religious beliefs are not always consistent with it.

There are also dialogical approaches of religious education that take a different stand from inter faith dialogue. Julia Ipgrave from Warwick University developed her approach while working in a multicultural primary school. She started her research with students from one school, combining research with a form of dialogical teaching (Ipgrave, 1998). As the second step, Ipgrave linked students from two schools in the same city and incorporated other teachers into the work (Ipgrave, 2001). Then she extended the research to link students from different parts of England using e-mail contacts (Ipgrave, 2003). Although Ipgrave, in her *Building E-Bridge: Inter faith Dialogue by E-mail* (Ipgrave, 2003a) and *Inter faith Dialogue by Email in Primary School* (McKenna et al. 2008), uses inter faith dialogue as a reference point, she does not see students as 'little representatives of the faith they belong to', but encourages them to work out solutions themselves rather than to accept the answers of authorities. Actually she does not fix children to a group of 'insiders' or 'outsiders' of a religion, but leaves it open.

> "*Neither is Dialogical RE limited to dialogue between members of the class from distinct religious traditions, such as a discussion group containing a Hindu, a Christian, a Muslim. Participants do not need to identify with any religious group or have a religious faith of their own.*" (Ipgrave, 2001, 18)

Usually religious education in Germany is confessional, but there are also some endeavours to bring different religious groups into common religious education, as for example in Hamburg federal state. With the help of Hamburg University a new approach has been developed – *dialogischer Religionsunterricht* [Dialogical Religious Education]. This approach explicitly opposes the inter faith dialogue, which is seen as 'dialogue from above' where leaders of faith communities share theological debates, while the classroom situation requires dialogue 'from below' and draws on students as ordinary people, not key persons of religious organisations. In emphasizing 'dialogue from below' the term 'neighbour religion' (Weisse, 1999, 181) is used instead of 'world religions' – neighbour in my classroom, village or global village – and touches upon the questions important for students themselves and social justice.

> "*The wisdom of religious traditions should be used in dialogue with neighbours where they form stimuli and inputs, but they should not become obstacles for addressing basic questions that emerge from the realities of coexistence and dialogue. Dialogue in the context of neighbour religions is not imposed or decreed from above, but emerges from below. This kind of dialogue relates to the relevant questions of the participants, in this case those of the students at school.*" (Knauth & Weisse, 2009, 8)

Heid Leganger-Krogstad has combined contextual and dialogical approaches. She did this initially to meet the needs of students in Northern Norway. Her primary interest was to incorporate the children's life world and concerns into teaching. She empowered children with basic ethnographic skills and gave them the opportunity to share their findings with each other (Leganger-Krogstad, 2001; 2003). In contrast to the dialogical approaches that see children as representatives of different world religions, Heid Leganger-Krogstad developed a dialogical approach to religious education in the Norwegian context of integrated religious education and made an even more clear distinction between inter faith dialogue and a dialogical approach in religious education.

> "*The ideal concept of dialogue in religious education ought not to be dialogue between religious traditions or between adult representatives. Instead, at school, dialogue should make use of the equal status that children have in their role as pupils, and use school as arena for open questions, experiments, reflection, criticism and information; dialogue should be seen as attitude and a working method.*" (Leganger-Krogstad, 2003, 181)

In such a way dialogue promotes new understanding and may change both oneself and the partner in dialogue. It cannot be viewed as an inter faith dialogue, but it happens in an interpersonal level, building identity and empowering for citizenship.

Similarly to the Norwegian dialogical approach, other dialogical approaches are also aimed at identity-formation and mutual respect. Although dialogue brings different perspectives into the classroom, the aim of *Dialogischer Unterricht* is not to mirror social divisions in society but rather to develop self-understanding, mutual understanding and respect:

"Dialogue in the classroom fosters respect for other religious communities, can confirm pupils' views or help them to make their own commitments whilst also allowing them to monitor their commitments critically." (Weisse, 2003, 194)

Weisse stresses that the starting point for dialogue should be common human experience, not similarities and differences of religions. The aim for such religious education is to understand others as well as oneself by practising skills of comparing and contrasting views. The *"individual positions are not found by mixing different views, but by comparing and contrasting them with one another"* (Weisse, 2003, 193). In doing so, participants may refer to their different religious backgrounds, but are not required to do it. Hamburg's approach puts great emphasis on social justice, peace, human rights and exploration of existential questions.

Ipgrave's dialogical approach could be seen as contributing both to children's personal development and to citizenship education:

"The very nature of religious thought – its engagement with 'big questions' and multiple answers it presents – makes the religious education class an ideal forum for the development of skills of dialogue and negotiation, and of the intellectual and moral awareness that contribute the citizenship ideal." (Ipgrave, 2003b, 147)

Additionally Ipgrave found that her approach raised children's self-esteem, developed critical and social skills, gave a voice for underachievers and empowered them for democratic citizenship (Ipgrave, 2003a; McKenna et al. 2008).

Both Ipgrave and Leganger-Krogstad have developed their approaches while working at school. Thus their approaches have evolved at the grass roots level and have direct pedagogical implications. Similarly to the teachers in Estonia (Schihalejev, 2009a), Heid Leganger-Krogstad believes that religion is a private matter and teachers should be concerned not to put students into vulnerable situations (Leganger-Krogstad, 2003). The risk-free zones could be created by different methods: role plays, drama, discussions through stories, and conversations from a particular view point.

On the basis of her research, Julia Ipgrave developed a threefold definition of dialogue (2001, 19; 2005, 40–41).

- Primary dialogue (context) is acknowledgement of diversity of experiences, viewpoints, understandings and ideas within the class. Primary dialogue can be achieved by e-mail contacts, quotations from people having very different views and traditions, including extracts from texts.
- Secondary dialogue (attitude) is the positive, open response to that context, promotion of an ethos in which children are willing to engage with difference, to share their own views and to learn from others. For students it in-

volves readiness to risk expressing their own ideas in the light of encountering a different view; this is not to avoid areas of disagreement between religious traditions, groups and individuals – the differences are made public and explicit. Secondary dialogue is achieved by school (class) ethos which values diversity and listening to others and in which students are willing to engage with differences by sharing their own views and learning from others. Students are encouraged to set up rules, to evaluate their own work, and also to formulate questions and their own opinions.

- Tertiary dialogue (activity) an act of verbal communication itself between children, drawing on primary and secondary dialogue. It is achieved by a variety of methods, strategies and exercises; students are encouraged to express, negotiate and justify their views. Stimuli for tertiary dialogue can vary from stories, case studies, quotations, pictures and video extracts; sorting tasks or sequence cards are also used to activate students' thinking skills and engagement with material.

Insights from these various approaches could be applied to the Estonian situation. For example, Ipgrave's distinction between different levels of dialogue is very valuable in the light of my empirical finding that the implementation of dialogue only as an activity may not work.

Even if personal faith-based contributions might be felt to be too private to start with, more distanced methods may contribute in creating risk-free zones for students. They could be enabled to enter into more explicit dialogue between different worldviews and more implicit dialogue between self and other.

6. CONCLUSIONS:
A POSSIBLE WAY FORWARD FOR RELIGIOUS EDUCATION IN ESTONIA

The main aim of my research was to establish the hindrances and potentials for developing tolerance towards religious diversity among 14–16 years old Estonian students in the context of school, and of religious education in particular.

Looking at religion in the context of education, I analysed the position of religion in education in Estonia in the second chapter of the book. My main aim was to introduce to the reader the contextual limitations and possibilities religious education has as it is organised in Estonia. Empirical studies, targeting students aged 14–16 years, looked into their own perceptions of religion and religious diversity, its potentials to promote dialogue or conflict. My study included a dual perspective of, on the one hand, the young people's own views and, on the other hand, analyses of observed teaching situations. The third chapter presented results of the qualitative study about young people's perception of religion and religious diversity. The fourth chapter explored the views of young people by the means of a quantitative study. Additionally I looked at the potentials and limitations to dialogue among and about religious and worldview differences in the context of religious education in schools. The fifth chapter dealt with my analysis of observed classroom interactions.

In the following discussion, I will triangulate the results of the different studies. Some of the results gained in many different phases of fieldwork are consistent with each other, pointing in a similar direction; others are helpful in gaining more a complex picture of the situation. Firstly, I will triangulate results of the qualitative and quantitative studies on the views of 14–16 years old students on religion and education. In doing this I will focus on students studying within different models of religious education. Secondly, I will examine results gained from classroom interaction in combination with the results from interviews with teachers. Finally, taking into consideration the results of the empirical studies, I will discuss possibilities for future developments with regard to religious education in Estonia, and consider possible pedagogies needed for strengthening active tolerance as well as developing an understanding of religions.

6.1 Triangulation of results from qualitative and quantitative studies on the views of students

The main criteria for selecting schools for the quantitative and qualitative surveys were similar. Geographical, demographic, and linguistic factors, religious ethos of the area, and organization of religious education were all taken into account in both surveys. I wanted to maintain a variety in the qualitative study, as its results allow the identification of patterns in students' responses with different experiences of religious education and in the use of different languages of study. The number of schools in the qualitative study was smaller and was added to by the quantitative study. This enabled me to compare groups with different models of studies about religion and their views on dealing with religious diversity. The qualitative study examined students who had not studied religious education and those who had studied it recently. The sample of quantitative study was comprised of four groups. In addition to those with no religious education and those who were studying the subject at the time of the survey, students with experience of religious education only in primary school were added to the quantitative sample together with a group who, although they did not have it as a separate subject, experienced some form of religious education through the integration of religious activity into the life of the school – such as visits to religious services or the work of a chaplain. Some of the students studied religious education in a school where it was optional and others were in schools where religion was taught as a compulsory subject. The inclusion of schools with diverse solutions to the question of teaching religion enabled the exploration of the views of students with different educational models for living in a pluralistic society. Geographical variety was enlarged by adding big schools, with presumed religious diversity, from Tallinn and Tartu, and smaller schools with presumed homogeneity from different 'border areas' – western islands, south-eastern villages, and a north-eastern industrial town.

6.1.1 Impact of studies on personal beliefs and views about religion

As indicated in section 2.2.1, one of the arguments used against religious education in Estonia is its potential to make children religious, or deliberately to encourage religious faith. In order to explore this question, I needed to ask 'What place does religion have in the lives of young people and how does education about religion influence their personal beliefs and views abut religion?' In the following, I will triangulate the results presented in chapters 3 and 4.

1. **Unobtrusive role of religion for young people**. The role of religion in students' lives and in their environment is not very visible for most students in Estonia. Religion belongs more to history and 'others' than to contemporary

time and 'oneself' for Estonian speaking students, and is regarded as a very private matter for Russian speaking students. The influences of religious communities for both ethnic groups are almost non-existent. Many students in both surveys found that religion was an irrelevant topic. Their direct experiences of religion were rare, usually through encountering endeavours of missionaries; thus religious people often seemed to them to be annoying and strange. Few students (15%) saw themselves as affiliated to a particular religious tradition, while most of them could think about religion only in abstract and impersonal terms, and found difficulties in defining their own worldview or religious affiliation.

However, Russian speaking students diverged greatly in their attitudes to religion in both surveys. For this group, religion was a personal matter, closely related to their identity, in an intimate and personal manner, almost irrespective of their religious affiliation. At the same time, religion had hardly any societal aspect for them, neither was it regarded as a means to belong to a group. Although the family was important for Russian speaking respondents, they also tended to rebel against the wider family's attitudes and beliefs more then the 'Estonian' sample, as the quantitative survey shows. Students tended to look for their own way of believing, but in this search they stayed close to a monotheistic belief and to Orthodox approaches, and were hardly aware of other religious traditions.

If I compare the results of the Estonian sample to other countries participating in the study (Valk et al., 2009), then students in Estonia were far less attached to religion than students from any other country. There were, for example, 3 times more religiously affiliated students in the Russian (St. Petersburg) sample, which was the next less affiliated country, while 65% of all the students in the Dutch and Spanish samples adhered to some religion. Also the importance of religion and frequency of attendance at different religious ceremonies was lower in the Estonian sample than in other countries, but the differences here were not so drastic. Many students tried to avoid expressing definite opinions. One of the reasons for this may be their insufficient knowledge about religion which inhibited their ability and willingness to express a point of view about their own convictions. The reluctance to express a point of view may also indicate the students' wish to be 'normal' or similar to 'everybody else', rather than being seen as part of a 'religious' minority. A further reason for avoiding fixed positions could be a tendency towards a relativistic view in which some truth is seen in a variety of different positions.

2. **Family and school as two main sources of information about religion**. Students valued families most highly as a source of information about religion but, at the same time, mentioned that they hardly ever spoke about religion at home. Only the students who studied religious education recently valued the school higher than the family as a source of information. In the qualitative

survey it was clear that students who valued school as a source of information about religion spoke more about different religions and plural ways of understanding it than others. It is impossible to assess, on the basis of the quantitative survey, the extent of the information they got from family or school, but it is very doubtful that parents with no education on religious issues could provide their children with balanced and rich information about it. Both surveys show that students, especially those without a religious affiliation, admitted that they do not know about religion, and that they were not interested in it – so the amount of information they have about religion is very limited. Thus, their understanding of religion is very likely to be fragmented and unsystematic, supporting a state of affairs where many prejudices about religions and religious people are held. For example, more students from Estonia than any other REDCo country agreed that they did not like people from other religions and fewer students from Estonia than any other REDCo country agreed that they respected people who are believers. Several countries which have an inclusive form of non-confessional religious education have recognized that teaching about religion, when it comes to fostering tolerance and respect, is a task of common state funded schools, and not only families and faith communities.

3. **Influences of religious education on one's personal perception of religion**. The personal relevance of religion seemed not to be directly correlated with the model of religious education that students experienced. Although there were no differences in terms of belonging or belief in God between the groups who had experienced different models of religious education, students who had studied religious education believed more in 'some sort of spirit or life force' and believed less in God and also held less atheistic views. This option was probably felt to be more flexible and less loaded with connotations students wanted to avoid in their own belief (such as anthropomorphism, for example). In general, views about the relevance of religion for one's own life were similar for students who had had experiences of different models of religious education. Nevertheless, some minor differences in the importance of religion, frequency of thinking about religion and about the meaning of life were present: students with experience of religious education tended to avoid more negative extreme positions. The students with experience of religious education tended to express more readiness to change their views about religion and to think that a person could be religious without belonging to any religious community. This evidence leads to the conclusion that studying religious education does not make students more religious but tends to help them to be more reflexive and more cautious in expressing negative or very fixed attitudes about religion at the personal level or about the religious beliefs of others, as discussed above.

3.a. **Impacts of religious education only in primary school on the personal views about religion**. The attitudes of those who had religious education only in primary classes showed some apparent contradictions in their responses.

185

For example, while students with experience of religious education in primary classes said that they attended religious services and prayed slightly more frequently, at the same time they considered religion to be nonsense more than other respondents did. One might observe that religious education studied **only** in primary schools is likely be an inadequate option, both in terms of the coverage of intellectual content and in terms of relating studies to the personal and social development of students.

3.b. **Impacts of religious education in secondary school on the personal views about religion**. Those students who had studied religious education at secondary level used and valued more knowledge-based sources in finding information about religion. Students who studied religious education tended to notice religious phenomena in their surroundings and in the lives of people around them. Moreover, they articulated more complex ideas about religion and religious people. They often found differences to be interesting and fascinating, while students who had had no religious education showed some frustration with religious stances different from their own. This shows that a combination of the knowledge students with experience of religious education have about different religions, and skills they acquire in handling issues of religion, can reduce their prejudices about religious issues and their fear of 'difference'.

In conclusion, the data reported in this study provide evidence that religious education does not make students more religious but that it does change values. Religion is not regarded as something to be afraid of or regarded as an irrelevance from the past, but as at least an acceptable choice for some people.

A further point is that in the schools and classes with no religious education, some students from a religious background had experienced the expression of prejudices about religious people. These prejudices currently do not get discussed in school and often stay unchallenged because of the often tacitly accepted private and silent 'taboo' position of religion in society and also because of the fragmented knowledge about religion of many students. The school could be a public institution that provides a 'semi-formal' space for giving students the possibility to encounter religious and worldview diversity. The fear in front of 'other' could be lessened by increasing familiarity with different religions.

6.1.2 Impact of studies on views about religion in society and about respect

According to the data of this study religion rarely had personal relevance to students' lives. Many students had no experience of religion in school or in wider society, so their attitudes towards religious diversity were often provisional and not based on personal experience. In general, students wished to have harmonious relations in society, but their predominant view was that, in such a society, religion does not have any place in public sphere. In general, students did not feel that public discussion about religion helps to create a harmonious society.

1. **Influences of religious education on the perception of societal dimension of religion**. As the students attending diverse models of religious education did not differ by their religious affiliation, it was interesting to see how the students' attitudes to religion and tolerance altered in different contexts. Many positive impacts of religious education in the direction of more tolerant positions to religious diversity which were found in the qualitative study were also present in the quantitative study. First, the students who had studied religious education agreed more that they had respect for believers. Both surveys showed that students who had studied religious education in upper grades valued religion as a societal force more highly than those who had not and that they valued tolerance and interpersonal competences more than those students who had not studied religious education. Both the qualitative and the quantitative surveys identified similar tendencies in assessing different means to improve peaceful co-existence. Those who had experienced religious education were more positive about living in a multireligious society and they were more committed to a variety of ways advancing non-violent co-existence of people from different religions than those who had not studied the subject. The statement 'I do not like people from other religions…' was most agreed with by students who had experienced no religious education and least by those with an integrated form of religious education. Somewhat unexpected was the finding that students without religious education believed less than the others that religion may cause some conflicts or that people of different religious backgrounds could not live together. One might interpret this finding as indicating that students with no conscious experience of religious diversity at school may be less aware of the potential for religion to be a factor in conflicts or have a limited understanding of how religion might cause conflicts.

2. **Influences of religious education in primary school on students' perception of the societal dimension of religion**. Here, on the basis of the quantitative study, there are some indications of hostile attitudes towards religion from students who had studied religious education only in primary classes. The students who had learned religious education only in primary school were more ready to see religion as violent and a source of aggression. One might interpret this finding as indicating that their thoughts about religion had not become complex and consistent with other aspects of their development. In contrast, students with recent religious education experience were more open to religious differences and more respectful towards religion than students without such experience.

3. **Explicit diversity as a stimulus for dialogue**. When students from the schools with integrated religious education, which emphasised the role of relig-

ion in their schools and allowed open discussion about religious convictions, encountered explicitly religious diversity at school, they tended to be more open to dialogue on religious issues than other students, in spite of the fact that they had some negative experiences with members of different religions. Perhaps it works both ways – if there is a need to have dialogue, one can learn it and become more ready for it. However, when students have skills needed for peaceful dialogue, they are more ready to use them and to see benefits in dialogue. In my interpretation, if young people are put into a situation in which religious diversity is visible and spoken about, they are likely to develop strategies supporting openness to otherness. From this perspective, schools should offer students an environment in which they can encounter religious diversity, and develop skills of dialogue. Students could profit from this not only in relation to their own personal development but also in seeing a more complex picture of religion and in acquiring social skills needed in contemporary pluralistic Europe. Meira Levinson, in her article about multicultural education and public schools, has stated: "... *it is so hard for students to learn to be mutually tolerant and respectful of other people, traditions, and ways of life unless they are actually exposed to them*" (Levinson, 1999, 114).

4. **(Ir)relevance of religion in daily conversations**. According to the students' accounts they had very few or no conversations about religion. The students who had a religious affiliation spoke about religion, but predominantly with people of a similar background (family, religious leaders, friends). Only those students who had studied religious education recently showed more interest in and readiness to start a conversation with people from different backgrounds.

What are the reasons for talking or not talking about religion? Students avoided the topic because they did not have the skills to enter into intelligent and respectful dialogue on religious issues. Students without any experience of religious education were less informed and believed more readily that religion was an embarrassing issue to talk about. They also believed more in the risk of being teased on religious grounds. However, students who had studied religious education in secondary school or, who had experienced integrated religious education, saw the positive effects of speaking about religion for understanding themselves and society. The students who had religious education only in primary classes spoke with friends about the stupidity and cruelty of religion and they were much more critical about the effects of talking about religion.

The correlation between low levels of religious education and a willingness to use religion as a criterion for exclusion and confrontation is one of the research findings. However, caution needs to be expressed in assuming that knowledge about religion alone will encourage positive attitudes or increase tolerance. As Robert Jackson warns: "*It is a mistake to assume that understanding and knowledge necessarily foster tolerance. There are some very well*

informed racists and bigots. I would argue, however, that knowledge and un-
derstanding are necessary but not sufficient conditions for the genuine removal
of prejudice" (Jackson, 2005, 11). Religion in Estonia is squeezed into a very
private and hidden sphere of life, being almost invisible in life or at school and
there is a culture of not talking about religion. There are two dangers here.
Firstly, prejudices may remain uncovered and secondly, the self-esteem of
students with a religious background is endangered if they are given no opportunity to reflect upon their own convictions and feelings about religion. The
school is a potentially a 'safe space' where respectful and intelligent dialogue
about religious and worldview issues can be learned and experienced. As the
research data indicate, this is unlikely to happen in other contexts, such as the
family.

6.1.3 Impact of studies on views about religion in school

1. **The school as a secular institution**. The school was not seen by respondents
as a place to practise religion. The students also rejected the idea that school
should foster religious beliefs. In addition more personal, although not strictly
religious, aims – such as developing moral values or one's own point of view –
were less agreed with than statements about acquiring knowledge. In the students' view religious education should help them to understand the world
around them rather than themselves. Most possibilities for how religion could
appear at school were rejected by many Estonian respondents. On the one hand
this shows some awareness of institutional limits within the public sphere,
depicting a school as fundamentally a secular institution for learning, and not a
place *to practise* religion. On the other hand, the lack of experiences of religion
also plays some role, since religious diversity is usually not visible. In schools
with integrated religious education, where religion and religious diversity were
more observable, religious rights were valued more highly than in other schools.

2. **Preferred models of religious education**. When students were asked
about favourable models of religious education they were inclined to choose
models most familiar to them. The knowledge-oriented approach of religious
education in combination with voluntary form of religious education was preferred by a majority of students, reflecting descriptive views of the *status quo*. If
young people in Estonia are asked about the necessity for a separate subject of
religious education, they tend to argue against it, especially if they personally
have not studied it. The students who studied religious education long ago, even
if they valued its outcomes, opposed the subject equally just as much as those
who had not studied it, since they felt that such an option could be a factor
contributing to segregation and exclusion. Only these who studied religious

education recently were in favour of the subject and considered that it should be available for all students, irrespective of their religious affiliation.

3. **The hopes and fears of religiously affiliated students**. According to the survey, religious education had a special interest for religiously affiliated students. They appreciated religious education classes as a place for self-reflection and an environment to acquire skills for articulating religious beliefs. While in the qualitative study the impression was given that students with religious affiliation were in favour of learning more about Christianity, the quantitative survey indicated that they saw more than other respondents how they could benefit personally from their studies. However, at school they wanted a different form of religious education to that given by religious communities. They valued outcomes of religious education which helped them to make personal ethical decisions and to build up own views, but they valued even more highly objective knowledge and learning respect towards others. Despite their expression of some positive attitudes towards religious education, their dominant feeling remained that such an option would be a factor in increasing segregation and exclusion, and so they would not choose it.

4. **Influences of experience of religious education on students' perception the subject**. The survey of the views of students showed that those with experience of religious education in secondary schools valued studies about religions and the outcomes of such studies for everyday life much more highly than others did as well as giving greater recognition to the importance of the societal dimension of religion. Such an attitude did not depend on whether they had chosen the subject themselves or the school made this choice for them.

In conclusion

1. Currently, there is a lack of balanced information about religion among students. Existing prejudices, together with regarding religion as a strictly private matter, are contributing to a situation in which religious students and students who are interested in religion feel segregation and exclusion.

2. The findings suggest that those schools that have integrated religion into their everyday life, making it more visible and less private, support students' readiness for respect and tolerance. The more hostile attitudes of those without any study of religion, except for dealing with religion in other subjects, can be detected throughout the questionnaire responses. Students both with and without a religious affiliation felt uncomfortable and insecure in encountering a different worldview and lacked the competences needed for mutual dialogue. Religious education in secondary schools, on the contrary, made students curious, developed readiness for discussing religious matters and also helped to educe students' self confidence to have and express a different opinion. My conclusion is that schools should offer students an environment

for meeting religious diversity, having dialogue and fostering relevant skills, be it in religious education, other subjects or extra-curricular activities.

3. Where there is no distinctive subject dealing with religion there may be some resistance among students to changing the system. However, students' attitudes are likely to change quickly if they find that the subject deals with different belief systems and helps them to understand the importance of religion in society and their surroundings.

6.2 Hindrances and potentials for developing tolerance in the context of school

In addition to the students' views, another important factor is the school and its pedagogical practices. In the following, I will focus on the limits and potentials detected in patterns of classroom interaction in lessons of religious education and the views held by teachers as elicited from interviews with teachers during the fieldwork on classroom interaction and from studies of teachers (Schihalejev, 2009a; 2009e).

1. **Teacher-centred pedagogies**. Estonian education in practice is rather traditional in style – the teacher is expected to have a strong regulative role, concentrating on transmitting knowledge, while students are expected to acquire skills easily measured by tests. According to observations of lessons and interviews with students during my classroom interaction study, the commonest method of teaching in different subjects is an oral introduction by the teacher, with students completing written answers in workbooks. The habit learned during many years at school is that the correct way to behave as a student is to give 'right' or expected answers, even in relation to issues of value. This habit may hinder open dialogue among representatives of different religious and secular worldviews. Such a dialogue is not likely to happen without stimulus and special efforts to foster it.

2. **Little space for exchange of ideas in the context of content-oriented education**. A limited amount of dialogue takes place during lessons; usually it is restricted to student – teacher conversation, more on the level of confrontation than of dialogue. The current approach to education emphasises knowledge more than personal development. Such an approach reaffirms already existing patterns of thought that discussion of religion is something to be confined to the private sphere.

3. **Expectations of students and teachers**. In the interviews teachers claim that they are interested in students' active role, participation, and debating with each other, but they also indicate that these methods usually do not work well in lessons. Students are not used to the student-centred approach. Moreover, teachers have not experienced how it works themselves and need help in learn-

ing the techniques of active learning pedagogies. In both the studies of teachers and students, there was a strong feeling that there is a wish for dialogue in lessons from both the student and teacher sides. Dialogue is seen as a valuable tool to understand better oneself, each other and the concepts under study. Unfortunately success is not always experienced. Students are able to dispute and appreciate being challenged by dialogue if it is done systematically and in a respectful manner but their contributions in the course of a lesson are determined by the way they are used to behaving as students. Even in a context where no representatives of a certain religion are present, dialogue and respect can be built up by challenging students to enter the logic of the religion being studied and to relate their contributions to their own lives. The dialogical approach has significant potential for success if the concept of 'being a student' is changed. It is relevant here to point out that Ruth Deakin-Crick, in her survey of research studies on citizenship education in Europe and beyond, shows that students respond positively especially in active learning situations where dialogue is possible. However, she also found that teachers cannot simply switch to this mode of learning: they need specific training in dialogical and active learning methods (Deakin-Crick, 2005).

4. **Cooperative learning methods**. One of the ways to break the teacher-centred approach which hinders dialogue between students and to promote dialogue at a level of together seeking together common ground is through using group work, where a common goal must be achieved. Work in pairs or small groups can contribute to an aspiration to understand each other; also it can deepen students' understanding of the problem being considered. As was detected in the schools studied, a dialogical approach gave some privilege to students with better linguistic and academic skills; also girls were more in favour of it. The potential in this case is to combine other methods with dialogue. I will touch upon them in the section 6.3.2.

6.3 Perspectives for future developments

Following from the findings of my research and wider European perspectives about religion in education I will offer some possible ways forward and will indicate suitable policies and pedagogies for studying religion in Estonian education. First I will discuss the status of religious education and then make suggestions about needs for teacher education.

6.3.1 The status of religious education

The perception of and actual outcomes of religious education. Religious education in Estonia is clearly non-confessional according to its aims and contents. Still, it cannot be classified as integrative but rather as separative, as discussed in section 2.2.3. There is still a lingering idea that knowledge about religions is not fully worthwhile and that the subject is basically only relevant to people from religious backgrounds, as the aim of religion in education is still generally considered to be to bring people to religion. The subject is often regarded in public discussions as if it were confessional. Also the subject's 'optional' status indicates that religious education is also regarded as confessional in the legislation. Education about religions and beliefs is not valued generally in society, otherwise this would be a study which all children would do. However, my study has shown that the subject in practice is non-confessional, not only according to its syllabus but also in relation to its actual outcomes. There is no evidence to support the view that the subject propagates religion; there is, however, evidence that it contributes to peaceful co-existence and to the well-being of people living in Estonian society.

The appropriateness of the model for the Estonian context. The non-confessional approach is proper in the highly secular Estonian context in which most students are non-religious in any terms. The school is a place where all students must be respected, secular as well religious. Even students with a religious background favoured the non-confessional model of religious education. However, its potential benefits are unlikely to be realized within the separative framework of a voluntary subject. Existing prejudices, together with regarding religion as a strictly private matter, are contributing to a situation where religious students and students who are interested in religion feel segregation and exclusion. Thus, a positive potential for the subject remains unrealized and can even cause further segregation.

This suggests two directions for future developments: to include a religious dimension in other subjects and/or to allow schools to teach inclusive religious education. The first direction rests on the fact that there are only a few schools and teachers to teach religious education. It is difficult to imagine that they could bring about a major change, especially in the short term. There is a challenge to support young people in developing their sophistication in understanding religions and worldviews, in helping to create a readiness and capacity for dialogue and in facilitating young people's ability to develop their own viewpoint on religious and worldview issues.

The second direction means that a school should be allowed to teach religious education as a mandatory subject for all students if the subject is consistent with the national syllabus for religious education. The right to opt-out should be indeed available in cases where the teaching is perceived as not being neutral by some students or parents, but on the same grounds as it should be available for other subjects that include some sort of teaching about religions and beliefs[24].

The European context. Estonia, being a member of the European Union and of the Council of Europe, and belonging culturally-historically to Europe, must take into account not only its inner developments but should also be outward looking. As discussed in section 1.1.1, in recent years at the European level it has been recognized increasingly that religion is not simply a matter for the private sphere. Key documents now recognize that education about religions within public education is necessary in order to have a population that is not ignorant of religious diversity. These points are clearly emphasized in *The Toledo Guiding Principles on Teaching about Religions and Beliefs in Public Schools* (OSCE, 2007) and in different documents of the Council of Europe (2004; 2005; 2007; 2008). The *Toledo Guiding Principles* are published by the Office for Democratic Institutions and Human Rights of the Organisation for Security and Co-operation in Europe, which includes 56 participant states. The Council of Europe, Europe's leading human rights institution, with a strong educational input, has 47 member states. Estonia is a member of both European institutions. Council of Europe documents point out that education systems need to recognize that religion is *at least* a part of human culture and that the variety of religious communities present in society contributes to its plurality. If that is the case, then in a plural society people need to understand religion and to create cohesion among its citizens: this is one of the messages of the Council of Europe's *White Paper on Intercultural Education* (2008) and in other key documents referenced above. There is a growing consensus among European educators that it is not worthwhile to ignore the role of religions in societies and in schools in particular.

> "6. *Education is essential for combating ignorance, stereotypes and misunderstanding of religions. Governments should also do more to guarantee freedom of conscience and of religious expression, to foster education on religions, to encourage dialogue with and between religions and to promote the cultural and social expression of religions.*" (Council of Europe, 2005)

Even in France, with its very strong and clear approach of *laïcité*, the place of religion in the public sphere and the need for the inclusion of religion in education have been of high relevance since the 1980s (Beraud et al., 2008, 52). The biggest shift in including religion in education has been since Régis Debray's report and requirement to include studies about religion in initial teacher training and also in-service training to change a 'laïcité of ignorance' into 'laïcité of understanding' (Debray, 2002, 43, as cited in Williame, 2007, 93).

---

24 In some European systems, there is a parental right of withdrawal, even from nonconfessional religious education. The pros and cons of a withdrawal clause are discussed in the *Toledo Guiding Principles* (OSCE, 2007, 68-73).

The *Toledo Guiding Principles* give broad suggestions for religious education and ideas which could be adapted to fit different national contexts. This document complements the Council of Europe's 'cultural argument' stressing that knowledge about religions and beliefs is an important part of education in the context of commitment to religious freedom and human rights. It draws on the principle of freedom of religion or belief and the framework of human rights. If there is religious freedom in a society, then it follows that society will be plural. The only way for a plural society to function peacefully, is through encouraging tolerance of difference and to educating its citizens for tolerance (OSCE, 2007, 76–77). Both the Council of Europe's 'cultural' argument and the OSCE's 'human rights' argument are very relevant to the Estonian situation. I believe that it is time for Estonia to take these arguments and recommendations seriously and to revise its current approaches to education about religion. This needs to be done in such a way that the distinctiveness of the Estonian context is recognized. I hope that the data from my research provide the necessary detail about the particular nuances of the Estonian situation for such a discussion to take place in a productive way.

REDCo findings which challenge policies for religious education in Estonia. There were several findings which challenged models and policies concerning education on religious issues in the Estonian educational system. My empirical findings show that some changes should be made in order to improve students' tolerance towards ways of life different from their own. The role of the school in giving a balanced picture is of great importance for guaranteeing freedom of religion or belief and activating mutual respect. The policy where religious education is taught only in primary classes or not at all can be seen to contribute to some hostile attitudes students held towards religion and representatives of different religions. Pushing religion only into the private sphere creates a situation where students are not educated about a phenomenon which is making a very significant impact globally and in Europe and may inadvertently marginalise students with a religious background. Leaving out any consideration of religion within education is not a neutral act: prejudices towards religious people are supported by **avoidance** of religious topics – if students do not have the possibility to talk and to know about each other's convictions, there is no challenge to their own presuppositions.

In most Estonian schools there is no religious education. According to my study, there is a need for inclusive religious education. I am not suggesting that all schools necessarily must include religious education as a separate subject. However, the students should be given possibilities to have some knowledge about world religions, to have opportunities to discuss religion in the contemporary world and know about their fellows' views in a more systematic way than is possible under present arrangements. The studies of religions, if handled as set out above, could precipitate more tolerant and open views.

An alternative for dealing with religious education as a distinctive subject is to make efforts to improve the studies of religion in other subjects. In this case major changes would need to be made in teacher education, and in the contents and text books of other subjects which would need to cover issues about religion and tolerance. If all that students need to know about religions, together with the relevant competences, could be acquired in such subjects as history, literature and civic education, then the teaching of these various subjects should be revised and improved to include broader and more explicit knowledge about different religions and their impact on the lives of individuals and societies. Such a change should also give space for reflecting upon one's own beliefs and attitudes. The challenge of this approach would be to include sufficient knowledge and understanding of religions in the teacher training courses of those who would have responsibility for teaching about religions.

6.3.2 Teacher education

Michael Fullan in his book *The New Meaning of Educational Change* argues that the implementation of any changes is dependent on teachers' involvement in these changes and this is rather unlikely to happen just by making some general recommendations or improving educational documents (Fullan, 2007, especially in chapter 7, but also elsewhere). I want to highlight that no changes in classroom practices are possible to make effectively without teachers' desire and willingness and without provision of the necessary competences. The crucial task is to prepare teachers of different subjects to treat religious topics relevant to their subject in a way that does not offend students with a religious background and which also counters stereotypical images of religions. Such a preparation should include not only knowledge about certain topics but also skills for managing classroom debates on contentious religious issues applicable to their subject, personal reflection and the promotion of active tolerance.

Pedagogical approaches. Although knowledge about religions is an important prerequisite for mutual understanding, the teaching should go beyond mere facts and promote the development of individual understanding and responses to a diversity of opinions. As could be followed from the results of the empirical research, there is a need for pedagogies that support an analytical, self-reflective and empathetic approach to learning about religion and enhancing active tolerance by encouraging engagement with, and not just awareness of, views other than one's own.

The crucial task is to introduce not only teaching methods but a whole pedagogical approach that gives more agency to students and introduces an ethos of pluralism and appreciation of different opinions. Good examples of implementing a dialogical approach to religious education can be found in different countries (see section 5.3). All of them follow the educational drive for the promotion of citizenship and preparation of young people for a plural and democratic society. Thus, to some extent, they are already compatible with the Estonian national syllabus. The dialogical approaches that depict students in their own right and not as representatives of a particular religion are of particular interest for the secular context of Estonian education. A dialogical approach, drawing on students' contributions, has potential for promoting students' identity formation, self-reflection, and analytical skills, and for fostering mutual respect and empowering students for citizenship.

Training in methods. Teacher training should include preparation in active learning and dialogical methods in order that teachers are able to allow and encourage students to be comfortable with difference; teachers also need to learn techniques for engaging with the diversity of personal experiences of the students. Such training would include skills to create an ethos and environment in which dialogue can be fostered instead of avoiding issues on religious topics. Dialogue is an approach that requires meeting the other, and also formulating one's own views and reflecting on them. It is possible to take advantage of the common school system to provide a genuine dialogical education that includes the religious dimension.

Teachers, either of religious education or of social studies, should acquire skills needed for improving more dialogical ways of learning and teaching by using systematically open questions and by varied methods that give more autonomy to students. In implementation of a dialogical approach special attention would need to be given for developing skills of creating risk-free zones for students who enter into dialogue about personal matters.

Dan Moulin argues that a single approach to religious education is not sufficient (Moulin, 2009, 154) and I agree with him. I am not suggesting that dialogical religious education is *the only* approach to religious education. However, the dialogical approach has the potential to reshape education about religion as it is practised in Estonia into a more student-centred activity, contributing to students' personal and social development as well as to the development of a more tolerant and cohesive society.

REFERENCES

Aavik, T., Keerus, K., Lõuk, K., Nõmper, A., Pevkur, A., Saarniit, L., Simm, K., Sutrop, M., Tõnissaar, M., Vaher, A., Volt, I. (2007) *Eetikakoodeksite käsiraamat* [Codes of Ethics, a Handbook] (Tartu: Tartu Ülikooli Eetikakeskus, Eesti Keele Sihtasutus).

Afdal, G. (2007) *Tolerance and Curriculum: Conceptions of Tolerance in the Multicultural Unitary Norwegian Compulsory School* (Münster: Waxmann).

Alaja, S., Palho, S., Sarsa, R. (1994) *Hea Karjane 3: Õpetaja raamat* [Good Shepherd 3: Teacher's book] (Tallinn: Logos).

Alaja, S., Palho, S., Sarsa, R. (1995) *Hea Karjane 4: Õpetaja raamat* [Good Shepherd 4: Teacher's book] (Tallinn: Logos).

Alasuutari, P. (1995) *Researching Culture: Qualitative Method and Cultural Studies* (London: Sage Publications).

Alberts, W. (2007) *Integrative Religious Education in Europe: A Study-of-Religions Approach* (Berlin / New York: Walter de Gruyter).

Alliance of Civilizations (2009) *Education about Religions and Beliefs Clearinghouse*, available online at: http://www.unaoc.org/content/view/252/224/lang,english/ (last accessed 17.04.2009).

Altnurme, L. (1997) *Eesti koolinoorte jumalapilt* [Estonian School Students' Image of God. Master thesis] (Tartu: Tartu Ülikool).

Altnurme, L. (Ed.) (2004) *Mitut usku Eesti* [Multi-Religious Estonia] (Tartu: Tartu University Press).

Altnurme, L. (2006) *Kristlusest oma usuni: uurimus muutustest eestlaste religioossuses 20. sajandi II poolel* [From Christianity to Personal Religion: Research on Religiosity of Estonians] (Tartu: Tartu University Press).

Altnurme, L. (Ed.) (2007) *Mitut usku Eesti II* [Multi-Religious Estonia II] (Tartu: Tartu University Press).

Avest, I. ter, Jozsa, D.-P., Knauth, T., Rosón, J., Skeie, G. (Eds.) (2009) *Dialogue and Conflict on Religion: Studies of Classroom Interaction in European Countries* (Münster: Waxmann).

Babbie, E. (2008) *The Basics of Social Research* (Boston: Thomson Wadsworth).

Barrows, H.S. (2000) *Stimulated Recall: Personalized Assessment of Clinical Reasoning* (Springfield: Southern Illinois University School of Medicine).

Beraud, C., Massignon, B., Mathieu, S. (2009) The school – an appropriate institution in France for acquiring knowledge on religious diversity and experiencing it firsthand?, in: Valk, P., Bertram-Troost, G., Friederici, M., Beraud, C. (Eds.) *Teenagers' Perspectives on the Role of Religion in their Lives, Schools and Societies: a European Study* (Münster: Waxmann), 131–163.

Bevans, S.B. (1992) *Models of Contextual Theology* (Maryknoll, New York: Orbis).

Bloom, B.S. (1953) The thought process in lectures and discussion, *Journal of General Education,* 7, 160–169.

Blumer, H. (1986) *Symbolic Ineractionism: Perspective and Method* (Berkley / Los Angeles / London: University of California Press).

Bohm, D. (1996) *On Dialogue* (London: Routledge).

Burr, V. (2003) *Social Constructionism* (London and New York: Routledge).

Campbell, D.T. (1957) Factors relevant to the validity of experiments in social settings, *Psychological Bulletin,* 54(4), 297–312.

Chidester, D.S. (2002) Religion education: learning about religion, religions and religious diversity, in: Asmal, K., James, W. (Eds.) *Spirit of the Nation: Reflections on South Africa's Educational Ethos* (Cape Town: New Africa Education), 91- 102.

Chidester, D. (2003) Global citizenship, cultural citizenship and world religions in education, in: Jackson, R. (Ed.) *International Perspectives on Citizenship, Education and Religious Diversity* (London / New York: RoutledgeFalmer), 31–50.

Churchill, R.P. (1997) On the differences between non-moral and moral conceptions of toleration: The case for toleration as an individual virtue, in: Razaavi, M.A., Ambuel, D. (Eds.) *Philosophy, Rreligion and the Question of Intolerance* (Albany: State University of New York Press).

Cicourel, A.V. (1974) *Cognitive Sociology: Language and Meaning in Social Interaction* (New York: Free Press).

Cohen, L., Manion, L., Morrison, K. (2007) *Research Methods in Education* (London: Routlege).

Cook, D. (2007) Stimulated recall and mental models: Tools for teaching and learning computer information literacy, *Journal of the American Society for Information Science and Technology,* 58 (3), 456–457.

Council of Europe (Ed.) (2004) *The Religious Dimension of Intercultural Education* (Strasbourg: Council of Europe Publishing).

Council of Europe (2005) *Recommendation N. 1720 on Religion and Education of the Council of Europe Parliamentary Assembly 4 October 2005* (Strasbourg: Council of Europe). Also available online at: http://assembly.coe.int/Main.asp?link=/Documents/AdoptedText/ta05/EREC1720.htm (accessed 24.04.2009).

Council of Europe (2007) *Draft Recommendation on the Religious Dimension of Intercultural Education: Principles, Objectives and Teaching Approaches* (Strasbourg: Council of Europe).

Council of Europe (2008) *White Paper on Intercultural Dialogue "Living Together as Equals in Dignity"* (Strasbourg: Council of Europe).

Crawford, M., Rossiter, G. (2006) *Reasons for Living: Education and Young People's Search for Meaning, Identity and Spirituality : a Handbook* (Camberwell, Vic.: Australian Council Educational Research Press).

Creswell, J.W. (2002) *Educational Research: Planning, Conducting, and Evaluating Quantitative and Qualitative Research* (London: Merrill, Prentice Hall).

Creswell, J.W. (2003) *Research Design: Qualitative, Quantitative and Mixed Methods Approaches* (Thousands Oaks: Sage Publications).

Danilson, L. (2007a) *Multikultuurne haridus ja religioon gümnaasiumi eesti kirjanduse õpikute näitel* [Multicultural Education and Religion in the Textbooks of Estonian Litarature for Upper Secondary School] (Tartu: Tartu Ülikool).

Danilson, L. (2007b) *Religiooniõpetuse integreerumise võimalustest kirjandusõpetusega* [Possibilities for Integration of Religious Education and Literature] (Tartu: Tartu Ülikool).

Deakin-Crick, R. (2005) Citizenship education and the provision of schooling: a systematic review of evidence, in: *International Journal of Citizenship and Teacher Education*, 1 (2), December, 56–75.

Debray, R. (2002) *L'enseignement du fait religieux dans l'école laïque* (Paris: Odile Jacob/Sceren-CNDP).

Denzin, N.K. (1989) *Interpretive Interactionism* (London: Sage).

Diez de Velasco, F. (2008) Religion, identity and education for peace: beyond the dichotomies confessional/non confessional and global/local, in: Jackson, R. and Fujiwara, S (Eds.) *Peace Education and Religious Plurality. International Perspectives* (London/New York: Routledge), 63–73.

Elstein, A.S., Shulman, L.S., Sprafka, S.S. (1978) *An Analysis of Medical Inquiry Process* (Cambridge: Harvard University Press).

Engelbrecht, K. (2008) Noored tutvustavad Eestit paganliku maana [Young people present Estonia as a heathen country], *Postimees, 12.04.2008.*

Estonian Council of Churches (2001) *Ühiskond, kirik ja religioonisotsioloogilised uuringud* [Society, Church and Sociological Research] (Tartu: Sõnasepp).

Estonian Council of Churches and the Government of the Republic of Estonia (2002) *Ühishuvide protokoll* [Protocol of Shared Interests], availble online at: http://www.ekn.ee/dokumendid/vv_ekn_yhishuvi_17.10.02.pdf (accessed 20.04.2009).

Estonian Institute (1997) *Russian Communities in Estonia. A Historical overview,* available online at: http://www.einst.ee/factsheets/russians/ (accessed 10.10.2008).

European Commission (2005) *Social Values, Science and Technology: Special Eurobarometer 225* (European Commission: Brussels). Also available online at: http://ec.europa.eu/public_opinion/archives/ebs/ ebs_225_ report_en.pdf (accessed 30.04.2008).

Eurydice (2008) *The Educational System in Estonia,* available online at: http://www.eurydice.org/ressources/eurydice/eurybase/pdf/0_integral/EE_EN.pdf (accessed 20.06.2008).

Flick, U. (2004) *Triangulation: Eine Einführung* (Wiesbaden: Verlag für Sozialwissenschaften).

Freire, P. (1972) *Pedagogy of the oppressed* (London: Penguin).

Friederici, M. (2009) From the research question to the sampling, in: Valk, P., Bertram-Troost, G., Friederici, M., Beraud, C. (Eds.) *Teenagers' Perspectives on the Role of Religion in their Lives, Schools and Societies: a European Study* (Münster: Waxmann), 13–22.

Fullan, M. (2007) *The New Meaning of Educational Change* (Columbia University: Teachers College Press).

Gadamer, H.-G. (1975) *Truth and Method* (London: Sheed and Ward).

Garfinkel, H. (1967) *Studies in Ethnomethodology* (Englewood Cliffs, NJ: Prentice-Hall).

Gass, S.M.; Mackey, A. (2000) *Stimulated Recall Methodology in Second Language Research* (Mahwah, NJ: Lawrence Erlbaum Associates).

Gergen, K.J. (2002) *An Invitation to Social Construction* (London: Sage).

Gray, J. (1991) Introduction, in: Mill, J.S. *On Liberty and Other Essays* (Oxford: Oxford University Press).

Grimmitt, M.H. (2000), The captivity and liberation of religious education and the meaning and significance of pedagogy, in: Grimmitt, M.H. (Ed.) *Pedagogies of Religious Education: Case Studies in the Research and Development of Good Peda-*

gogic Practice in RE (Great Wakering, Essex, UK: McCrimmons Publishing Co.Ltd), 7–23.

Hackett, R.I.J. (2007) Foreword, in: Alberts, W. *Integrative Religious Education in Europe: A Study-of-Religions Approach* (Berlin and New York: Walter de Gruyter).

Halman, L., Luijkx, R., Zundert, M. (2005) *Atlas of European Values* (Leiden: Brill).

Hansen, H. (2001) Religioonisotsioloogilise küsitluse "Elust, usust ja usuelust II" tulemused [The results of the sociological survey "Of life, Faith and Religious Life II], in: Eesti Evangeelne Allianss *Kristlik kogudus ja postmodernne maailm* (Tallinn: Logos), 65–76.

Hansen, H. (2002) *Luterlased, õigeusklikud ja teised* [Lutherans, Orthodoxes and others] (Tallinn: OÜ Teabetrükk).

Headland, T.N., Pike, K.L., Harris, M. (Eds.) (1990) *Emics and Etics: The Insider/Outsider Debate* (Newbury Park: Sage).

Heinapuu, O. (2004) Kas tahame rohkem sallimatust ja vägivalda? [Do we want more intolerance and violence?], *Postimees* 11.03, 11.

Heininen, S., Mauranen, M.-L., Mäkituuri, M., Peltola, L. (1990) *Kiriku ajalugu ja teave* [Church History and Knowledge] (Keuruu: Otava).

Henderson, L., Tallman, J. (2006) *Stimulated Recall and Mental Models: Tools for Teaching and Learning Computer Information Literacy* (Lanham, ML: Scarecrow Press).

Henley, P. (2001) Film-making and ethnographic research, in: Prosser, J. (Ed.) *Image-based Research* (London: RoutledgeFalmer), 42–59.

Heyd, D. (1996) Introduction, in: Heyd, D. (Ed.) *Toleration: An Elusive Virtue* (Princeton: Princeton University Press).

Holstein, J., Gubrium, J. (2002) Active interviewing, in: Weinberg, D. (Ed.) *Qualitative Research Methods* (Malden, MA: Blackwell), 112–126.

Hull, J. M. (2001) The contribution of religious education to religious freedom: A global perspective, in: The International Association for Religious Freedom (Ed.) *Religious Education in Schools: Ideas & Experiences from around the World* (London), 1–8.

Ilja, V. (2006) *Vennastekoguduse ajalugu Liivimaal (Lõuna-Eesti) 1766–1817* V [The History of Moravian Church in Livland (Sothern Estonia) 1766–1817] (Tallinn: Logos).

Ipgrave, J. (1998) *Religius Education and Muslim Students* (London: Teacher Training Agency).

Ipgrave, J. (2001) *Pupil-to-Pupil Dialogue in the Classroom as a Tool for Religious Education*, Warwick Religions and Education Research Unit Occasional Papers 2 (Coventry: University of Warwick).

Ipgrave, J. (2003a) *Building E-Bridges. Interfaith Dialogue by E-mail* (Birmingham: Christian Education Publications).

Ipgrave, J. (2003b) Dialogue, citizenship and religious education, in: Jackson, R. (Ed.) *International Perspectives on Citizenship, Education and Religious Diversity* (London/New York: RoutledgeFalmer), 147–168.

Ipgrave, J. (2005) Pupil-to-pupil dialogue as a tool for religious education in the primary classroom, in: Jackson, R., McKenna, U. (Eds.) *Intercultural Education and Religious Plurality,* Oslo Coalition Occasional Papers 1 (Oslo: the Oslo Coalition on Freedom of Religion or Belief), 39–42.

Isaacs, W. (1999) *Dialogue and the Art of Thinking Together* (New York: Doubleday).

Jackson, R. (1997) *Religious Education: An Interpretive Approach* (London: Hodder and Stoughton).

Jackson, R. (2004a) Intercultural education and religious diversity: Interpretive and dialogical approaches from England, in: Council of Europe (Ed.), *The Religious Dimension of Intercultural Education* (Strasbourg: Council of Europe Publishing), 39–50.

Jackson, R. (2004b) *Rethinking Religious Education and Plurality: Issues in Diversity and Pedagogy* (London: RoutledgeFalmer).

Jackson, R. (2005) Intercultural education, religious plurality and teaching for tolerance: Interpretive and dialogical approaches, in: Jackson, R & McKenna, U. (Eds.) *Intercultural Education and Religious Plurality: Oslo Occasional Papers (1)* (Oslo: The Oslo Coalition on Freedom of Religion or Belief), 5–13.

Jackson, R. (2007) European institutions and the contribution of studies of religious diversity to education for democratic citizenship, in: Jackson, R., Miedema, S., Weisse, W., Willaime, J.-P. (Eds.) *Religion and Education in Europe: Developments, Contexts and Debates* (Münster, Waxmann), 27–56.

Jackson, R. (2008a) *REDCo Deliverable D 2.1: Report on the validity and changes of the interpretive approach: Findings on the basis of this theory and adaptation of the interpretive approach on the basis of the triangulation* (Hamburg: Universität Hamburg).

Jackson, R. (2008b) Teaching about religions in the public sphere: European policy initiatives and the interpretive approach, *Numen: International Review for the History of Religions*, 55 (2/3), 151–182.

Jackson, R., Miedema, S., Weisse, W., Willaime, J.-P. (Eds.) (2007) *Religion and Education in Europe: Developments, Contexts and Debates* (Münster: Waxmann).

Jackson, R., Nesbitt, E. (1993) *Hindu Children in Britain* (Stoke on Trent: Trentham).

Jackson, R., Skeie, G. (2009) *REDCo Milestone M 2.2. Triangulation of theoretical and empirical results* (Hamburg: Universität Hamburg).

Jansen-Mann, E. (2007) *Religioossete teemade käsitlemine gümnaasiumi ajalooõpetuse õpikutes Inimõiguste deklaratsiooni perspektiivis* [Dealing with religious issues in textbooks of history for upper secondary school] (Tartu: Tartu Ülikool).

Jõks, A. (2006a) *Letter of the Chancellor of Justice to the headmaster of Hugo Treffner's Gymnasium*, June 2006, available online: http://www.oiguskantsler.ee/.files/78.doc (accessed 20.04.2009).

Jõks, A. (2006b) *Verbatim Report of the Riigikogu [the Parliament of Estonia] sitting 05.06.2006,* available online at: *http://web.riigikogu.ee/ems/stenograms/2006/06/t06060517–05.html#P185_61226* (accessed 05.06.2009).

Josza, D.-P. (2007) *Confessional versus Non-confessional RE* (Hamburg: Unpublished paper for REDCo quantitative study).

Josza, D.-P. (2008) Religious education in North-Rhine Westphalia: Views and experiences of students, in: Knauth, T., Jozsa, D.-P., Bertram-Troost, G. & Ipgrave, J. (Eds) *Encountering Religious Pluralism in School and Society – A Qualitative Study of Teenage Perspectives in Europe* (Münster, Waxmann), 173–206.

Jürgenstein, T. (1997) *Piibliõpik ja dogmaatika alused* [Bible Studies and Dogmatics] (Tallinn: Tallinna Raamatu trükikoda).

Jürgenstein, T. (2006) Kõige ohtlikumad teadmised [The most dangerous knowledge], *Eesti Päevaleht*, 20.06.2006, available online: http://www.epl.ee/?artikkel=324022 (accessed 20.04.2009).

Jürgenstein, T., Ruut, R., Friedenthal, T.-E. (1999) *Kiriku ajalugu ja tänapäev. Kristlik eetika (Religiooniõpetuse õpik gümnaasiumile)* [Church History and Contemporary Life. Christian Ethics] (Tallinn: Koolibri).

Jürgenstein, T., Schihalejev, O. (2005) *Gümnaasiumi religiooniõpetuse tuumkursuse "Inimene ja religioon" õppematerjalid* ["A Human and Religion". Teaching-Learning Resources for Upper Secondary School]. Available at http://intranet.hot.ee/ Gymnamaterjal.

Kalamees, K., Koorits, V. (2008) Kiisler surub koolidesse religiooniõpetust [Kiisler pushes religious education into schools], *Postimees*, 14.11.2008.

Kankaanpää, U.-M., Nisonen, R., Töllinen, M. (1994) *Hea Karjane 1: Õpetaja raamat* [Good Shepherd 1: Teacher's book] (Tallinn: EELK Pühapäevakooli Ühendus, Logos).

Kankaanpää, U.-M., Nisonen, R., Töllinen, M. (1995) *Hea Karjane 2: Õpetaja raamat* [Good Shepherd 2: Teacher's book] (Tallinn: EELK Pühapäevakooli Ühendus).

Kilemit, L. (2000) *Eesti usuliikumiste suhtumine ühiskonda* [The attitude of Estonian Religious Movements towards Society. Master thesis] (Tartu: Tartu Ülikool).

Kilemit, L., Nõmmik, U. (2003) Konfessionslosigkeit in Estland. Die gegenwärtige Situation: Ein Kreuzungspunkt der Geschichte, in: C. Gärtner, D. Pollack, M. Wohlrab-Sahr (Eds) *Atheismus und religiöse Indifferenz. Veröffentlichungen der Sektion "Religionssoziologie" der Deutschen Gesellschaft für Soziologie 10* (Opladen: Leske&Budrich), 215–227.

Kilemit, L., Nõmmik U. (2002) Über Religion im heutigen Estland. Zu den Ergebnissen einer religionssoziologischen Umfrage. *Trames*, No 4, Vol 6, 297–321.

Kivine, M., the National Audit Office of Estonia (2004) *Ülevaade üldhariduse probleemidest*. Raport nr 2–5/04/20, [Overview of the Problems of General Education. Raport] (Tallinn: National Audit Office of Estonia). Also available online at: http://www.riigikontroll.ee/upload/failid/ka_7062-eriraport-uldhariduse-probleemid_h.kivilo_24.05.2004_lopp.pdf (accessed 21.06.2008).

Kivirähk, A. (2006) Majamaniakid ja usundiõpetus [House-maniacs and religious education], *Ärileht*, 04.11.

Knauth, T. (2007) *Approaching the Concept of Incidents and their Analysis. Conceptual Remarks and Example,* unpublished paper presented in the REDCo-conference on video-taping and analysis of incidents of classroom interaction; June 18 2007, Vrije Universiteit Amsterdam.

Knauth, T. (2008) Better together than apart: Religion in school and lifeworld of students in Hamburg, in: Knauth, T., Jozsa, D.-P., Bertram-Troost, G. & Ipgrave, J. (Ed.). *Encountering Religious Pluralism in School and Society – A Qualitative Study of Teenage Perspectives in Europe* (Münster: Waxmann), 207–246.

Knauth, T., Jozsa, D.-P., Bertram-Troost, G., Ipgrave, J. (Eds.) (2008) *Encountering Religious Pluralism in School and Society – A Qualitative Study of Teenage Perspectives in Europe* (Münster: Waxmann).

Knauth, T., Leutner-Ramme, S., Weiße, W. (2000) *Religionsunterricht aus Schülerperspektive.* (Münster: Waxmann).

Knauth, T., Weisse, W. (2009) Neighbour-religions, in: *REDCo Deliverable 2.2. Report on the Relevance of the Approaches "Neighbour-Religions", "Citizenship-Edu-*

204

cation", *"Nonfoundational Education"*, *and "Identity-formation* (Hamburg: Universität Hamburg), 5–12.

Kodelja, Z., Bassler, T. (2004) *Religion and Schooling in Open Society: A Framework for Informed Dialogue* (Slovenia: Open Society Institute). Also available online at: http://www.soros.org/initiatives/esp/articles_publications/publications/relign_20041201/religion_20041201.pdf (accessed 25.03.2009).

Kozyrev, F., Schihalejev, O. (2008) Religion and education in Estonia and Russia – resemblance and differences, in: Knauth, T., Jozsa, D.-P., Bertram-Troost, G., Ipgrave, J. (Eds.) *Encountering Religious Pluralism in School and Society – A Qualitative Study of Teenage Perspectives in Europe* (Münster: Waxmann), 309–326.

Küng, H. (1991) *Global Responsibility: in Search of New World Ethic* (London: SCM Press).

Laks, S. (2007) *Religiooni kajastamine ajalooõpikutes* [Dealing with Religion in History Textbooks] (Tartu: Tartu Ülikool).

Lauristin, M. (2008) Non-Estonians as part of the population and citizenry of Estonia, in: Heidmets, M. (Ed.) *Estonian Human Development Report 2007* (Tallinn: Eesti Ekspress Kirjastus), 46–47.

Leganger-Krogstad, H. (2001) Religious education in a global perspective: A contextual approach, in: Heimbrock, H.-G., Scheilke C. T., Schreiner, P. (Eds.) *Towards Religious Competence: Diversity as a Challenge for Education in Europe.* (Münster: LIT Verlag), 53–73.

Leganger-Krogstad, H. (2003) Dialog among young citizens in a pluralistic religious education classroom, in: Jackson, R. (Ed.) *International Perspectives on Citizenship, Education and Religious Diversity* (London/New York: RoutledgeFalmer), 169–190.

Levinson, M. (1999) *The Demands of Liberal Education* (Oxford and New York: Oxford University Press).

Liiman, R. (2001) *Usklikkus muutuvas Eesti ühiskonnas* [Religiosity in the Changing Estonian Society] (Tartu: Tartu University Press).

Liiv, E. (2002) Usuvabadusest Eesti moodi ehk elame luterlik-kristlikus riigis [Religious freedom in Estonian way or we live in a Lutheran-Christian state], *Kultuur ja Elu*, 4, 29–32.

Lukas, T. (2008) *Online-intervjuu: lugejate küsimustele vastas haridusminister Lukas* [Online interview: to readers' questions answers the Minister of Education Lukas], available online at: www.hm.ee/index.php?popup=download&id=6277 (accessed 20.04.2009).

Lyle, J. (2003) Stimulated recall: a report on its use in naturalistic research, *British Educational Research Journal* 29(6), 861–878.

MacIntyre, A. (1985) *After Virtue. A Study in Moral Theory* (London: Duckworth).

Masso, A., Vihalemm, T. (2004) Kollektiivsed identiteedid siirdeaja Eestis [Collective identities in transformational Estonia], in: Kalmus, V., Lauristin, M., Pruulmann-Vengerfeldt, P. (Eds.) *Eesti alevik 21. sajandi algul* [Estonian Hamlet in the Beginning of the 21st Century] (Tartu: Tartu University Press), 45–56.

Mauranen, M.-L. (1990) *Maailma usundid* [World Religions] (Keuruu, Otava).

McKenna, U., Ipgrave, J., Jackson, R. (2008) *Interfaith Dialogue by Email in Primary School* (Münster: Waxmann).

Meade, P., McMeniman, M. (1992) Stimulated recall: An effective methodology for examining successful teaching in science, *Australian Educational Researcher* 19(3), 1–18.

Ministry of Education and Research of the Republic of Estonia (2007) *Education and Research in Estonia* (Tartu: Ministry of Education and Research of the Republic of Estonia).

Ministry of Education and Research (2009) *Lasteasutuste pedagoogid haridustaseme järgi* [Pedagogical staff according to the level of education], available online at http://www.hm.ee/index.php?048055 (accessed 12.12.2008).

Moran, G. (2006) Religious education and international understanding, in: Bates, D., Durka, G., Schweitzer, Fr. (Eds.) *Education, Religion and Society: Essays in honour of John M. Hull* (Routledge: Research in Education Series), 38–48.

Moulin, D. (2009) A too liberal religious education? A thought experiment for teachers and theorists, *British Journal of Religious Education*, 31 (2), 153–165.

Nesbitt, E. (2004) *Intercultural Education: Ethnographic and Religious Approaches* (Brighton: Sussex Academic Press).

Niglas, K. (2004) *The Combined Use of Qualitative and Quantitative Methods in Educational Research* (Tallinn: TPÜ Kirjastus). Also available online at: http://www.ear.ee/e-rmtk/sotsiaalt.htm (accessed 13.04.2009).

Niit, K.-K. (2002) Sotsiaalsed aksioomid – üldised veendumused selle kohta, kuidas maailmas asjad käivad [Social axioms – general beliefs on how the things work], in: Valk, A. (Ed.) *Eesti ja eestlased võrdlevas perspektiivis. Kultuuridevahelisi uurimusi 20. sajandi lõpust* (Tartu: Tartu University Press), 60–73.

Nõmmela, K. (2007) *Rakvere gümnaasiumite õpilaste, lastevanemate, õpetajate ja koolijuhtide suhtumine religiooniõpetusse* [The Perceptions of Religious Education by Students, Parents, Teachers and Head Teachers from Rakvere] (Tartu: Tartu Ülikool).

O'Brien, J. (1993) Action research through stimulated recall, *Research in Science Education* 23(1), 214–221.

OECD (2001) *Reviews of National Policies for Education Estonia* (Paris: OECD Publishing).

OSCE (2007) *The Toledo Guiding Principles on Teaching about Religion or Belief* (Warsaw: Organisation for Security and Co-operation in Europe).

Ouellet, F. (2006) Religious education and citizenship in postmodern societies, in: de Souza, M., Engebretson, K., Durka, G., Jackson, R., McGrady, A. (Eds.) (2006). *International Handbook of the Religious, Moral and Spiritual Dimensions of Education.* (2 Vols) (Dordrecht, The Netherlands: Springer Academic Publishers), 363–374.

Paesüld, A. (2005) *Religiooniõpetuse õpetajatest aastal 2004* [About Teachers of Religious Education in Year 2004] (a research paper in religious education) (Tartu: Tartu Ülikool).

Pärkson, K. (2006) *Religiooniõpetus gümnaasiumiõpilaste isiksusliku arengu toetajana Tartu Tamme Gümnaasiumi õpilaste nägemuse põhjal* [Religious Education as a Facilitator of Personal Development According to the Students from Tartu Tamme Gymnasium] (Tartu: Tartu Ülikool).

Peltola, L., Pihkala, L., Sinnemäki, M. (1989) *Dogmaatika ja eetika* [Dogmatics and Ethics] (Keuruu: Otava).

Pihkala, L., Peltola, L., Virta, M.-L. (1991) *Piibliõpik* [Bible Study] (Keuruu: Otava).

Pike, K.L. (1967) *Language in Relation to a Unified Theory of Structure of Human Behaviour* (The Hague: Mouton).

Pink, S. (2001) *Doing Ethnography: Images, Media and Representation in Research* (London: Sage).

Plaat, J. (2003) *Saaremaa kirikud, usuliikumised ja prohvetid 18.–20. sajandil* [Churches, Religious Movements and Prophets in Saaremaa in the 18th–20th Centuries] (Põltsamaa: Vali Press)

Põder, K. (2007) *Religioossete teemade kajastamine põhikooli ühiskonnaõpetuse õpikutes* [Dealing with Religious Topics in Textbooks of Civic Education for Upper Secondary School] (Tartu: Tartu Ülikool).

Polio, C., Gass, S., Chapin, L. (2006) Using stimulated recall to investigate native speaker perceptions in native–nonnative speaker interaction, *Studies in Second Language Acquisition* 28, 237–267.

Ponomariova, G., The Society of Old Believer Culture and Development (2003) *Russian Old Believers in Estonia*, available online at http://www.starover.ee/, (accessed 18.04.2008).

Rawls, J. (1971) *A Theory of Justice* (Cambridge: Harvard University Press).

REKK (2009), *Religiooniõpetuse ainekava esimene versioon, 12.01.2009* [The First Draft of the Syllabus for Religious Education], available online at: https://www.oppekava.ee/ainekavad_sotsiaalained (accessed 12.05.2009)

Remmel, A.-S. (2005) *Ateistlike tõekspidamiste elujõulisusest Tartu gümnaasiumiõpilaste näitel* [The Perservance of Atheistic Views, Example of Students from Tartu Gymnasiums] (Tartu: Tartu Ülikool).

Reps, M. (2006) *Verbatim Report of the Riigikogu [the Parliament of Estonia] sitting 05.06.2006*, available online at: http://web.riigikogu.ee/ems/stenograms/2006/06/t06060517–04.html#P118_33847 (accessed 05.06.2009).

Riigi Statistika Keskbüroo (1935) *Rahvastiku koostis ja korteriolud. 1.III 1934 rahvaloenduse andmed. Vihk II* = Composition démographique de la populationn et logements. Données du recensement e 1. III 1934. Vol. II (Tallinn: Riigi trükikoda). Also available online at: http://dspace.utlib.ee/dspace/handle/10062/4439 (accessed 21.04.2009)

Riigi Teataja [State Herald] 1992, 12, 192, available online at: http://www.riigiteataja.ee/ert/act.jsp?id=30588 (accessed 21.04.2009).

Riigi Teataja [State Herald] I 1999, 24, 358, available online at: https://www.riigiteataja.ee/ert/act.jsp?id=77246 (accessed 21.04.2009)

Riigi Teataja [State Herald] I 2002, 20, 116, available online at: http://www.riigiteataja.ee/ert/act.jsp?id=162998&replstring=33 (accessed 21.04.2009)

Riigi Teataja [State Herald] I 2009, 2, 4, available online at: http://www.riigiteataja.ee/ert/act.jsp?id=13198443 (accessed 07.09.2009).

Rouch, J. (1995) The camera and man, in: Hockings, P. (Ed.) *Principle of Visual Anthropology* (New York: Mouton de Gruyter), 79–98.

Ruus, V.-R., Veisson, M., Leino M. (2007) Õpilaste edukus, toimetulek ja heaolu koolis [Students' success, management and wellbeing at school], in: Kuurme, T. (Ed.) *Eesti kool 21. sajandi algul: kool kui arengukeskkond ja õpilaste toimetulek* (Tallinn: TLÜ Kirjastus), 59–72

Rüütel, I., Tiit, E.-M. (2005) Eesti kooliõpilaste väärtushinnanguist ja huvialadest [Estonian students' values and hobbies], *Akadeemia*, 11, 2401–2442.

Saar, A. (2005) *Religiooniõpetuse kvalitatiivuuringu tulemuste esitluse materjale* [Materials for the Presentation about the Results of the Poll among Upper Secondary School Students] (Tallinn: SaarPoll).

Sandel, M.J. (1998) *Liberalism and Limits of Justice* (Cambridge: Cambridge University Press).

Schihalejev, O. (2008a) Kohtumine endast erinevaga – õpilaste arusaam [Meeting difference – students' perspectives], in: Valk, P. (Ed.) *Töid religioonipedagoogikast I* (Tartu: Tartu Ülikooli Kirjastus), 123–156.

Schihalejev, O. (2008b) Meeting diversity – students' perspectives in Estonia, in: Knauth, T., Jozsa, D.-P., Bertram-Troost, G. & Ipgrave, J. (Eds.) *Encountering Religious Pluralism in School and Society – A Qualitative Study of Teenage Perspectives in Europe* (Münster: Waxmann), 247–278.

Schihalejev, O. (2009a) Challenges in creating respect for diversity: Teachers' perspectives, in: van der Want, A., Bakker, C., Avest, ter I., Everington, J. (Eds.) *Teachers Responding to Religious Diversity in Europe. Researching Biography and Pedagogy* (Münster: Waxmann), 41–54.

Schihalejev, O. (2009b) Comments on Russia from an Estonian perspective, in: Valk, P., Bertram-Troost, G., Friederici, M., Beraud, C. (Eds.) *Teenagers' Perspectives on the Role of Religion in their Lives, Schools and Societies: A European Study* (Münster: Waxmann), 350–353.

Schihalejev, O. (2009c) Dialogue in religious education lessons – possibilities and hindrances in the Estonian context, in: *British Journal of Religious Education*, 31 (3), 277–288.

Schihalejev, O. (2009d) Options beside 'and no religion too' – Perspectives of Estonian youth, in: Valk, P., Bertram-Troost, G., Friederici, M., Beraud, C. (Eds.) *Teenagers' Perspectives on the Role of Religion in their Lives, Schools and Societies: A European Study* (Münster: Waxmann), 79–120.

Schihalejev, O. (2009e) Portraits of the Estonian respondents, in: van der Want, A., Bakker, C., ter Avest, I., Everington, J. (Eds.) *Teachers Responding to Religious Diversity in Europe: Researching Biography and Pedagogy* (Münster: Waxmann), 149–160.

Schihalejev, O. (2009f) Prospects for and obstacles to dialogue in religious education in Estonia, in: Avest, I. ter; Jozsa, D.-P.; Knauth, T.; Rosón, J.; Skeie, G. (Eds.) *Dialogue and Conflict on Religion: Studies of Classroom Interaction in European Countries* (Münster: Waxmann), 62-85.

Schihalejev, O., Kaljulaid, K. (2003) *Religiooniõpetuse I kooliastme tuumkursuse "Vanavanemate pärand" õppematerjalid* ["Grandparents' Heritage" Teaching-Learning Resources for the First School Stage]. Available at http://religiooniopetus.ee/ index_files/Ikooliaste.htm.

Schihalejev, O., Kaljulaid, K. (2004a) *Religiooniõpetuse II kooliastme tuumkursuse "Eetika" õppematerjalid* ["Ethics" Teaching-Learning Resources for the Second School Stage]. Available at http://religiooniopetus.ee/index_files/IIkooliaste.htm.

Schihalejev, O., Kaljulaid, K. (2004b) *Religiooniõpetuse III kooliastme tuumkursuse "Maailma religioonid" õppematerjalid* ["The Wolrld Religions" Teaching-Learning

Resources for the Third School Stage]. Available at http://religiooniopetus.ee/ index_files/IIkooliaste.htm.

Schreiner, P. (2000) *Religious Education in Europe: A Collection of Basic Information about RE in European Countries* (Muenster: Comenius Institut).

Schreiner, P. (2002) Religious education in the European context, in: Broadbent, L. Brown, A. (Eds.) *Issues in Religious Education* (London/ New York: RoutledgeFalmer), 86–98.

Schreiner, P. (2007) Religious education in European context, in: Kuyk, E., Jensen, R., Lankshear D.W., Leoh Manna, E., Schreiner, P. (Eds.) *Religious Education in Europe* (Oslo: IKO & ICCS), 9–16.

Schweitzer, F. and Boschki, R. (2004) What children need: co-operative religious education in German schools: results from an empirical study, in: *British Journal of Religious Education*, 26 (1), 33–44.

Searle, J.R. (1995) *The Construction of Social Reality* (New York: The Free Press).

Silvermann, D. (1993) *Interpreting Qualitative Data: Methods for Analyzing Talk, Text and Interaction* (London: Sage).

Simmel, G. (2002) The Stranger, in: Weinberg, D. (Ed.) *Qualitative Research Methods* (Malden: Blackwell), 30–34.

Sirge, K. (2008) *Noored ja usk Setumaal aastal 2008: hetkeseis ja jätkusuutlikkus* [Youth and Belief in Setumaa in 2008: Status Quo and Continuity] (Tartu: Tartu Ülikool).

Skovdahl, K., Kihlgren, L.A., Kihlgren, M. (2004) Dementia and aggressiveness: stimulated recall interviews with caregivers after video–recorded interactions, *Journal of Clinical Nursing* 13(4), 515–525.

Soom, K. (2007) *Täiskasvanute leeritöö Eesti Evangeelses Luterlikus Kirikus ja selle arengustrateegia koostamine* [Adult Confirmation in the Estonian Evangelical Lutheran Church and its Development Strategy] (Doctoral thesis) (Tartu : Tartu Ülikooli Kirjastus).

Statistical Office of Estonia (2002) *2000. aasta rahva ja eluruumide loendus: IV Haridus, usk*. [2000 Population and Housing Census: IV Education, Religion] (Tallinn: Statistikaamet). Also available online at: http://pub.stat.ee/ (accessed 16.04.2009).

Statistics Estonia, *Eestlaste osatähtsus rahvastikus* [The Proportion of Estonians in Population] http://www.stat.ee/29847, (accessed 02.04.2009)

Statistics Estonia, *2000 Population and Housing Census* http://www.stat.ee/population-census-2000 , (accessed 02.04.2009)

Sterkens, C. (2001) Interreligious learning: The problem of interreligious dialogue in primary education, in: *Empirical Studies in Theology 8* (Leiden: Brill).

Strauss, A., Corbin, J. (1990) *Basics of Qualitative Research: Grounded Theory Procedures and Technique* (London: Sage).

Tamminen, K., Vesa, L., Pyysiäinen, M. (1998) *Kuidas õpetan usuõpetust? Usundididaktika käsiraamat* [How Do I Teach Religious Education? A Handbook for Didactics of Religious Education] (Tallinn: Argo Kirjastus, REKK).]

Toompuu, P. (2007) *Eesti noorte teispoolsuskujutelmad XI klassi õpilaste näitel* [The Perceptions of Other-World by Youth from 11th Form] (Tartu: Tartu Ülikool).

Toots, A., Plakk, M., Idanurm, T. (2004) *Infotehnoloogia Eesti koolides: Trendid ja väljakutsed:* Uuringu „Tiiger luubis" 2000–2004 lõppraport [Infotechonology in Estonian Schools: Tendencies and Challenges] (Tallinn: Tiigrihüppe SA).

Uibopuu, M. (2007) *Religiooni kajastamine gümnaasiumi filosoofia õpikutes* [Dealing with Religion in Textbooks of Philosophy for Upper Secondary School] (Tartu: Tartu Ülikool).

Undrits, A. (2006) *Answer by e-mail for a request from EHIS (Estonian Education Information System) to Olga Schihalejev*, 14.09.2006.

Vaher, K. (2009) *Answer by e-mail for a request from EHIS (Estonian Education Information System) to Olga Schihalejev*, 28.01.2009.

Valk, A. (2002a) Sissejuhatus [Introduction], in: Valk, A. (Ed.) *Eesti ja eestlased võrdlevas perspektiivis. Kultuuridevahelisi uurimusi 20. sajandi lõpust* [Estonia and Estonian in a Comparative Perspective. Intercultural Researches from the End of the 20th Century] (Tartu: Tartu University Press), 7–13.

Valk, P. (1997) *Ühest heledast laigust Eesti kooli ajaloos: Usuõpetus Eesti koolides aastatel 1918–1940* [About an Unrevealed Spot in the History of Estonian Education: Religious Education in Estonian Schools in 1918–1940] (Tallinn: Logos).

Valk, P. (2000) From the Soviet atheism to the national identity: a specific background for the religious education in Estonia, *Panorama: International Journal of Comparative Religious Education and Values* 12 (1), 78–93.

Valk, P. (2002b) *Eesti kooli religiooniõpetuse kontseptsioon* [Concept of Religious Education for Estonian Schools] (Tartu: Tartu University Press).

Valk, P. (2003). Religious education through the eyes of pupils, teachers and headmasters, in: Mietrich, M., Kulmar, T. (Eds) *Die Bedeutung der Religion für Gesellschaften in Vergangenheit und Gegenwart: Fünften gemeinsamen Symposiums der Evangelisch-Theologischen Fakultät der Universität Tartu, der Estnischen Studiengesellschaft für Morgenlandkunde und der Deutschen Religionsgeschichtlichen Studiengesellschaft; Estland; 2.–3.11.2001* (Münster: Ugarit Verlag; Forschungen zur Anthropologie und Religionsgeschichte; 36), 239–252.

Valk, P. (2006) Churches and European integration: A challenge for religious education in the post-Soviet context. *Kirchliche Zeitgeschichte* 19(1), 166–186.

Valk, P. (Ed.) (2007a) *Religiooniõpetuse õpetamisest* [About Teaching Religious Education] (Tallinn: Riiklik Eksami ja Kvalifikatsiooni Keskus).

Valk, P. (2007b) Religious education in Estonia, in: Jackson, R., Miedema, S., Weisse, W., Willaime, J.-P. (Eds.) *Religion and Education in Europe: Developments, Contexts and Debates* (Münster, Waxmann), 159–180.

Valk, P. (Ed.) (2008) *Töid religioonipedagoogikast I* [Papers on Religious Education I] (Tartu: Tartu Ülikooli Kirjastus).

Valk, P., Bertram-Troost, G., Friederici, M., Beraud, C. (Eds.) (2009) *Teenagers' Perspectives on the Role of Religion in their Lives, Schools and Societies: A European Study* (Münster: Waxmann).

Vavilov, T. (2007) *Kristlike mõistete kasutamine neljanda ja kaheksanda klassi laste poolt* [Actuation of Christian Terms by Children from the Fourth and the Eights Forms] (Tartu: Tartu Ülikool).

Veisson, M., Pallas, L., Ruus, V. R., Ots, L. (2007) Erinevusi ja sarnasusi Eesti Vabariigi eesti ja vene õppekeelega koolide koolikultuuris, õpilaste edukuses, heaolus, huvides ja toimetulekus [The similarities and differences in school culture, students achievements, well-being and managing by the students from Estonian- and Russian-medium schools], in: Kuurme, T. (Ed.) *Eesti kool 21. sajandi algul: kool kui arengukeskkond ja õpilaste toimetulek* (Tallinn: TLÜ Kirjastus), 73–95.

Villems, R. (2008) *Speech of the President of the Academy on General Assembly of Estonian Academy of Sciences*, 10.12.2008, available online at: http://www.akadeemia.ee/_repository/File/TEGEVUS/ETTEKANDED/ RV%2010.12.08.pdf (accessed 01.02.2009).

Walzer, M. (1997) *On Toleration* (New Haven: Yale University Press).

Walzer, M. (1998) Education, democratic citizenship, and multiculturalism, in: Weiner, E. (Ed.) *The Handbook of Interethnic Coexistence* (New York: Continuum Publishing), 153–161.

Want, A. van der, Bakker, C., Avest, I. ter, Everington, J. (Eds.) (2009) *Teachers Responding to Religious Diversity in Europe: Researching Biography and Pedagogy* (Münster: Waxmann).

Weisse, W. (2007) The European research project on religion and education 'REDCo': An introduction, in: Jackson, R., Miedema, S., Weisse, W., Willaime, J.-P. (Eds.) *Religion and Education in Europe: Developments, Contexts and Debates* (Münster / New York / München / Berlin: Waxmann Verlag GmbH), 9–25.

Weisse, W. (1999) Ökumenische Theologie und interreligiöse Dialogerfahrungen. Anstöße für die Religionspädagogik, in: Weiße, W. (Ed.) *Vom Monolog zum Dialog. Ansätze einer dialogischen Religionspädagogik, 2*, (Münster: Waxmann), 181–202.

Willaime, J.P. (2007) Different models for religion and education in Europe, in: Jackson, R., Miedema, S., Weisse, W., Willaime, J.-P. (Eds.) *Religion and Education in Europe* (Münster : Waxmann), 57–66.

Wimberley, J. (2003) Education for intercultural and interfaith dialogue: A new initiative by the Council of Europe, *Prospects*, XXXIII (2), 199–209.

APPENDICES

Appendix 1: Questionnaire for qualitative study (English version)

Religion in education: A contribution to Dialogue or a factor
of Conflict in transforming societies of European
Countries

Code: ....

Age..........
Boy... Girl...
School: ....
Form: ....
Religion/denomination/worldview: ....
Born in which country..
Citizenship of which country.......................................
Parents born in which country...
Mother.......................Father..........................
Languages spoken in family-life ....

We'd like to ask you some questions concerning religion or faith. We just like to get to know your opinion; it is important for us to know what you personally think about these issues. If possible, please write down your answer in complete sentences. Thank you very much for your cooperation!

1. *If you hear the words a) Religion and b) God: what comes to your mind?*
   a) ***Please write down 3 to 6 words, which you feel relevant for "religion".***

   b) ***Please write down 3 to 6 words which you feel to be relevant to "God".***

   c) ***How important is religion/God for your personal life? Can you write down one whole sentence (or even more), which could illustrate your position?***

2. *How did you get to know about religions?*
   Please <u>underline</u> one or several of the following possibilities:
   family, friends, school, media, places of worship? (Or other possibilities?
   Please write it down: ....)

   Could you explain, how that was (what you experienced, what you got as information)?

3. **Do you talk about religion with your friends?**
   If no, why not? Please explain: .....

   If yes, what is interesting in talking about religion? And on which occasions do you have such talks?

4. **What are your experiences with your own religion and with the religions of others?**
   Could you please write down examples of good and/or bad experiences?

5. **Do you think that people from different religions can live together?**
   Please explain, what you think (and add an example).

6. *Imagine you are a person who can decide on school-matters*
   Should there be a place for religion at school? Please explain, why, or why not

7. *If religion is taught at school: What do you think students should learn about religions?*
   Please write down three wishes!

8. *Religion at school! Please write down your opinion in view of the following two questions:*
   a) **Should the teachers have a religious faith? Please write down your opinion**

   b) **Should all pupils be taught together, irrespective of differences in belief or world views? Or should the pupils be separated when it comes to religion at school? Please give your opinion in general and add an example, why you have that opinion!**

You've already written down a lot about the significance of religion. But it might be possible that our questions have left out something very important. So is there something else you would like to tell us about? Please write it down, whatever it is.

Appendix 2: Questionnaire for qualitative study (Estonian and Russian versions)

**Religioon ja haridus: panus dialoogiks või
konfliktifaktor
Euroopa muutuvates ühiskondades**

Kood: __ __ __ __ __ __ __

Vanus: ___
Poiss: ___ *Tüdruk:* ___
Kool: _____
Klass: ___
Religioon / konfessioon / usutunnistus / maailmavaade: _____
Millises riigis sündinud: _____
Millise riigi kodanik: _____
Vanemate päritolu maa: ema: _____ *isa:* _____
Kodus kõneldavad keeled: _____

Soovime esitada mõned küsimused, mis puudutavad religiooni ja usku. Soovime teada Sinu arvamust, meile on oluline teada, mida Sina isiklikult arvad antud teemadest. Kui võimalik, kirjuta oma vastused täislausetega. Täname koostöö eest!

1. ***Kui sa kuuled sõna „religioon" või „Jumal", mis mõtteid see sinus tekitab?***
   a) Kirjuta palun 3 kuni 6 sõna, mis on asjakohased sõna "religioon" puhul.

   _____

   _____

   b) Kirjuta palun 3 kuni 6 sõna, mis on asjakohased sõna "Jumal" puhul.

   _____

   _____

   c) Kui oluline on religioon sulle isiklikult? Kas saaksid kirjutada ühe täislause (või enamgi), mis selgitaks sinu seisukohta?

   _____

   _____

2. ***Kuidas said teada religioonide kohta?*** *Jooni alla üks kuni mitu järgmistest võimalustest:*
   perekond, sõbrad, kool, meedia, jumalateenistuse paigad,

midagi muud .... (palun kirjuta üles)
Kuidas Sa selle kohta (religioon, Jumal) teada said, mis see oli ja kuidas Sa seda kogesid.

_____

_____

3. Kas te sõpradega räägite religioonist?
Kui ei, siis miks? Palun selgita:

_____

_____

Kui jah, siis mis teeb religioonist kõnelemise huvitavaks? Ja mis puhkudel te kõnelete neil teemadel?

_____

_____

4. Millised on sinu kogemused sinu enda ja teiste inimeste religiooniga?
Too palun näiteid heast ja/või halvast kogemusest!

_____

_____

5. Kas sinu arust saavad erinevate religioonide esindajad elada kõrvuti?
Palun selgita, mida arvad (ja lisa näide).

_____

_____

6. Kujuta ette, et oled isik, kes saab otsustada kooli puudutavate küsimuste üle. *Kas koolis peaks olema ruumi religioonile? Selgita, miks (mis mõttes) peaks või ei peaks.*

_____

_____

_____

7. Kui koolis õpetatakse religiooni: mida peaksid õpilased õppima religioonide kohta?

Palun kirjuta kolm soovi!

_____

_____

_____

8. Religioon koolis. Palun kirjuta oma arvamus järgmise kahe küsimuse suhtes:

a) Kas õpetajad peaksid olema usklikud? Palun selgita oma arvamust!

_____

_____

_____

b) *Kas kõik õpilased peaksid saama ühiselt religiooni puutuvat õpetust, olenemata nende usust või maailmavaatest? Või peaksid olema erinevad rühmad, vastavalt õpilase usulisele tõekspidamisele? Palun esita oma arvamus üldiselt ning lisa näide, miks sa nii arvad!*

_____

_____

_____

Oled juba kirjutanud palju religiooni tähendusest. Kuid on võimalik, et meie küsimused ei käsitlenud mõnda olulist tahku. Kui on midagi veel, millest tahaksid meile rääkida, siis kirjuta palun siia!!!

_____

_____

Täname koostöö eest!

Анкета

Ваш возраст: ___

Ваш пол: ___

Школа: _____

Класс: ___

Ваша религия / конфесия / мировозрение: _____

Место рождения: _____

Гражданином какой страны Вы являетесь: _____

Место рождения – мать: _____ отец: _____

На каком языке (языках) Вы разговариваете дома: _____

Когда Вы слышите слово «религия», с чем оно связано для Вас, каково Ваше представление о религии?

_____

_____

а)   Напишите 3–6 слов, имеющих отношение к слову «религия»

_____

_____

и 3–6 слов, имеющих отношение к слову «Бог»

_____

_____

б) Насколько важна религия (Бог) в Вашей жизни? Попробуйте выразить Вашу точку зрения в одном или нескольких предложениях

_____

_____

_____

1. *Где Вы получили первые знания о религии?*
   Подчеркните один из вариантов *(в семье; от друзей; в школе; из теле- и радиопрограмм; в церкви или религиозной общине)* **или назовите свой**

_____

_____

Как это случилось? Что Вы узнали? Что оказалось для Вас наиболее важным?

_____

_____

_____

Вы говорите о религии (Боге) со своими друзьями?
(Да / нет)_____
Если нет, то почему нет? Если да, то в каких случаях возникают такие разговоры и что вас интересует в них?

_____

_____

_____

Что Вы можете сказать о личном опыте встречи с религиозными явлениями и религиозными людьми (общей и разной с Вами веры)?
Постарайтесь привести пример положительного и отрицательного опыта

_____

_____

_____

2. *Могут ли люди разных вероисповеданий уживаться вместе?*
Поясните, как Вы себе это представляете, и приведите пример

_____

_____

_____

6. _Представьте себя директором школы. Включили бы Вы преподавание религии в школьную программу?_ (Да / нет)

_____

_____

Поясните, почему

_____

_____

Если бы религия преподавалась в школе, с чем именно надо было бы знакомить учащихся? **Запишите три пожелания**

_____

_____

7. *Представим, что в школе есть уроки религии. Как Вы считаете:*
   а) Должен ли преподаватель религии быть верующим и почему?

_____

_____

_____

б) Надо ли учить всех вместе, независимо от различий вероисповедания и убеждений, или разделять учащихся на этих уроках? (Сформулируйте вашу точку зрения и поясните ее)

_____

_____

_____

Спасибо за все, чем Вы поделились с нами! Может быть, наши вопросы обошли стороной что-то важное, о чем Вы хотели бы сказать. Пожалуйста, добавьте все, что считаете нужным

_____

_____

Сообщите, если считаете нужным, Вашу религиозную (вероисповедную) принадлежность

Questionnaire on Religion and School

A survey of attitudes regarding religion among students of your age was conducted last year in Europe. This questionnaire has been designed on the basis of that survey. It aims to find out how students from eight European countries see the role of religion in school and in society in general. We would like your help in this research. We are interested in your personal views. Maybe some of the questions seem irrelevant to you and your context. Do not worry about this – the role of religion in different European countries is different. Choose the answer which fits you best.

If you have any problems understanding the questions, please ask for help. Please write your personal remarks, comments and additions on the last page of the questionnaire.

Thank you for your cooperation!
REDCo team

Filled by researchers:

MS	Country	Date	Model of RinE	Code

PART I. Religion in school

*When it comes to religion in school, European countries are different in several ways from each other. There are countries where religious education classes are compulsory for all students; and countries where such lessons are optional or not provided at school at all. There are countries in which religious education classes are taught from the point of view of a particular religion and others which mainly teach **about** religions.*

Topics about religion may come up in several subjects, e.g. literature or history, or may come up incidentally in general school life.

1. How many years have you studied Religious Education at school? ☐
2. Do you participate in Religious Education classes during this school year? Yes / No

❖ What are your experiences of religion in school? How much do you agree, that:

		Strongly agree	Agree	Neither agree or disagree	Dis-agree	Strongly disagree
3.	At school, I get knowledge about different religions.	1	2	3	4	5
4.	At school, I learn to have respect for everyone, whatever their religion.	1	2	3	4	5
5.	At school, I have opportunities to discuss religious issues from different perspectives.	1	2	3	4	5
6.	I find topics about religions interesting at school.	1	2	3	4	5
7.	I find religions as topic important at school.	1	2	3	4	5
8.	Learning about different religions at school helps us to live together.	1	2	3	4	5
9.	Learning about religions at school helps me to make choices between right and wrong.	1	2	3	4	5
10.	Learning about religions at school helps me to understand current events.	1	2	3	4	5
11.	Learning about religions at	1	2	3	4	5

		Strongly agree	Agree	Neither agree or disagree	Dis-agree	Strongly disagree
	school helps me to learn about myself.					
12.	Learning about religions leads to conflicts in the classroom	1	2	3	4	5

❖ Religion could appear in the school in many different ways. Imagine you are a person in authority who can decide on school matters. How far would you agree with the following positions?

		Strongly agree	Agree	Neither agree or disagree	Dis-agree	Strongly disagree
13.	At school meals, religious food requirements should be taken into account	1	2	3	4	5
14.	Students should be able to wear	… discreet ones (e.g. small crosses, etc on necklace)	1	2	3	4	5
15.	religious symbols at school…	… more visible ones (e.g. head-scarves)	1	2	3	4	5
16.	Students can be absent from school when it is their religious festivals.	1	2	3	4	5
17.	Students should be excused from taking some lessons for religious reasons.	1	2	3	4	5
18.	Schools should provide facilities for students to pray in school.	1	2	3	4	5
19.	Voluntary religious services (e.g. school worship, prayers) could be a part of school life	1	2	3	4	5

❖ To what extent do you agree, that learning about different religions helps:

		Strongly agree	Agree	Neither agree or disagree	Dis-agree	Strongly disagree
20.	To understand others and live peacefully with them.	1	2	3	4	5
21.	To understand the history of my country and of Europe.	1	2	3	4	5
22.	To gain a better understanding of current events.	1	2	3	4	5

23.	To develop my own point of view.	1	2	3	4	5
24.	To develop moral values.	1	2	3	4	5
25.	To learn about my own religion.	1	2	3	4	5

❖ What is your position regarding different models of religious education in school?

		Strongly agree	Agree	Neither agree or disagree	Dis-agree	Strongly disagree
26.	Religious Education should be optional.	1	2	3	4	5
27.	Students should study Religious Education separately in groups according to which religion they belong to.	1	2	3	4	5
28.	There should be no place for religion in school life.	1	2	3	4	5
29.	Religious Education should be taught to Students together, whatever differences there might be in their religious or denominational background.	1	2	3	4	5
30.	There is no need for the subject of Religious Education. All we need to know about religion is covered by other school subjects (e.g. literature, history etc).	1	2	3	4	5
31.	Religious Education should be taught sometimes together and sometimes in groups according to which religions students belong to.	1	2	3	4	5

❖ To what extent do you agree that at school students should:

		Strongly agree	Agree	Neither agree or disagree	Dis-agree	Strongly disagree
32.	Get an objective knowledge about different religions.	1	2	3	4	5
33.	Learn to understand what religions teach.	1	2	3	4	5

34.	Be able to talk and communicate about religious issues.	1	2	3	4	5
35.	Learn the importance of religion for dealing with problems in society.	1	2	3	4	5
36.	Be guided towards religious belief.	1	2	3	4	5

PART II. You and Religion

37. **How important is religion to you?** *Please, choose a suitable position for yourself on the following scale:*

Not at all important		0	1	2	3	4		very important

38. **Which of these statements comes closest to your position?**

1	There is a God
2	There is some sort of spirit or life force
3	I don't really think there is a God or any sort of spirit or life force.

❖ How often do you:

		About every day	*About every week*	*About once a month*	*Less than once a month*	*Never*
39.	think about religion	1	2	3	4	5
40.	read sacred texts (e.g. Bible, Qur'an) for yourself	1	2	3	4	5
41.	look on the internet for religious topics	1	2	3	4	5
42.	pray	1	2	3	4	5
43.	attend religious events (acts of worship, youth groups, etc)	1	2	3	4	5
44.	think about the meaning of life	1	2	3	4	5

❖ How important are the following things to get information about different religions:

		Very important	*Important*	*Little bit important*	*Not important*	*Not important at all*
45.	Family	1	2	3	4	5

		Strongly agree				
46.	School	1	2	3	4	5
47.	Friends	1	2	3	4	5
48.	Faith community	1	2	3	4	5
49.	Books	1	2	3	4	5
50.	Media (e.g. newspapers, TV)	1	2	3	4	5
51.	Internet	1	2	3	4	5

❖ Your peers in Europe have explained their positions regarding religion in different ways. To what extent do you agree with their statements?

		Strongly agree	Agree	Neither agree or disagree	Dis-agree	Strongly dis-agree
52.	"Religion helps me to cope with difficulties."	1	2	3	4	5
53.	"Religion helps me to be a better person."	1	2	3	4	5
54.	"Religion is important to me because I love God."	1	2	3	4	5
55.	"I respect other people who believe."	1	2	3	4	5
56.	"Religion is nonsense."	1	2	3	4	5
57.	"Religion determines my whole life."	1	2	3	4	5
58.	"Religion is important in our history."	1	2	3	4	5
59.	"You can be a religious person without belonging to a particular faith community."	1	2	3	4	5
60.	"Sometimes I have doubts – is there a god or not?"	1	2	3	4	5
61.	"What I think about religion is open to change."	1	2	3	4	5

PART III. You and others

The following questions deal with your opinions regarding the role religions play in different relationships and contexts.

❖ How often do you speak with others about religion?

		About every day	About once a week	About once in a month	Less than once in a month	Never
62.	Family	1	2	3	4	5
63.	Friends	1	2	3	4	5
64.	Classmates	1	2	3	4	5
65.	Other students at school	1	2	3	4	5
66.	Teachers	1	2	3	4	5
67.	Religious leaders	1	2	3	4	5

❖ People around you

		Yes	No	I don't know about their views or religion
68.	Most of my friends have the same views about religion as me	1	2	3
69.	Most of the students in my class have the same views about religion as me	1	2	3
70.	I have friends who belong to different religions.	1	2	3
71.	I have family members who belong to different religions.	1	2	3
72.	I have students in my class who belong to different religions.	1	2	3
73.	My parents have totally different views about religion from me.	1	2	3
74.	At school, I go around with young people who have different religious backgrounds.	1	2	3
75.	After school, I go around with young people who have different religious backgrounds	1	2	3
76.	At school, I prefer to go around with young people who have the same religious background as me.	yes	no	
77.	In my spare time, I prefer to go around with young people who have the same religious background as me.	yes	no	

❖ To what extent do you agree with the following statements your peers have made?

		Strongly agree	Agree	Neither agree or disagree	Dis-agree	Strongly disagree
78.	"I like to know what my best friend thinks about religion"	1	2	3	4	5
79.	"It doesn't bother me what my friends think about religion."	1	2	3	4	5
80.	"I have problems showing my views about religion openly in school."	1	2	3	4	5
81.	"A student who shows his/her religious belief openly in school, risks being mocked."	1	2	3	4	5
82.	"Religious people are less tolerant towards others."	1	2	3	4	5
83.	"Without religion the world would be a better place."	1	2	3	4	5
84.	"Religion belongs to private life."	1	2	3	4	5
85.	"Religion is a source of ag-gressiveness."	1	2	3	4	5
86.	"Religion is something one inherits from one's family."	1	2	3	4	5

❖ Students of your age have mentioned different reasons why religion is or is not a topic to discuss. To what extent do you agree with their views?

		Strongly agree	Agree	Neither agree or disagree	Dis-agree	Strongly disagree
87.	"To me talking about religion is interesting because people have different views."	1	2	3	4	5
88.	"Talking about religion helps to shape my own views."	1	2	3	4	5
89.	"I and my friends talk about how stupid religion is and what cruel-ties are carried out in its name."	1	2	3	4	5
90.	"Talking about religion helps us to understand others."	1	2	3	4	5
91.	"In my view, talking about religion is embarrassing."	1	2	3	4	5

92.	"Religion doesn't interest me at all – we have more important things to talk about."	1	2	3	4	5
93.	"In my view, talking about religion only leads to disagreement."	1	2	3	4	5
94.	"Talking about religion helps me to live peacefully together with people from different religions."	1	2	3	4	5
95.	"I don't know much about religion and thus I can't have an opinion."	1	2	3	4	5
96.	"For me talking about religious topics is boring."	1	2	3	4	5
97.	"Talking about religion helps me to understand better what is going on in the world."	1	2	3	4	5

❖ Imagine that a student of a different religious faith wants to convince you that his/her religion is the best one. How do you react?

		That's exactly my reaction	That could be my reaction	I would never react like that
98.	I try to ignore him/her	1	2	3
99.	I try to discuss with him/her about his/her opinions	1	2	3
100.	I try to convince him that s/he is wrong	1	2	3
101.	I try to explain that my own opinions about religion are the best ones.	1	2	3
102.	I listen but their views do not influence me.	1	2	3

❖ When discussing how people of different worldviews and religions can live together, other young people have made following statements. How far do you share the following views?

		Strongly agree	Agree	Neither agree or disagree	Dis-agree	Strongly disagree
103.	"Disagreement on religious issues leads to conflicts."	1	2	3	4	5
104.	"Respecting the religion of others helps to cope with differences."	1	2	3	4	5
105.	"I don't like people from other	1	2	3	4	5

	religions and do not want to live together with them."					
106.	"People with different strong religious views cannot live together."	1	2	3	4	5

❖ There are people from different religions living in every country. What do you think would help them to live together in peace?

		Very important	Quite important	Not important	Cannot say
107.	If people share common interests	1	2	3	4
108.	If they know about each other's´ religions	1	2	3	4
109.	If they personally know people from different religions	1	2	3	4
110.	If they do something together	1	2	3	4
111.	If everyone keeps to their own religion in private	1	2	3	4
112.	If the state has strong laws about the role of religion in society.	1	2	3	4

Finally we would like to ask some questions about you.
113.   What is your age?
114.   What is your gender?
115.   In which country were you born?
116.   In which country was your mother born?
117.   In which country was your father born?
118.   In which country do you hold citizenship?
119.   What are the main languages spoken at your home?
120.   What profession has your mother?
          ....
121.   What profession has your father?
          ....
122.   Does your father have a certain religion or worldview? Yes / No / I do not know
123.   If 'yes, which one? ....
124.   Does your mother have a certain religion or worldview? Yes/ No / I do not know
125.   If 'yes', which one? ....
126.   Do you have a certain religion or worldview? Yes / No
127.   If 'yes', which one? ....

If you have personal comments, additions or remarks, please, write them here:
Thank you for your cooperation!

Appendix 4: Questionnaire for quantitative study (Estonian version)

Religioon ja kool
Ankeetküsitlus

Möödunud aastal toimus Euroopas uuring, mille raames selgitati koolinoorte suhtumist religiooniga seotud küsimustesse. Käesolev ankeet on selle uuringu jätkuks ja see viiakse läbi kaheksas Euroopa riigis. Meie eesmärgiks on uurida, kuidas Euroopa noored näevad religiooni rolli hariduses ja ühiskonnas laiemalt. Palume selle uuringu läbiviimiseks ka Sinu abi. Oleme Sinu seisukohtadest neis küsimustes väga huvitatud.

Võib-olla tunduvad mõned küsimused Sulle Eesti kontekstis kummalistena. See pole probleem – religiooni roll erinevates Euroopa riikides ongi väga erinev. Vali lihtsalt vastusevariant, mis on Sinu vastusele kõige lähemal.

Kui mõni küsimus jääb arusaamatuks, palu julgelt abi ankeedi läbiviijalt. Kui soovid ankeedi küsimustele lisada oma kommentaare, selgitusi ja mõtteid, saad seda teha ankeedi viimasel leheküljel.

Täname sind koostöö eest!
REDCo meeskond

Täidab ankeedi läbiviija:

MS	Country	Date	Model of RinE	Code

I OSA. Religioon koolis.

Religioonil on erinevate Euroopa riikide koolides erinev roll. On riike, kus religiooniõpetus on kõigile õpilastele kohustuslik õppeaine, teisal on see valikaine, mõnes riigis pole eraldi religiooniõpetuse tunde üldse. Erinev võib olla ka religiooniõpetuse õpetamine – mõnel pool keskendub see konkreetse religiooni tundmaõppimisele, teisal tutvustatakse erinevaid religioone. Religiooniga seotud teemad tulevad esile ka mitmetes teistes ainetes nagu näiteks kirjanduses, ajaloos vm. Religiooniga seotud küsimused võivad ilmneda ka igapäevases koolielus.

1. Mitu aastat oled Sa koolis religiooniõpetust õppinud?

2. Kas Sa käesoleval aastal õpid religiooniõpetust? Jah Ei

❖ Millised on Sinu kogemused religioonist koolis? Kuivõrd Sa nõustud, et:…

		Täiesti nõus	Nõus	Pole nõus ega vastu	Ei ole nõus	Pole üldse nõus
3.	Koolis saan ma teadmisi erinevate religioonide kohta.	1	2	3	4	5
4.	Koolis õpin ma lugupidavalt suhtuma kõigi religioonide esindajatesse.	1	2	3	4	5
5.	Koolis saan ma arutleda religiooniga seotud küsimuste üle erinevatest vaatepunktidest lähtuvalt.	1	2	3	4	5
6.	Minu meelest on religioonidega seotud teemade käsitlemine koolis huvitav.	1	2	3	4	5
7.	Minu meelest on oluline, et koolis käsitletaks religiooniga seotud teemasid.	1	2	3	4	5
8.	Erinevate religioonide tundmaõppimine koolis aitab kaasa rahumeelsele kooselule.	1	2	3	4	5
9.	Erinevate religioonide tundma-õppimine aitab mul teha oma elus valikuid õige ja väära vahel.	1	2	3	4	5
10.	Erinevate religioonide tundmaõppimine aitab mul mõista kaasaegseid sündmusi.	1	2	3	4	5
11.	Erinevate religioonide tundmaõppimine aitab mul mõista iseennast.	1	2	3	4	5

12.	Erinevate religioonide tundmaõppimine tekitab klassis konflikte.	1	2	3	4	5

❖ Religioon võib koolis ilmneda mitmel moel. Kujutle, et Sul on võimalik otsustada mitmeid kooliga seotud korralduslikke küsimusi. Kuivõrd oleksid Sa nõus järgmiste seisukohtadega?

		Täiesti nõus	Nõus	Pole nõus ega vastu	Ei ole nõus	Pole üldse nõus
13.	Koolitoidu menüü peaks arvestama õpilaste religioossete tõekspidamistega.	1	2	3	4	5
14.	Õpilastel peaks olema õigus koolis kanda religioosseid sümboleid …	tagasihoidlikke (nt. väike rist, ripats jmt)	1	2	3	4	5
15.		silmatorkavamaid (nt. pearätid jmt)	1	2	3	4	5
16.	Õpilastel peaks olema õigus oma religiooni pühade ajal koolist puududa.	1	2	3	4	5
17.	Õpilastel peaks olema õigus keelduda mõnedest tundidest religioossetel põhjustel.	1	2	3	4	5
18.	Koolis peaks olema ruum palvetamiseks.	1	2	3	4	5
19.	Vabatahtliku osalusega jumalateenistus võib olla koolielu osaks.	1	2	3	4	5

❖ Kuivõrd Sa nõustud, et erinevate religioonide tundmaõppimine aitab:

		Täiesti nõus	Nõus	Pole nõus ega vastu	Ei ole nõus	Pole üldse nõus
20.	Mõista teisi ja elada nendega rahumeelselt koos.	1	2	3	4	5
21.	Mõista oma maa ja Euroopa ajalugu.	1	2	3	4	5
22.	Mõista paremini kaasaegseid sündmusi.	1	2	3	4	5
23.	Kujundada oma seisukohti.	1	2	3	4	5
24.	Kujundada kõlbelisi tõekspidamisi.	1	2	3	4	5

25.	Tundma õppida oma religiooni.	1	2	3	4	5

❖ Kuidas Sa suhtud erinevatesse religiooniõpetuse mudelitesse?

		Täiesti nõus	Nõus	Pole nõus ega vastu	Ei ole nõus	Pole üldse nõus
26.	Religiooniõpetuse õppimine peaks olema vabatahtlik.	1	2	3	4	5
27.	Õpilased peaksid õppima religiooni-õpetust eraldi rühmades vastavalt nende religioossele taustale.	1	2	3	4	5
28.	Religioonil ei tohi koolis olla mingit kohta.	1	2	3	4	5
29.	Religiooniõpetust peaksid kõik õpilased õppima koos, olenemata õpilaste usulisest või konfessionaalsest taustast.	1	2	3	4	5
30.	Religiooniõpetust eraldi õppe-ainena pole vaja. Kõike, mida on vaja religiooni kohta teada, käsitletakse teistes ainetes (nt kirjandus, ajalugu jt)	1	2	3	4	5
31.	Religiooniõpetust peaks õpetama osaliselt koos ja osaliselt rühmades vastavalt õpilaste usulisele taustale.	1	2	3	4	5

❖ Mil määral Sa nõustud, et õpilased peaksid koolis:

		Täiesti nõus	Nõus	Pole nõus ega vastu	Ei ole nõus	Pole üldse nõus
32.	saama objektiivseid teadmisi maailma religioonidest.	1	2	3	4	5
33.	õppima mõistma, mida religioo-nid õpetavad.	1	2	3	4	5
34.	saama rääkida ja arutleda religiooniga seotud teemadel.	1	2	3	4	5
35.	õppima nägema, kuidas reli-gioon mõjutab ühiskonna elu.	1	2	3	4	5
36.	saama usulist kasvatust.	1	2	3	4	5

II OSA. Sina ja religioon

37. **Kui oluline on Sinu jaoks religioon?** *Palun vali alljärgneval skaalal Sinu suhtumist väljendav number.*

täiesti ebaoluline	0 - 1 - 2 - 3 - 4 väga oluline

38. **Milline järgmistest väidetest on kõige lähemal Sinu arusaamadele?**

1	Usun, et Jumal on olemas.
2	Usun, et on olemas mingi kõrgem vaim või elu juhtiv jõud.
3	Usun, et pole olemas ei jumalat, kõrgemat vaimu ega elu juhtivat jõudu.

❖ Kui sageli Sa:

		Pea iga päev	Umbes iga nädal	Umbes kord kuus	Harvem kui kord kuus	Mitte kunagi
39.	mõtled religiooniga seotud küsimuste üle	1	2	3	4	5
40.	loed lihtsalt huvist pühakirja (nt Piiblit Koraani jmt)	1	2	3	4	5
41.	otsid internetist materjali religiooniga seotud teemade kohta	1	2	3	4	5
42.	palvetad	1	2	3	4	5
43.	külastad usulisi talitusi (nagu nt jumalateenistusi, noorteõhtuid jne)	1	2	3	4	5
44.	mõtled elu mõttest	1	2	3	4	5

❖ Kui oluline on Sulle erinevate religioonide kohta info saamiseks:

		Väga oluline	Oluline	Mingil määral oluline	Pole oluline	Pole üldse oluline
45.	Perekond	1	2	3	4	5
46.	Kool	1	2	3	4	5
47.	Sõbrad	1	2	3	4	5
48.	Kogudus või usuline ühendus	1	2	3	4	5
49.	Raamatud	1	2	3	4	5
50.	Meedia (ajalehed, TV jne)	1	2	3	4	5
51.	Internet	1	2	3	4	5

❖ Sinu eakaaslased Euroopas on põhjendanud oma suhtumist religiooni mitmeti. Mil määral Sa nõustud siintoodud seisukohtadega?

		Täiesti nõus	Nõus	Pole nõus ega vastu	Ei ole nõus	Pole üldse nõus
52.	"Religioon aitab mul raskustega toime tulla."					
53.	"Religioon aitab mul olla parem inimene."					
54.	"Religioon on minu jaoks oluline, sest ma armastan Jumalat."					
55.	"Ma respekteerin inimesi, kes usuvad."					
56.	"Religioon on mõttetus."					
57.	"Religioon kujundab kogu mu elu."					
58.	"Religioon on olnud oluline meie ajaloos."					
59.	"Inimene võib olla usklik ka nõnda, et ta pole seotud ühegi kindla usulise rühmaga."					
60.	"Mõnikord ma kahtlen, kas Jumal on olemas või mitte."					
61.	"See, mida ma religioonist arvan, võib muutuda."					

III OSA. Sina ja teised.

Järgmised küsimused on seotud Sinu arusaamadega selle kohta, milline roll on religioonil erinevates inimsuhetes ja olukordades.

❖ Kui sageli Sa kõneled religioonist:

		Peaaegu iga päev	Umbes iga nädal	Umbes kord kuus	Harvem kui kord kuus	Mitte kunagi
62.	pereliikmetega	1	2	3	4	5
63.	sõpradega	1	2	3	4	5
64.	klassikaaslastega	1	2	3	4	5
65.	teiste koolikaaslastega	1	2	3	4	5

66.	õpetajatega	1	2	3	4	5
67.	vaimulikega	1	2	3	4	5

Sind ümbritsevad inimesed.	Jah	Ei	Ma ei tea nende seisukohti või religiooni
68. Enamik minu sõpru jagab minu vaateid religiooni kohta.	1	2	3
69. Enamik minu klassikaaslasi jagab minu vaateid religiooni kohta.	1	2	3
70. Mul on sõpru, kes on seotud minust erineva religiooniga.	1	2	3
71. Mul on pereliikmeid, kes on seotud minust erineva religiooniga	1	2	3
72. Mul on klassikaaslasi, kes on seotud minust erineva religiooniga	1	2	3
73. Minu vanemate vaated religioonile on täiesti teistsugused kui minul.	1	2	3
74. Koolis suhtlen ma kaaslastega, kellel on minust erinev usuline taust.	1	2	3
75. Väljaspool kooli suhtlen ma erineva usulise taustaga noortega.	1	2	3
76. Koolis eelistan ma lävida kaaslastega, kelle usuline (maailmavaateline) taust on samasugune kui minul.	Jah	Ei	
77. Vabal ajal eelistan ma läbi käia noortega, kelle usuline (maailmavaateline) taust on samasugune kui minul.	Jah	Ei	

❖ Mil määral Sa nõustud järgmiste seisukohtadega, mida on esitanud Sinu eakaaslased Euroopas?

		Täiesti nõus	Nõus	Pole nõus ega vastu	Pole nõus	Pole üldse nõus
78.	"Mind huvitab, mida mu parim sõber religioonist mõtleb."	1	2	3	4	5
79.	"Mulle ei lähe korda, mida mu sõbrad religioonist arvavad."	1	2	3	4	5
80.	"Minu jaoks on oma religioossete tõekspidamiste väljanäitamine koolis problemaatiline."	1	2	3	4	5
81.	"Õpilane, kes väljendab koolis avalikult oma usku, võib saada pilkealuseks."	1	2	3	4	5
82.	"Usklikud inimesed on teiste suhtes vähem sallivad."	1	2	3	4	5
83.	"Ilma religioonita oleks maailm	1	2	3	4	5

	parem."				
84.	"Religioon on eraasi."	1	2	3	4	5
85.	"Religioon on agressiivsuse allikas."	1	2	3	4	5
86.	"Religioon saadakse kaasa perekonnast."	1	2	3	4	5

❖ Sinu eakaaslased on nimetanud erinevaid põhjusi, miks nad religioonist räägivad või ei räägi. Mil määral Sa nende põhjendustega nõustud?

		Täiesti nõus	Nõus	Pole nõus ega vastu	Pole nõus	Pole üldse nõus
87.	"Inimeste erinevad seisukohad teevad religioonist kõnelemise huvitavaks"	1	2	3	4	5
88.	"Religioonist kõnelemine aitab mul kujundada oma seisukohti."	1	2	3	4	5
89.	"Räägime sõpradega sellest, kui nõme on religioon ja milliseid julmusi on selle nimel korda saadetud."	1	2	3	4	5
90.	"Religioonist kõnelemine aitab meil teisi mõista."	1	2	3	4	5
91.	"Minu arust on religioonist rääkimine piinlik."	1	2	3	4	5
92.	"Religioon ei huvita meid üldse – meil on palju olulisemaid jututeemasid."	1	2	3	4	5
93.	"Minu meelest viib religioonist rääkimine vaid vaidlusteni."	1	2	3	4	5
94.	"Religioonist kõnelemine aitab kaasa rahumeelsele kooselule eri religioonide esindajatega."	1	2	3	4	5
95.	"Ma ei tea religioonist eriti palju ega oska seepärast neis asjus kaasa rääkida."	1	2	3	4	5
96.	"Minu jaoks on religioonist rääkimine igav."	1	2	3	4	5
97.	"Religioonist kõnelemine aitab mul maailmas toimuvat paremini mõista."	1	2	3	4	5

❖ Kujuta ette, et keegi usklik õpilane püüab sind veenda, et tema usk on kõige õigem. Kuidas Sa reageeriksid?

		Reageeriksin täpselt nii	Võib-olla reageeriksin nii	Ma ei reageeriks kunagi nii
98.	Püüan temast mitte välja teha.	1	2	3
99.	Püüan temaga tema seisukohti arutada.	1	2	3

100.	Püüan teda veenda, et ta eksib.	1	2	3
101.	Püüan talle selgeks teha, et hoopis minu seisukohad religiooni küsimustes on õiged.	1	2	3
102.I	Ma kuulan ta ära, aga tema seisukohad ei mõjuta mind.	1	2	3

❖ Arutledes selle üle, kuidas erinevate religioonide esindajad saaksid rahumeelselt elada, on Su eakaaslased pakkunud välja järgmisi ideid. Mil määral Sa nendega nõustud?

		Täiesti nõus	*Nõus*	*Pole nõus ega vastu*	*Ei ole nõus*	*Pole üldse nõus*
103.	"Erimeelsused religioossetes küsimustes viivad konfliktideni."	1	2	3	4	5
104.	"Teiste inimeste religiooni austamine aitab erinevustega toime tulla."	1	2	3	4	5
105.	"Mulle ei meeldi teist usku inimesed ja ma ei taha nendega kõrvuti elada."	1	2	3	4	5
106.	"Rangete religioonide esindajad ei saa koos elada."	1	2	3	4	5

❖ Igal maal elab erinevate religioonide esindajaid. Mis aitaks Sinu meelest neil rahumeelselt koos elada?

		Väga oluline	*Mingil määral oluline*	*Ei ole oluline*	*Ei oska öelda*
107.	Kui inimestel on ühiseid huvisid.	1	2	3	4
108.	Kui nad tunnevad üksteise religioone.	1	2	3	4
109.	Kui neil on teiste religioonide esindajate hulgas isiklikke tuttavaid.	1	2	3	4
110.	Kui nad teevad midagi üheskoos.	1	2	3	4
111.	Kui igaüks hoiab oma usu vaid enda teada.	1	2	3	4
112.	Kui riigis on ranged seadused, mis panevad religiooni rolli ühiskonnas selgelt paika.	1	2	3	4

Lõpetuseks soovime esitada mõned küsimused Sinu enda kohta.

Kui vana Sa oled?

Sinu sugu: | mees | naine |

113. Mis maal oled Sa sündinud?
_____

114. Mis maal on Su ema sündinud?
_____

115. Mis maal on Su isa sündinud.?
_____

116. Mis riigi kodakondsus Sul on?
_____

117. Mis keeltes te kodus omavahel suhtlete?
_____

118. Mis elukutse on Sinu emal?
_____

119. Mis elukutse on Sinu isal?
_____

120. Kas Su isa on seotud mõne kindla religiooni või maailmavaatega?

| Jah | Ei | Ei tea |

Kui jah, siis millisega? _____

121. Kas Su ema on seotud mõne kindla religiooni

| Jah | Ei | Ei tea |

Kui jah, siis millisega? _____

122. Kas Sina oled seotud mõne kindla religiooni või maailmavaatega?

| Jah | Ei |

123. Kui jah, siis millisega? _____

Kui Sa soovid lisada oma kommentaare, mõtteid, selgitusi, kirjuta palun need siia:

Täname Sind koostöö eest!

Appendix 5: Questionnaire for quantitative study (Russian version)

Религия и образование

Вопросник

В прошлом году в Европе проводилось исследование отношения учащихся Вашего возраста к религии. На основе выполненного исследования разработан данный вопросник. Его цель – выяснить, как учащиеся из восьми европейских стран, видят роль религии в образовании и в общественной жизни в целом.

Мы рассчитываем на Вашу помощь в этом исследовании. Нас интересует, что думаете лично Вы. Может быть, некоторые вопросы покажутся Вам мало подходящими в Вашем контексте. Не беспокойтесь, роль религии в разных европейских странах не одинакова. Выберите наиболее подходящий вариант ответа.

Если у Вас возникнут трудности с пониманием вопросов, пожалуйста, обращайтесь за помощью. Вы можете оставить личные замечания, комментарии и дополнения на последней странице вопросника.

Спасибо за участие!
Исследовательская группа REDCo

(заполняется исследователями)

PT	Country	Date	Model of RinE	Code

Часть I. Религия в школе

Применительно к преподаванию религии в школе, между Европейскими странами существуют некоторые различия. Есть страны, в которых уроки религиозного образования обязательны для посещения, в других странах такие уроки посещаются по желанию или вообще не проводятся в школе. В некоторых странах религии учат с точки зрения определенного вероучения. В других учащимся даются общие знания о религиях.

Вопросы, связанные с религией, могут подниматься на занятиях другими предметами, например литературой или историей. Время от времени их может ставить перед учащимися сама школьная жизнь.

Сколько лет Вы обучали религию в школе?

1. Посещаете ли Вы уроки религиозного образования в этом учебном году?

Да | Нет

❖ Каков ваш опыт встречи с религией в школе? Насколько Вы согласны, что:…

		Совершенно согласен	Согласен	Не то не другое	Не согласен	Категорически не согласен
3.	В школе я получаю знания о разных религиях	1	2	3	4	5
4.	В школе я учусь уважать всех людей независимо от их религии	1	2	3	4	5
5.	В школе у меня есть возможность обсуждать религиозные вопросы с разных точек зрения	1	2	3	4	5
6.	Темы школьной программы, связанные с религиями, представляются мне интересными	1	2	3	4	5
7.	Религии представляются мне важной темой школьной программы	1	2	3	4	5

8.	Изучение разных религий в школе помогает нам жить вместе	1	2	3	4	5
9.	Изучение религий в школе помогает мне выбирать между злом и добром	1	2	3	4	5
10.	Изучение религий в школе помогает мне понимать происходящие события	1	2	3	4	5
11.	Изучение религий в школе помогает мне лучше узнать самого себя	1	2	3	4	5
12.	Изучение религий приводит к конфликтам в классе	1	2	3	4	5

Религия может присутствовать в школе в разных формах. Представьте себя лицом, уполномоченным принимать решения по школьным вопросам.

❖ Насколько Вы согласились бы со следующими положениями?

			Совершенно согласен	Согласен	Не то не другое	Не согласен	Категорически не согласен
13.	При организации школьного питания следует учитывать религиозные требования к пище.		1	2	3	4	5
14.	Учащимся должно быть позволено ношение религиозной	не бросающейся в глаза (напр., маленький крестик)	1	2	3	4	5
15.	символики	более заметной (напр., головные платки)	1	2	3	4	5
16.	Учащиеся могут пропускать занятия в те дни, когда у них религиозные праздники		1	2	3	4	5
17.	Учащимся должно быть позволено не посещать не-		1	2	3	4	5

	которые уроки по религиозным мотивам					
18.	Школа должна предоставить учащимся возможность молиться в школьном помещении	1	2	3	4	5
19.	Добровольные религиозные службы (общешкольные молитвы, богослужения) могут быть частью школьной жизни	1	2	3	4	5

❖ Насколько Вы согласны с тем, что изучение разных религий помогает:

		Совершенно согласен	Согласен	Не то не другое	Не согласен	Категорически не согласен
20.	Понимать других и жить с ними в мире	1	2	3	4	5
21.	Понимать историю своей страны и Европы	1	2	3	4	5
22.	Обрести лучшее понимание происходящих событий	1	2	3	4	5
23.	Развивать собственную точку зрения	1	2	3	4	5
24.	Развивать нравственные ценности	1	2	3	4	5
25.	Больше узнать о своей религии	1	2	3	4	5

❖ Как Вы относитесь к разным моделям религиозного образования в школе?

		Совершенно согласен	Согласен	Не то не другое	Не согласен	Категорически не согласен
26.	Религиозное образование должно предлагаться как курс по выбору	1	2	3	4	5
27.	Занятия религиозным образованием должны проводиться раздельно, в соответствии с религиозной принадлежностью учащихся	1	2	3	4	5
28.	Религии в школе не место	1	2	3	4	5

29.	Учащиеся должны заниматься религиозным образованием вместе, независимо от религиозных и конфессиональных различий между ними	1	2	3	4	5
30.	В религиозном образовании как отдельном предмете нет необходимости. Все, что мы должны знать о религии, входит в содержание других учебных предметов (литературы, истории и др.)	1	2	3	4	5
31.	Занятия религиозным образованием должны проводиться иногда вместе, а иногда раздельно в соответствии с религиозной принадлежностью учащихся	1	2	3	4	5

❖ Насколько Вы согласны с тем, что школьники должны:

		Совершенно согласен	Согласен	Не то не другое	Не согласен	Категорически не согласен
32.	Получать объективные знания о разных религиях	1	2	3	4	5
33.	Научиться понимать, чему учат религии	1	2	3	4	5
34.	Уметь говорить и объясняться на религиозные темы	1	2	3	4	5
35.	Узнать о значении религии для решения общественных проблем	1	2	3	4	5
36.	Получить наставление в вере	1	2	3	4	5

Часть II. Вы и религия

37. **Насколько важна для Вас религия?** *Выберите, пожалуйста, соответствующую оценку по приведённой ниже шкале:*

| совершенно не важна | 0 | 1 | 2 | 3 | 4 | очень важна |

38. **Какое из следующих утверждений Вам ближе?**

1	Бог есть
2	Существует что-то вроде духа или жизненной силы
3	Я не думаю, что существует Бог, дух или какая-то жизненная сила.

❖ Как часто Вы:

		Почти каждый день	Почти каждую неделю	Пример-но раз в месяц	Реже чем раз в месяц	Никогда
39.	думаете о религии	1	2	3	4	5
40.	читаете для самого себя священные тексты (напр. Библию или Коран)	1	2	3	4	5
41.	ищете в интернете что-нибудь на религиозные темы	1	2	3	4	5
42.	молитесь	1	2	3	4	5
43.	посещаете религиозные собрания (богослужения, молодежные группы и др.)	1	2	3	4	5
44.	думаете о смысле жизни	1	2	3	4	5

❖ Насколько важны для Вас следующие источники сведений о разных религиях?

		Очень важны	Важны	Важны в малой степени	Не важны	Совсем не важны
45.	семья	1	2	3	4	5
46.	школа	1	2	3	4	5
47.	друзья	1	2	3	4	5
48.	религиозная община	1	2	3	4	5
49.	книги	1	2	3	4	5
50.	СМИ (напр., газеты телевидение	1	2	3	4	5
51.	интернет	1	2	3	4	5

❖ Ваши сверстники в Европе по-разному объясняли свое отношение к религии. Насколько Вы согласны с их высказываниями?

		Совершенно согласен	Согласен	Не то не другое	Не согласен	Категорически не согласен
52.	«Религия помогает мне справляться с трудностями»	1	2	3	4	5
53.	«Религия помогает мне становиться лучше»	1	2	3	4	5
54.	«Религия важна для меня потому, что я люблю Бога»	1	2	3	4	5
55.	«Я уважаю других верующих»	1	2	3	4	5
56.	«Религия – это вздор»	1	2	3	4	5
57.	«Религия определяет всю мою жизнь»	1	2	3	4	5
58.	«Религия имеет важное значение в нашей истории»	1	2	3	4	5
59.	«Можно быть религиозным человеком и не принадлежа к определенной религиозной общине»	1	2	3	4	5
60.	«Иногда я сомневаюсь, существует ли Бог или его нет»	1	2	3	4	5
61.	«То, что я думаю о религии, открыто для пересмотра»	1	2	3	4	5

Часть III. Вы и другие

Следующие вопросы касаются вашего мнения о том, какую роль играют религии в разных человеческих отношениях и ситуациях.

❖ Как часто вы говорите о религии ...

		Почти каждый день	Примерно раз в неделю	Примерно раз в месяц	Реже, чем раз в месяц	Никогда
62.	В семье	1	2	3	4	5
63.	С друзьями	1	2	3	4	5
64.	С одноклассниками	1	2	3	4	5
65.	С другими учащимися в школе	1	2	3	4	5
66.	С учителями	1	2	3	4	5
67.	С религиозными служителями	1	2	3	4	5

Ваши окружающие.		Да	Нет	Не знаю об их взглядах и религии
68.	Большинство моих друзей разделяет мои взгляды на религию	1	2	3
69.	Большинство моих одноклассников разделяет мои взгляды на религию	1	2	3
70.	У меня есть друзья, принадлежащие другой религии	1	2	3
71.	В моей семье есть родственники, принадлежащие другой религии	1	2	3
72.	В моем классе есть учащиеся, принадлежащие другой религии	1	2	3
73.	У моих родителей совершенно иные взгляды на религию, чем у меня	1	2	3
74.	В школе я общаюсь с ребятами разных религиозных традиций	1	2	3
75.	После школы я общаюсь с ребятами разных религиозных традиций	1	2	3
76.	В школе я предпочитаю общаться с ребятами той же религиозной традиции, что и моя	нет	да	
77.	В свободное время я предпочитаю общаться с ребятами той же религиозной традиции, что и моя	нет	да	

❖ *Насколько Вы согласны со следующими высказываниями Ваших сверстников?*

		Совершенно согласен	Согласен	Не то не другое	Не согласен	Категорически не согласен
78.	«Я хотел бы узнать, что мой лучший друг думает о религии»	1	2	3	4	5
79.	«Мне безразлично, что мои друзья думают о религии»	1	2	3	4	5
80.	«Мне трудно в школе открыто выражать свои религиозные взгляды»	1	2	3	4	5
81.	«Учащийся, открыто показывающий в школе свою религиозную веру, рискует стать объектом насмешек»	1	2	3	4	5
82.	«Религиозные люди менее терпимы по отношению к другим»	1	2	3	4	5

83.	«Без религии мир стал бы лучше»	1	2	3	4	5
84.	«Религия – личное дело каждого»	1	2	3	4	5
85.	«Религия – источник агрессии»	1	2	3	4	5
86.	«Религия – это то, что передается по наследству в семье»	1	2	3	4	5

❖ Учащиеся Вашего возраста назвали разные причины, по которым религия является или не является предметом для обсуждения. Насколько Вы согласны с их позициями?

		Совершенно согласен	Согласен	Не то не другое	Не согласен	Категорически не согласен
87.	«Мне интересно разговаривать о религии, потому что у людей разные точки зрения»	1	2	3	4	5
88.	«Разговоры о религии помогают мне выработать собственную точку зрения»	1	2	3	4	5
89.	«Я и мои друзья говорим о том, какая глупая вещь религия и какие жестокости совершались от ее имени»	1	2	3	4	5
90.	«Разговоры о религии помогают понять других»	1	2	3	4	5
91.	«По-моему, говорить о религии как-то неловко»	1	2	3	4	5
92.	«Религия меня совершенно не интересует – у нас есть более важные темы для разговоров»	1	2	3	4	5
93.	«По-моему, разговоры о религии ведут только к разногласиям»	1	2	3	4	5
94.	«Разговоры о религии помогают мне жить в мире с представителями других религий»	1	2	3	4	5

95.	«Я мало, что знаю о религии, и поэтому у меня нет своего мнения по этому вопросу»	1	2	3	4	5
96.	«По мне, разговаривать на религиозные темы скучно»	1	2	3	4	5
97.	«Разговоры о религии помогают мне лучше понять, что происходит в мире»	1	2	3	4	5

❖ Представьте, что учащийся другого вероисповедания захочет убедить вас, будто его религия самая лучшая. Как вы отреагируете?

		Это именно то, как я поступлю	Такая реакция возможна	Я бы так никогда не поступил
98.	Попытаюсь не обращать внимания	1	2	3
99.	Попытаюсь обсудить с ним/ней его/ее позицию	1	2	3
100.	Попытаюсь убедить его/ее, что он(а) не прав(а)	1	2	3
101.	Попытаюсь объяснить, что мои религиозные представления лучше	1	2	3
102.	Выслушаю, но эти взгляды на меня не повлияют	1	2	3

❖ Обсуждая вопрос о том, как люди разных религий и мировоззрений могут уживаться друг с другом, молодые люди из разных стран сделали следующие заявления. Насколько Вы разделяете их взгляды?

		Совершенно согласен	Согласен	Не то не другое	Не согласен	Категорически не согласен
103.	«Разногласия в религиозных вопросах ведут к конфликтам»	1	2	3	4	5
104.	«Уважение к религии других людей поможет ужиться с различиями»	1	2	3	4	5
105.	«Я не люблю людей иной религиозной принадлежности и не хочу жить с ними рядом»	1	2	3	4	5

106.	«Люди со строгими, но отличающимися религиозными взглядами не могут ужиться вместе»	1	2	3	4	5

❖ В каждой стране живут люди разных религий. Как Вы думаете, что может помочь им жить мирно?

		Очень важно	Довольно важно	Не важно	Не могу сказать
107.	Если у них будут общие интересы	1	2	3	4
108.	Если они будут знать о религии друг друга	1	2	3	4
109.	Если они будут лично знакомы с представителями других религий	1	2	3	4
110.	Если они будут что-нибудь делать сообща	1	2	3	4
111.	Если каждый будет исповедовать свою религию частным образом	1	2	3	4
112.	Если государство строго регламентирует роль религии в обществе	1	2	3	4

Напоследок мы хотели бы задать несколько вопросов лично о Вас:

113. Ваш возраст

114. Ваш пол   М   Ж

115. Место рождения (государство, республика) _____

116. В какой стране родилась Ваша мать? _____

117. В какой стране родился Ваш отец? _____

118. Гражданином какой страны Вы являетесь? _____

119. На каком языке (языках) Вы разговариваете дома? _____

120. Профессия Вашей матери _____

121. Профессия Вашей матери _____

122. Исповедует ли Ваш отец какую-нибудь религию?

Да	Нет	Не знаю

123. Если да, то какую?   _____

124. Исповедует ли Ваша мать какую-либо религию?

Да	Нет	Не знаю

125. Если да, то какую?   _____

126. Исповедуете ли Вы какую-нибудь религию?

Да	Нет

127. Если да, то какую?   _____

Если Вы хотите что-либо дополнить или пояснить, пожалуйста, оставьте Ваши заметки здесь

_____

_____

Спасибо за участие!

Appendix 6: Desired and actual sample for quantitative study

School	Students	LE/LR	SC/ST /SR	M/P/A	G/B NS/NM/ NB	AN/AW/ AS	RE	Comments
A	24	LE	SR	M	B, NS	AS	REA+	REDCo school, RE 8 years
E	18	LE	SR	M	B, NS	AS	RE-	As school A, but without RE
C	54	LE	ST	M	G, NM	AW	REG+	REDCo, RE in 10, no RE in 9
D	45	LE	SC	M ; A	G, NB	AS	REG+/v	REDCo, selective school one class has RE, the other not
F	29	LE	SC	P	B, NS	AS	REA+	Diverse by religion, open catholic
G	30	LE	SR	M	G, NS	AS	RE-	Looked for Estonian orthodox students
H	21	LR	SR	M	G, NS	AS	REBv	Old believers, 'settled' Russians
I	104	LE	SC	M	B, NM	AN	REB+, REI	Catholic approach. Privately founded, but egalitarian
J	109	LE	SC	P	G, NB	AN	REI	Private, 'rich'
K	129	LE	SR	M	G, NB	AN	REGv	Selective RE in 10, no RE before
L	107	LE	SR	M	G, NB	AN	REG+	RE for all in 10, no RE in basic school
M	55	LE	SC	M	G, NB	AN	RE-	An 'ordinary' school without RE
N	70	LR	SC	M	G, NB	AN	RE-	Russian humanitarian school
O	75	LR	SC	M	G, NB	AN	RE-	Russian ordinary school
P	53	LR	SC	M ; A	G, NB	AN	RE-	Selective school
Q	15	LE	ST	M	G, NB	AW	RE-	Chaplain at school
R	104	LE	SR	M	G, NB	AS	RE12v	Rural school, students have not studied RE
S	70	LE	SR	M	G, NM	AS	REBv	Rural school, some students have studied RE
T	29	LE	SR	M	B, NS	AS	RE9+	RE in grade 9
U	35	LE	SR	M	G, NM	AW	REB+	RE in grades 1–6, but our respondents have not studied RE
V	32	LE	SR	M	B, NS	AW	REI	No RE, but similar to School U
TOTAL schools		LE 17 LV 4	SC 8 ST 2 SR 11	P 2, M 19 A2	B 6, G 15 NS 7, NM 4, NB 10	AN 8, AW 4, AS 9.	RE-7, REI 3 REA 2 REB 5, REG 5	
Total students	1208	LE 989 LV 198	SC 540 ST 69 SR 599	P 138 M 1070 A 45	B 236, G 992 NS 183, NM 287, NB 738	AN 701, AW 370, AS 136.		

Desired sample	1200	LE 840 LV 360	SC 600 ST 100 SR 500	P 150 M 1050 A 50	B 200, G 1000 NS 200, NM 250 NB 750	AN 600 AW 400 AS 200	

The following codes are used to describe the clusters:

- Letters are used for the schools: A, C for schools where qualitative study about the views of students was done, C and D for schools where classroom interaction was studied, E-V for other schools
- Estonian-medium school (LE) – Russian-medium school (LR).
- Settlement: City (SC, over 50 000) – town (ST, 10000–50000) – rural schools (SR, under 10 000).
- Municipal (M) – private (P) – highly selective academic schools (A).
- Small (under 250) (NS) – middle (up to 500) (NM) – big schools (over 500) (NB)
- Basic school (B) – Gymnasium (G)
- Area: northern (AN) – western (AW) – southern (AS)

RE is integrated (REI) – RE is only in first years (REB) – RE in gymnasium (REG) – RE in all classes (REA) – no RE (RE-); + almost all take part, v optional RE.

Appendix 7: Coding tables for classroom interaction

Table 7: Symbols used in tables

Time (start, end)	Method	Topic	Type of the task/question	Incident suspicious unit?
0–1 min ✋	Lecture 📖	Topic	Closed question/task; memorising facts 🗺	Decrease of interest ↓
1–5 min ✌	Work in pairs ♋	"Question", also quote in quotation marks	Half-open/understanding the concepts 🖋	Average interest ⇔
5–10 min ✍	Frontal reply ♎		Open/self-reflective 🖋	Difficult to decide about interest; ever-changing ⇵
10–20 min 🖐	Group work ❖		Example ☞	Active participation, Increased interest ↑
	Individual work ✍			Students are puzzled; mess in the class; tensions 💣
	Film ☻			

Table 8: The second lesson about Judaism

Time	Method	Topic: Judaism	Type, activity	Comments Incident suspicious unit?
0–7 ✍	📖	Introduction		
7–11.40 ✌	Individual reading of the TB ✍	"What problems can raise the idea of a chosen nation? "	🖋 ↓	Decrease in interest due to different speed?
11.40–16 ✌	♎		5 different opinions	💣 potential conflict
16–24 ✍	📖	Messiah	↓ ☞ a student sprawls	Funny examples about Estonian "phenomenon of a chosen nation" ☺ Is it boring or can it interpreted in some other way (e.g.,

Time	Method	Topic: Judaism	Type, activity	Comments Incident suspicious unit?
				lesson takes place after lunch)?
25–31 ✎	Individual reading ✎	Religious life: synagogue		Difficult to grasp what they are doing
32–35 ✌	📖	Contradiction between text and photo: "You shall not make any image or likeness..."	↑ ⇔	Problems in textbook – contradiction increases the attention
35–39 ✌	Discussion ✌	"Why is God not depicted in imagery in Judaism?"	🗨 ↑	Every time an increase of interest during pair discussion is evident
39–45 ✎	♎		8 different opinions 🗨, ☞	One of the most multiple responses and several volunteers. Can it be seen as a dialogue, potential dialogue, no dialogue?

Appendix 8: Portraits of teachers

Heli

Biography

Heli has been a teacher of RE, philosophy and ethics in a medium-sized town for two years. Last year she started teaching history and civics for 16–19 year old students. She had no religious upbringing. She became Christian after finishing secondary school; influenced by a free church, and now she is a member of the Baptist Church. She has studied at *Kõrgem Usuteaduslik Seminar* (Higher Theological Seminary of the Union of Evangelical Christian and Baptist Churches of Estonia, HTSB) and continues her studies at TI, on the masters course for RE teachers.

Her first experience as a teacher was during her last year in gymnasium – on a teachers' day she was teaching some lessons and liked it very much. She has not decided yet if being a teacher is right for her, because she has had some problems maintaining class discipline. She values her religious background as a key to teaching RE, and to understanding religion.

Perception of diversity

She sees her students as very diverse, mainly in their attitude to religion – they can be interested or not interested or have prejudices. She says that she does not believe that there are students who are totally resistant to the subject; they take it with humour and try to integrate new knowledge in their own way.

> *"Very versatile, I find, nowadays. Well, certainly there is a contingent who are very interested, well, if we speak about religious education, such religious topics. For many, the biggest part are those who have several prejudiced questions and ...comments. There are some, certainly, who are not interested maybe at all, but they are so quiet usually, they have not been very outspoken. They have been rather curious, yes, and I respond to them gladly, as much as I can. But they are different indeed."*

But motivation is not the most important aspect of diversity; the most important distinction for her as a teacher is in students' learning styles. She thinks about this when planning her lessons.

She does not ask about religious diversity directly within the class, but some students write in essays about their religious beliefs. She says that they are more open when they write than orally. She thinks that the atmosphere in class is not encouraging or that students are embarrassed in front of one another. She also believes that most students have not yet developed their own worldview.

Aims

She sees the aim of RE as the acknowledgement of plurality and respect for other opinions.

> "[The aim of RE is] *that there would not develop an view that there is only my opinion and a wrong opinion. So I find that my role would be the same – that children start to understand that in addition to their opinion there could exist more different opinions what are not false but are also – beside his own position there is another right position, which could be equally true. And it is certainly wise to use those students' convictions in a lesson. So that it is not me who is speaking, not me who speaks only my versions, but there are new (ideas) and new ways of thought come and things that I probably do not know. That they themselves would get to know each other's worldviews.*"

She believes that the main aims of RE are to help children to identify their own worldview, to look for answers to existential questions, and to become more tolerant of people with different worldviews.

Strategy

She tries to answer the questions and react to comments. Instead of discouraging questions, she tries to use questions to encourage additional questions.

To satisfy the needs of different learning styles she tries to use different teaching-learning methods, and to have a variety of them available. Here one can notice the strong influence of her recent studies; she says "As in didactics we have been taught..." She finds that by work in groups one can only benefit from diversity present in a class, and get to know students who think differently. To encourage more personal contributions and to accommodate different learning styles she uses pictures, drama, and poetry. In order to help students to understand another point of view, she sometimes asks them to defend a position with which they disagree.

Some children think more analytically; others think more practically, so she tells stories from everyday life, invites members of different religions to class, or shows documentaries about religion, to supplement lectures and textbooks.

Relation

Heli almost never asks students about their religious convictions. She admits that it is not in accordance with her experience at school but rather with her own past experience as a Christian, when she was hurt by other people when she revealed her views. However, she does not avoid discussing her beliefs when students ask. Since she did not have strong religious convictions when she was a teenager, she does not expect many of her students to have them.

"Maybe I identify myself again with the age group, when I was approximately at that age. In some ways you have a mess in your head still – what is this world about? I have a feeling that there are a few who know what they think to be true."

She has found that she benefits most from active learning, so she prefers methods that enable students to be active learners. Her lessons are very much 'learning about', as the official curriculum in public schools demands. Helping students to grow in the spiritual sense is very much seen as a duty of religious communities, not of schools, except for religious schools. Heli has tried to overcome this gap by asking students their opinions so that they become more aware of their own emerging worldview.

Peter

Biography

Peter works in a selective, academically high level Gymnasium. He had no religious upbringing at home; religious issues became interesting for him during military service in Afghanistan and studies at university. He is a member of the Lutheran Church. He has two university degrees: one in Biology and one in Theology, both from Tartu University. Now he is studying a masters course in religious education. He was a teacher of Biology for three years and later he worked as a teacher of RE and Philosophy for over ten years. He teaches RE to 16–19 years old students. He is valued highly, has been selected as the teacher of the year 2006. He is married and has three children.

Perception of diversity

When asked to describe students, he starts with common qualities – they are smart and multi-talented as good in humanities as in the sciences. In Peter's view they have surprisingly many prejudices towards religious people. A religious person means for students *"a Christian fundamentalist who believes in creation in seven days"*. That is the reason why they do not regard their RE teacher as a 'real believer'.

When asked about diversities Peter names Jehovah's Witnesses and then Adventists and Satanists. The reason to highlight them is their different views on issues.

Peter likes diversity. He stresses his good and friendly relations with students from very different religious backgrounds, including some who identify themselves as Satanists. He interprets this as a transient passage of life, a part of a sincere search for truth and meaning he can see and admire. According to his experience these young students will not stay as Satanists for long, after finishing Gymnasium; in his experience, in 3–4 years they are unlikely still to be Satanists.

Some ethnic differences (Russians, exchange students from Denmark and Germany) do not affect teaching and, even if they have some influence on relations among students, this is not strong. There are sometimes students who are reserved and some of these maybe do not possess such high academic ability as others do.

Aims

The main aim of the subject is breaking prejudices towards religion as such, showing that religion is worthy of being regarded as normal. His aim is not to make students religious but rather he hopes that after studying religion they can make more aware and intentional choices on these issues.

> "*I try to bring them to the point that they are able to make adequate religious choices in their life. In a word ... In a word, the aim is to give to students such a luggage of knowledge and skills that they could in their life make reasoned, not only religious, but every kind of decisions for shaping their future life.*"

Peter believes that he can help students to develop in their religious thinking (in Fowler's terms) regardless of whether they are Christians, atheists, Satanists or do not have any religion. Also he wants students to be able to reflect and find arguments for and against their own opinions on religious issues. In this respect, even if he teaches a lot in terms of 'learning about', he incorporates many reflective exercises and disputes which give enough space to 'learning from' aims of RE. In this respect the content of the subject becomes important as a resource for personal growth.

Strategy

Peter tries to work individually with students who are reserved by nature or do not have as high academic ability as other students. He told me about a girl who writes him letters even now, many years later, and who has become a teacher. He encourages the students who do not want to make statements orally by setting their written thoughts as examples and he tries to compose teams for group work in such a way that their voice would be heard as well. Although he values personal reflection highly, Peter does not encourage students to be too open about their own convictions in the lesson as he does not want to make them vulnerable.

> "*I do not prohibit it. But I do not encourage them. It is such an era now of dissing[25] each other. From time to time it is searched for possibilities to diss. And*

---

25 an insult or put-down; to put (someone) down, or show disrespect by the use of insulting language or dismissive behaviour.

afterwards it is regretted. If the dissing takes place on the religious grounds, maybe even regretted afterwards, but someone will remember it for the rest of his life. I have been cautious in that question."

His strategy towards Jehovah's witnesses is of softening judgments about them and teaching material in such a way that their views are not classified as marginal. Satanists expect from Peter that he is critical of them but he surprises them by praising their honest search.

Relation

He sees clearly his role as a teacher of RE for students with no religious background, as he used to be, and with a long process of search for religious answers. He does not have any ambitions to convert children to any religion, but rather to show religion as a normal part of life:

> *"That religion is not idealised, that it is not thought that only angels deal with it... But it is understood that it is a serious sphere of life, there are ideas to be taken seriously, problems, serious issues about religion and culture – it is a sphere of life which cannot be easily erased..."*

He understands his vocation in helping his students – most of them very competent and ambitious – to come to terms with important philosophical life issues. He also wants to convey such values as respect and tolerance and this is something he shows to all his students regardless of their personal faith or relation to religious phenomena. In addition, he desires them to have a new awareness about religion – as a field of human life that deals with important issues that should be respected and taken seriously.

Appendix 9: Transcription of the incident 'Image'

Time	Act of speech	Remarks
34.26	Riho: *Eeee. Those Jews don't represent God in an image because it is written in the Holy Scripture. And if it is written in the Holy Scripture, then it is true indeed...*	(others laugh)
34.36	Peter: *Uh-huh, it is in that sense very, very Scripture-centred or very...Yes, if in a religion's holy scripture – in the central place – if it is written there that it is prohibited to represent God in an image, then it is of course a requirement in that religion. Certainly. Very good – it is a very good **religious** answer.* (writes) *Scripture says so...but...for some Judaists and for some bystanders, this answer is most likely satisfying. But generally there is an opinion that what stands in the Holy Scripture – at least Judaists think so – it is also reasonable. It can be reasoned also in other ways. Are...what are these other possible reasons? Very good, very good solution. Usually the most direct or the first answer is not given here. Excellent!* (x5) *Please, next one...*	
36.03	Carola: *I think that there is a fear [representing the] image [God] in the wrong way.*	
36.08	Peter: *Fear to err. But which way is right?*	
36.12	Carola :*I think that nobody knows...* (Mark*: God is not used in imagery in Christianity either.)*	whisper
36.22	Peter: *Fear to err...Does anybody have an idea what kind of misrepresentations those are, which are they afraid of?*	
36.32	Nelly: *For example if...they would humanise God, but at the same time God should be something higher, something else and if they do as an ordinary human being...* (Gitta*: But if they would make an image of a frog?)*	Side-talk
36.50	Peter: *...But what a deal! – Later, let's take Christianity arising from Judaism. And here God is in the image. Let's take Michelangelo ...*	
37.03	Nelly: *But, may I, may I, may I? Is God's image in Christianity? There is only Jesus Christ's image everywhere!*	
37.10	Peter: *Let's take Michelangelo...I have it even with me...* (Nelly*: Those artists are just a different topic* Mark*: He did not hear you...)*	Side-talk
37.15	Peter: *Remember – such a famous Michelangelo...in Sixtus' chapel – opa – Look at that, even the screen protests against using God's image....Here is a small fragment of that painting, Creation, by Michelangelo. But it is not Christ, it is God indeed. And in the same way, let's say, on icons, if the Trinity is depicted on icons, God is there.*	Screen does not open

37.52	Laura: *Maybe they don't want contradictions? Probably there would be very many different perceptions about God if God would be depicted.*	
38.00	Peter: *Perhaps it brings forth…different perceptions, that turn into contradictions. Does anybody have more ideas? Yes?*	
38.23	Maria: *They are afraid that those [images] are destroyed. It would be too severe.*	
38.29	Peter: *Wait, in what way are they destroyed?*	
38.32	Maria: *That those who are against Judaism, they would destroy [them]…*	
38.36	Peter: *Uh-huh, in this sense, to think so far, that such an extermination would be a bad sign, a bad sign for religion? Rocking religion's foundation.*	
38.50	Paula: *I thought that if those idols and pictures are made, then they would worship them, not God anymore.*	
38.58	Peter: *That is an important accusation, what is usually made, yes – that which is depicted is not worshiped anymore, but the idol itself is worshiped instead. Yes. One more can have a turn. Does anybody have something?*	
39.12	Rita: *That God is so important for them that it is said here, that Jews do not name even God's name Jahve. Maybe by that they try to show [they are] subordinate.*	

Religious Diversity
and Education in Europe

edited by Cok Bakker,
Hans-Günter Heimbrock, Robert Jackson,
Geir Skeie, Wolfram Weisse

Volume 18

Aurora Alvarez Veinguer, Gunther Dietz,
Dan-Paul Jozsa, Thorsten Knauth (Eds.)
Islam in Education in European Countries
Pedagogical Concepts and Empirical Findings

2009, 160 pages, pb, 19,90 €, ISBN 978-3-8309-2282-7

This book aims to illustrate that there are already rich and diverse experiences throughout Europe of how to integrate Islam into the national and regional school systems, particularly in primary, but also in secondary education. Accordingly, this book provides some analyses of the ways in which Islam is integrated in education in certain regions of Spain, the Netherlands, France and England. These analyses are paralleled by empirical findings concerning the role of religion in the life of young Muslims, their views concerning religion in school, and the impact of religion in education and society.

Volume 17

Jenny Berglund
Teaching Islam
Islamic Religious Education in Sweden

2010, 254 pages, pb, 29,90 €, ISBN 978-3-8309-2277-3

This study explores the formulation of Islamic Religious Education (IRE) at three Swedish Muslim schools that offer extracurricular IRE from one to three hours per week. Its aim is to contribute knowledge of how IRE is formed as a confessional school subject within the framework and under the jurisdiction of the Swedish school system. Here findings indicate that IRE functions to infuse pupils with a sense of connectedness to both the common Islamic tradition and Swedish society—and attempts to confirm connections between these two entities as well.

MÜNSTER · NEW YORK · MÜNCHEN · BERLIN

Waxmann

Volume 16

Ina ter Avest, Dan-Paul Jozsa, Thorsten Knauth,
Javier Rosón, Geir Skeie (Eds.)

Dialogue and Conflict on Religion

Studies of Classroom Interaction in European Countries

2009, 316 pages, br., € 29,90, ISBN 978-3-8309-2272-8

Regarding teaching about religions and worldviews, there is a gap between the
ambitions of educational policies and our knowledge about what really happens
in the classroom. Research on classroom interaction about religion is not very far
developed. There is a growing awareness, however, that research on pupils' perspectives on religion in education is needed in order to develop sustainable approaches for future education.
In this book we present studies of classroom interaction that focus on the micro-
sociological level of research. The studies presented open up a rather unexplored
field of international comparative research on religion in education and the role of
diversity for classroom interaction, giving deeper insights into what happens in
classrooms, displaying varieties of interactive patterns and relating these to their
specific contexts.

Volume 15

Dan-Paul Jozsa, Thorsten Knauth, Wolfram Weiße (Hrsg.)

Religionsunterricht, Dialog und Konflikt

Analysen im Kontext Europas

2009, 464 Seiten, br., 34,90 €, ISBN 978-3-8309-2251-3

Religiöse Pluralität in der Gesellschaft ist zu einem zentralen Thema in der Öf-
fentlichkeit und im akademischen Diskurs geworden. Hierbei spielt der Dialog
zwischen den Kulturen und Religionen eine zunehmend große Rolle. Eines der
wichtigen Felder, in denen der Dialog eingeübt werden kann, ebenso aber auch
die Grenzen des Dialogs und mögliches Potenzial für Konflikte vermessen werden können, ist die Schule. Genau hierum ging es in dem europäischen Großfor-
schungsprojekt REDCo: „Religion im Erziehungswesen. Ein Beitrag zum Dialog
oder ein Konfliktfaktor in sich verändernden Gesellschaften europäischer Staa-
ten".
Dieser Band informiert über die Forschungsansätze von REDCo und stellt die
wichtigsten Ergebnisse dar. Da sich die Publikation an deutschsprachige Adressa-
tinnen und Adressaten richtet, stehen die auf Deutschland bezogenen Analysen
im Zentrum. Der europäische Rahmen wird in allen Teilen allerdings gebührend
beachtet.

Waxmann

Volume 14

Siebren Miedema (Ed.)

Religious Education as Encounter
A Tribute to John M. Hull

2009, 152 pages, pb, € 19,90, ISBN 978-3-8309-1894-3

If we need an adequate vignette to characterize the contribution of the world wide famous religious educator Professor John M. Hull, a good one might be religious education as encounter. This volume is a tribute to John Hull; it is systematically focusing on religious education as encounter. It brings together contributions from leading scholars in the international field of Religious Education and addresses a great variety of perspectives regarding the concept of encounter in religious education.

Volume 13

Julia Ipgrave, Robert Jackson, Kevin O'Grady (Eds.)

Religious Education Research
through a Community of Practice
Action Research and the Interpretive Approach

2009, 238 pages, pb, 24,90 €, ISBN 978-3-8309-2158-5

This book brings together a group of teachers and teacher educators who have researched their own students' learning in schools and universities as part of the REDCo Project. Combining the methods of action and practitioner research with the key concepts of Robert Jackson's interpretive approach, the book illustrates the collaborative research of a group of professionals working together as a community of practice. The book is highly relevant to the work of teachers and teacher trainers in the field of religions and education, to researchers in this field, and to all interested in action research, practitioner research and communities of practice.

Volume 12

Wilna A.J. Meijer, Siebren Miedema,
Alma Lanser-van der Velde (Eds.)

Religious Education in a World of Religious Diversity

2009, 208 pages, pb., 24,90 €, ISBN 978-3-8309-2193-6

This volume brings together a selection of papers presented at the 15th Session of the International Seminar on Religious Education and Values (ISREV) in 2006, addressing the theme 'Religious Education in a World of Religious Diversity'.
The authors were invited to combine the concept of diversity with the dimensions of temporality, of time and history in reworking their contributions for this book. What does the inherent historicity mean for religious education as well as for (the concept) religion and religious diversity? The contributions represent the global

MÜNSTER · NEW YORK · MÜNCHEN · BERLIN

Waxmann

character of the concern with religious diversity in relation to religious education, and originate respectively from the following countries: Canada (Bhikkhu, English), United States (Moran), Latvia (Ilishko), Russia (Kozyrev), Germany (Pirner), South Africa (Roux, du Preez, Ferguson), Japan (Omori), Australia (de Souza), Turkey (Selçuk), and the Netherlands (Meijer, Miedema).

Volume 11

Geir Skeie (Ed.)

Religious Diversity and Education

Nordic Perspectives

2009, 236 pages, pb., 29,90 €, ISBN 978-3-8309-2154-7

This book addresses issues related to the increasing religious plurality in the Nordic countries. This is a challenge to many religious groups including historically dominant Lutheran national churches, both nationally and locally. A rich variety of research perspectives are presented under three headings: Theoretical and methodical perspectives; The world of the students; Teachers and textbooks.
Nordic religious education research here proves to be internationally oriented in terms of theoretical perspectives, while also contributing to the debate by important empirical studies. Examples of issues covered in the book are unintended learning, dialogue, gender, life interpretation, spirituality, identity and values.

Volume 10

Wilna A.J. Meijer

Tradition and Future of Islamic Education

2009, 200 pages, pb., 24,90 €, ISBN 978-3-8309-2131-8

The relation between Islam and the West is the topic of an ongoing debate that often leaves us with a choice between two mutually exclusive worlds: the modern West with its enlightenment and science, or else Islam and Islamic education, characterised by orthodoxy and tradition. In the hope of promoting dialogue instead of polarisation, the author, trained in the West, searches for the ideas and ideals of education, schooling and learning within Islam. Which educational culture was part of the highly developed intellectual culture of classical Islam? Current-day modernist Muslim intellectuals take inspiration from this rich intellectual tradition of Islam. The perspective on the future of Islamic education in the modern context utilizes their ideas. Hermeneutics is applied to the rereading and reinterpretation of the source texts of Islam.

MÜNSTER · NEW YORK · MÜNCHEN · BERLIN

Waxmann

MÜNSTER · NEW YORK · MÜNCHEN · BERLIN

Volume 9

Ina ter Avest (Ed.)

Education in Conflict

2009, 140 pp, pb., 19,90 €, ISBN 978-3-8309-2072-4

Under what conditions can people with different outlooks on life and different ethnic backgrounds live together in peace? In the Netherlands, as in other European countries, this question has been at the centre of public debate for some time and recently has focused in particular on religious diversity.

There are several positions, but they all see differences between groups as an essential problem. In this book, the authors take a different approach. The term conflict literally means 'clashing together'. Wherever people come together, their interests and beliefs are sure to clash. And, conversely, clashes only occur when there is something shared to quarrel about.

Five Dutch researchers share their exploration of the paradoxical situation that we cannot survive without the other, because we only really learn about ourselves when we come into contact with others. At the same time it is problematic to live with the other since our lives clash with the life of the other and we try to shield ourselves and draw boundaries.

Volume 8

Anna van der Want, Cok Bakker,
Judith Everington, Ina ter Avest (Eds.)

Teachers Responding to Religious Diversity in Europe
Researching Biography and Pedagogy

2009, 211 pp., pb., € 24,90, ISBN 978-3-8309-2119-6

Currently, all European societies are experiencing a transformation process towards greater cultural and religious pluralisation. Through a qualitative approach, we follow the different strategies of teachers to cope with religious diversity in the classrooms of six European countries, from Estonia to France, from Norway to England, from Germany to the Netherlands. The juxtaposition of biographical information on the teachers, together with their views on religious diversity and their strategies in responding to it, provides a well-rounded impression of the attitudes of teachers in Europe.

The readers can access the findings of the analyses of the respective national contexts and the European comparison. At the same time, they are able to study portraits of all of the teachers interviewed in the course of the project so that the collation of data is complemented by insight into the human perspective and the influence of national contexts.

Volume 7

Pille Valk, Gerdien Bertram-Troost,
Markus Friederici, Céline Béraud (Eds.)

Teenagers' Perspectives on the Role of Religion in their Lives, Schools and Societies
A European Quantitative Study

2009, 448 pp. , pb., € 34,90, ISBN 978-3-8309-2118-9

The quantitative study presented in this book is part of the research effort by the REDCo project. The book offers valuable interpretations and inspirations on the question how the students in the 14–16 year age group in Europe see the (ir)relevance of religions for dialogue and conflict in their daily lives, in the school environment, and in society as a whole.

Volume 6

Ursula McKenna, Julia Ipgrave, Robert Jackson

Inter Faith Dialogue by Email in Primary Schools
An Evaluation of the Building E-Bridges Project

2008, 136 pp., pb., € 19,90, ISBN 978-3-8309-1980-3

Although the book will be of immediate value to the participants in the UK and to others who might develop the approach, it will also inspire international researchers and curriculum developers concerned with children's dialogue. The findings of the study contribute valuable data to the European Commission research project ›Religion in Education: A contribution to dialogue or a factor of conflict in transforming societies of European countries?‹ (REDCo), to which the authors of this report are contributors.

Wolfram Weisse
Professor of Religious Education, University of Hamburg,
and Co-ordinator of the EC research project REDCo

Volume 5

Thorsten Knauth, Dan-Paul Jozsa,
Gerdien Bertram-Troost, Julia Ipgrave (Eds.)

Encountering Religious Pluralism in School and Society
A Qualitative Study of Teenage Perspectives in Europe

2008, 416 pages, pb., € 29,90, ISBN 978-3-8309-1972-8

Waxmann

MÜNSTER · NEW YORK · MÜNCHEN · BERLIN

Europe's religious plurality has filtered into the consciousness of the younger generation. They recognise the importance of getting to know about a wide range of religious traditions and worldviews and many consider school to be an excellent venue for this learning.

In the present volume we present an empirical qualitative study of religion in the lives and schooling of young people in Europe. The participating countries are Russia, Estonia, Norway, Germany, England, The Netherlands, France and Spain. For the first time, large-scale qualitative findings are presented on the importance of religion and attitudes towards religious diversity and religious education among European school students.

Volume 4

Cok Bakker, Hans-Günter Heimbrock (Eds.)

Researching RE Teachers. RE Teachers as Researchers

2007, 252 pages, pb., € 24,90, ISBN 978-3-8309-1786-1

The quality of religious education in schools is highly influenced by the quality of teacher practice. Especially in times of cultural change and pluralisation we need better knowledge about the actual practice in schools. The contributions of this volume present the results of a research project on religious education teachers in Europe set up by the ENRECA group during the last years.

But who is teacher and who is researcher? On the one hand, there are academics researching religious education in schools. On the other hand, there are teachers in religious education who reflect on their own teaching continuously. What kind of relationships do they have, yielding which kind of cooperation?

This project takes teachers in RE as objects and at the same time perceives practicing teachers as ›reflective practitioners‹.

Volume 3

Robert Jackson, Siebren Miedema,
Wolfram Weisse, Jean-Paul Willaime (Eds.)

Religion and Education in Europe

Developments, Contexts and Debates

2007, 286 pages, pb., € 24,90, ISBN 978-3-8309-1765-6

Recent events have resulted in the return of religion as a subject of discussion, both in the public and social domains, and at national as well as at European levels. This shift has a direct impact on the debates about the relationship between religion and education.

This book is the initial outcome of the REDCo-project. The project includes ten studies from eight different European countries, plus some collaborative thematic studies. This volume reports the first thematic study, which assesses current issues in religious education and related fields in Europe.

Volume 2

Geir Afdal

Tolerance and the curriculum

Conceptions of tolerance in the multicultural unitary
Norwegian compulsory school

2006, 365 pages, pb., € 29,90, ISBN 978-3-8309-1704-5

Being tolerant is considered important by most people. Tolerance is about navigating in societies of increased differences – societies where neighbours, colleagues, groups of people, even children and spouses are of different opinions and live in a different way. Besides, the ›navigator‹, or the self, is experienced as more complex and changing than ever before. The larger the differences in a society, the more pressing is the issue of tolerance.

But what does, however, tolerance mean? It is an ideal most people can agree with. But the process of identifying it more precisely often leads to confusion and disagreement. This study raises the question of what tolerance means in a specific multicultural context, namely education. What does tolerance mean to teachers? And does tolerance mean the same for teachers as it is defined in national curricula and in theories of tolerance?

Volume 1

Erna Zonne

Interreligiöses und interkulturelles Lernen an Grundschulen in Rotterdam Rijnmond

Eine interdisziplinäre religionspädagogische Studie des Umgangs
mit der Pluralität der Weltanschauungen

2006, 382 Seiten, br., 29,90 €, ISBN 978-3-8309-1652-9

Religiöse Pluralität der Gesellschaft ist in allen europäischen Ländern ein Faktum. Diese Gegebenheit stellt auch die Grundschulen vor Herausforderungen im Hinblick auf interreligiöse Erziehung. In dieser empirischen Studie werden Ausschnitte von der Wirklichkeit in der niederländischen Schule beschrieben, um zu verdeutlichen, wie und unter welchen Umständen beim Unterrichten mit dem gleichen interkulturellen und interreligiösen Schulbuch die Begriffe ›Religion‹ und ›Verantwortung für religiöse Bildung‹ durch die Lehrkräfte normativ ausgefüllt werden.

Waxmann

MÜNSTER · NEW YORK · MÜNCHEN · BERLIN